THE STING

NIGEL BLUNDELL
THE STING
TRUE STORIES OF THE WORLD'S GREATEST CONMEN

JOHN BLAKE

3, Bramber Court, 2 Bramber Road,
London W14 9PB, England

www.blake.co.uk

First published in paperback in 2004

ISBN 1 84454 049 9

All rights reserved. No part of this publication may be reproduced, stored in a retrieval system, or in any form or by any means, without the prior permission in writing of the publisher, nor be otherwise circulated in any form of binding or cover other than that in which it is published and without a similar condition including this condition being imposed on the subsequent publisher.

British Library Cataloguing-in-Publication Data:

A catalogue record for this book is available from the British Library.

Design by www.envydesign.co.uk

Printed in Great Britain by BookMarque

1 3 5 7 9 10 8 6 4 2

© Text copyright Nigel Blundell

Papers used by John Blake Publishing are natural, recyclable products made from wood grown in sustainable forests. The manufacturing processes conform to the environmental regulations of the country of origin.

Every attempt has been made to contact the relevant copyright-holders, but some were unobtainable. We would be grateful if the appropriate people could contact us.

Dedication

To a Great Old Rogue

(who, lest he use this as the opportunity for a libel action, shall remain anonymous!)

CONTENTS

Introduction....xiii

CUNNING CONMEN, FRAUDSTERS, VAGABONDS AND VILLAINS

Peter Foster	Wily Wizard of Oz	3
Charles Van Doren	Quiz Show Cheat	19
Charles Ingram	'Millionaire Major'	25
Daniel Faries	Jail Cell Tycoon	33
John Stonehouse	Vanishing Politician	45
Thérèse Humbert	The Locked Chest	51
D.B. Cooper	Mystery Skyjacker	59
Anthony Williams	Laird of Tomintoul	67
Harry Benson	Racing 'Certainties'	75
Horatio Bottomley	Flamboyant Felon	81
Bernie Cornfeld	Seriously Rich	87
Rosemary Aberdour	She Was No Lady	91
John Blunt	South Sea Bubble	101
Victor Lustig	The Bouncing Czech	107
Collins, Lowe and Furguson	Three King Cons	115

ARTFUL FAKERS, FORGERS, CHARLATANS AND CHEATS

Art Forgers: Past Masters		125
Thomas Chatterton	Poetic Licence	137
Yves Chaudron	The Missing *Mona Lisa*	147
Frances Griffiths and Elsie Wright	The Cottingley Fairies	151
Edward Simpson	'Flint Jack's' Finds	155
Thomas Goudie	Gambling Clerk	161
Konrad Kujau	The Hitler Diaries	167
George Hull	Giant Faker	177
William Ireland	From Bard to Verse	181
Clifford Irving	Howard Hughes Con	195
Tom Keating	'Sexton Blakes'	201
Charles Dawson	Piltdown Man	209
Bidwell Gang	Robbing the Bank	213
George Psalmanazar	'Native of Formosa'	219
Heinrich Schliemann	Greek Mythology	225
Hans van Meegeren	Works of Idle Hans	231

DARING RASCALS, ROGUES, INTERLOPERS AND IMPOSTERS

Frank Abagnale	The High-Flying Fake	243
Joyce McKinney	Kinky Kidnapper	249
Count Saint-Germain	Ageless Mystery Man	257
Anna Anderson	Romanov Fortune Seeker	265
Maundy Gregory	Honours for Sale	271
Mary Baker	Princess Caraboo	275

Arthur Orton	Tichborne Claimant	283
Phineas T. Barnum	One Born Every Minute	291
The Alchemists	Fool's Gold	299
Virginia Woolf and Friends	The Emperor of Abyssinia	303
Cynthia Payne	Madame Cyn	307
Wilhelm Voigt	Captain of Köpenick	315
Philip Arnold and John Slack	The 'Drunk' Prospectors	319
Reverend Harold Davidson	Into the Lions' Den	323
Giuseppe Balsamo	Count Cagliostro	329
The Trodmore Syndicate	The Race That Never Was	337
Donald Crowhurst	Man Overboard	343
Jim Bakker and Jimmy Swaggart	A Fall From Grace	347

INTRODUCTION

'You can fool all the people some of the time, and some of the people all the time, but you can't fool all the people all of the time.'

That quotation is properly attributed to President Abraham Lincoln. But, true to the nature of the characters in this book, it was later stolen by Phineas T. Barnum, one of the greatest tricksters of all time. The flamboyant showman was certainly not shy in claiming the words as his own. And in Barnum's case, just as in all the others in these pages, no quote better describes the art of deception.

Eventually all hoaxers, fraudsters and tricksters are exposed and sometimes caught. But not before they have succeeded in making a fool of someone, and gaining from the victim's downfall. And the richer or more self-important the victim, the easier to dupe.

Tricksters rely on that constant human frailty – GREED. A fool and his money are easily parted. A greedy fool is an even better bet for the confidence trickster. But those who are already wealthy yet desire to have even more are the conman's prime target.

There are, of course, other powerful motives for those

XIV ◀■ THE STING

who roam on to the wrong side of the law. Lust is a strong one. Laziness is another. Ambition often plays a part. And many illicit acts are committed for no other reason than a driving sense of adventure. These various motives link the disparate bunch of characters in this book. Gathered together here is an array of rascally conmen, artful tricksters, fantastic fakers and roguish pranksters. And there are some even less savoury characters who fall into the category of outright vagabonds and villains.

In this latter category are the crafty crooks who, when it comes to crime, think BIG! For them, acquiring wealth or notoriety means leading a life that many of us can sometimes only secretly envy. They may be villains but their exploits are remembered long after their more virtuous victims are forgotten.

For it is not so much what they do but the style in which they do it. As Robert Louis Stevenson said: 'The Devil, depend upon it, can sometimes do a very gentlemanly thing.' The characters brought together in this book have, contrary to appearances, all proved themselves less than gentlemen or ladies. They may not be honourable or honest. Indeed, in some cases their nefarious activities are quite reprehensible. Yet their deeds – whether dark, deceitful or dastardly – are often the very essence of enterprise and adventure.

They have one thing in common: the astonishingly brazen way in which they have pulled off their various crimes while pulling the wool over the eyes of the rest of us. It would be wrong to condone their antics but it is impossible not to admire their artifice.

From Joyce McKinney, the happy hooker who kidnapped a lover and conned a court, to the mystery men who ran a horse race without a single horse; from ancient alchemists who claimed to have the Midas touch, to the greediest gold-diggers of the Wild West; from the wily woman who fooled the world that she was a princess, to the conniving count who sold the Eiffel Tower not once but twice – they're all phoneys or philanderers who had a field day.

Together they make up an astonishingly diverse gallery of the World's Most Cunning Conmen, Fraudsters, Vagabonds and Villains, the World's Most Artful Fakers, Forgers, Charlatans and Cheats, and the World's Most Daring Rascals, Rogues, Interlopers and Impostors.

Cunning Conmen, Fraudsters, Vagabonds and Villains

PETER FOSTER
WILY WIZARD OF OZ

If Peter Foster did not exist, it would be hard for anyone to invent him, even as a character in fiction; the role would be just too implausible. And yet someone has to be holder of the inglorious title 'The World's Greatest Living Conman' and that dishonour deservedly belongs to Peter Clarence Foster, an affable but, at first sight, unimpressive Australian who somehow has the gift to persuade even the most sceptical and cynical individuals to part with their natural caution – and ultimately their money.

Foster's craft is seemingly effortless, which is the mark of a great confidence trickster. While appearing not to have a care in the world, he will be coolly, cunningly, perfectly planning a plot to ensnare his next victim. No detail is too small and no target too big for him. He has hoodwinked get-rich-quick merchants, charity workers, prisoners in jail, warders in charge of them, shopkeepers, hotels, credit-card companies, beautiful models, hard-headed businessmen, lawyers and politicians. At the pinnacle of his career, he even sucked Britain's Prime Minister and his family into his web of deceit. And it was all done so effortlessly, with a cheeky smile and a merry quip, a glass of champagne in hand.

Peter Foster, it has to be said, is a likeable guy. The king of conmen generally holds court surrounded by his old cronies back home on Australia's Gold Coast, the glittering Queensland holiday haunt of bikini-clad beauties and bleached-haired surfers. Foster could have been one of the latter but his ambition drove him at an early age away from the golden beaches and into the wheeler-dealering backstreets of the town of Surfers Paradise. He could have become a respectable businessman, rich through honest dealings, but that was not his way. 'It's not that he couldn't make a living out of running a legitimate business,' says an old school friend. 'It was just more fun for him to try to beat the system. He's a likeable bastard really.'

Former friends at Aquinas Catholic College on the Gold Coast, where the young Peter was 'heavily into horse racing', recall the family returning from a trip to the Philippines with 15-year-old Peter laden down with fake designer watches to sell to classmates. That was the start of his career as a conman.

He promoted pop concerts and boxing bouts but fell foul of the law in 1983, when he was fined £75,000 for trying to defraud an insurance company out of £40,000, and the following year, when he was declared bankrupt after trying to market a 'magic' method of quitting smoking. With his reputation sullied in Australia, he sought a broader stage for his grand game and in January 1986, at the age of 24, he flew to Britain seeking to ride to riches on someone else's coat tails. His unwitting target was no less than the country's most desired pin-up, Samantha Fox, famous at the time for her nubile body, which graced the pages of tabloid newspapers, calendars and posters.

He wooed and won Sam, not just to make himself the most envied lover boy in Britain but also because he needed a celebrity sponsor to launch his latest 'miracle' slimming potion, Bai Lin Tea. He signed her up to promote the dodgy brew, she fell in love with him and over the next 10 years they travelled the world in style, from Australia to Tokyo to Africa's safari country. He bought her jewellery, a sporty car and a magnificent home and claimed to be deeply in love with her but the cheat was seeing other women on the side. When Sam found out, she dumped him, later referring to him only as 'the Rat'.

Foster's company, Slimweight, ended up in voluntary liquidation after Bai Lin Tea was labelled a sham by TV hostess Esther Rantzen on her top-rated show *That's Life*. But he bounced back with a new diet scam, hiring Britain's 1998 Young Slimmer of the Year, Michelle Deakin, to back the new product. Nineteen-year-old Michelle was persuaded to launch the Deakin Diet by claiming that she had won her title by taking Foster's cheap pills filled with guar gum. The naive Liverpool girl fell for his soft sell after he wooed her with champagne parties, rides in his Rolls-Royce and flights in a private jet. But her claim to have lost weight through the conman's pills was a lie.

As Foster faced trial on trades description charges and the Bai Lin venture collapsed, he fled to Australia in 1987 and settled in the Golden Gate apartments in Surfers Paradise, Queensland. With him was his mother, Louise Polleti, whom many of those who know Foster believe is the only woman he is really close to. 'She is a fearsomely strong character and has total influence over him,' says an Australian journalist who knows them. 'She treats him as her little boy and, to her, he can do no wrong.'

An ex-friend of the family adds: 'Louise runs Peter's life for him and he hardly makes a move without his mother's say-so. When they are together they bicker all the time but when apart they are on the phone constantly.'

Louise Polleti, who is of Italian extraction, is long separated from the conman's father, Clarence 'Clarrie' Foster, who ran a Queensland hotel before the couple divorced. After Foster senior died in 1998, his widow would vie with her son to get through as much money as possible. The pair regularly fall out over money, which the mother manages to blow in casinos at an even swifter rate than her son can spend it on wine, women and song.

When living in Surfers Paradise, Foster even has to hide his cash to stop his mother stealing it. According to a former friend and neighbour, he began secreting undeclared money from his various scams in a tin in the garden, wrapping it in a plastic bag and burying it in the flower beds. On one occasion Louise Polleti knew he had $A35,000 in cash and pleaded with her son to give it to her so that she could go gambling. When he refused, she pretended to go shopping but instead crossed the broad Nerang River, which flowed past their rented mansion, and sat with a pair of binoculars on the far bank. Three hours later Foster emerged to dig up the tin, add some extra cash and bury it again. The next time he looked in it, it was empty. His mother had gambled and lost the lot.

This cheating and stealing from one another can work both ways, as we shall shortly see, for Foster once got his mother jailed by gambling away money set aside to pay a fine she faced. Most of the time, however, Louise is immensely supportive of her son in his dodgy dealings. She was particularly proud when he made untold millions out of selling Bai Lin Tea franchises in Britain, taking £5,000 from each of about 100 would-be distributors before the pyramid-selling scam collapsed with debts of £700,000. Mother and son celebrated with an unprecedented spending spree.

In 1989 Foster turned up in California, establishing a base in Beverly Hills to peddle another useless slimming product, Chow Lo Tea. Having run up huge advertising debts and served four months in jail for false claims, he again went on the run. After persuading the Australian consulate in Los Angeles to issue him with a passport, he flew to the Caribbean, then to Australia, much to the annoyance of LA city attorney Jim Hahn, who described him as 'a con artist peddling snake oil'.

Back in Queensland, Foster devised Biometrics Contour Treatment, which he claimed shrank girls' thighs. He sold a string of franchises before (and after) the Trade Practices Commission banned his business, accusing him of misleading and deceptive conduct.

Foster was now running out of places to which to flee. In 1994 he returned to Britain, supposedly 'to wipe the slate clean' over his previous UK diet scams, including Bai Lin Tea, and pay two outstanding fines, each of about £25,000, one against himself and one against his mother as chairman of one of his companies. He paid only his own and spent the rest on gambling, women, wining and dining.

He very publicly kissed and made up with Samantha Fox, saying that 'letting her go was the biggest mistake I ever made'. According to Foster, he resumed his affair with her and even planned marriage – claims which shocked Fox fans because since their last romance she had given up nude modelling, started a singing career and a lesbian relationship and had become a born-again Christian. Whether or not his nuptial plans for Ms Fox were genuine, the playboy's hidden agenda was to involve her in his next diet scam. Sam was having none of it and the rekindled romance quickly fizzled out.

Other products were dreamed up. There was Thigh Tone

1, then Body Right Pro, which Pamela Anderson, star of American TV series *Baywatch*, was conned into backing. A video was made with a shaky hand-held camera in which Pamela appeared to support the product, and this was about to be used to persuade British punters to buy distributorships when police again pounced. Foster was remanded in custody on the earlier Deakin Diet offences under the Trades Description Act.

At Liverpool Crown Court in January 1996 he was told by the judge: 'I have formed a very unfavourable view of you as someone whose champagne lifestyle meant that, as long as you cut a dash or make a splash, you were happy to do so. It may fairly be said that the party is now over.'

In fact the party was only just beginning, although it did not look like it at the time to Foster. Sentenced to two years jail, after which he was to be deported, he was incarcerated in Liverpool's ultra-tough Walton Prison and later in the fortress-like Winson Green, Birmingham. His mother immediately flew from Australia to comfort her son in jail but never got past Heathrow Airport. When Polleti's plane touched down, she was arrested for non-payment of her £25,000 fine and spent four weeks, including Christmas, in Holloway Prison. She was eventually freed after her other child, Jill, organised a whip-round back in Queensland.

Forgiven by his doting mother, Foster launched an appeal which reduced his two-year sentence to 18 months so that, with remission, he needed to serve only nine months. Happily for him, he was moved to Sudbury Open Prison, Derbyshire, where his tales of sun, fun and sex in the fast lane made his fellow inmates green with envy – though later they were red with rage after he took some of them for a ride with his phoney promises.

Foster was regularly allowed out with a prison officer to

raise funds for the jail's own anti-drugs charity, Outreach, but in August 1996 he walked through the gates and never returned. Why he should go on the run only 10 days before he was due to be freed was at first a mystery. The answer, it was later revealed, was that he feared fresh fraud charges were being prepared against him in relation to Thigh Tone 1.

His disappearance from Sudbury was a severe embarrassment for prison officers who had trusted him to work outside the jail on their Outreach scheme. It was damaging to former inmates whom he had persuaded to work for him on his next planned diet scam and who now feared their parole would be cancelled. It was financially disastrous to businessmen whom he had already persuaded to hand over money for the project, including, astonishingly, a fellow prisoner at Sudbury who had given him £13,000. And it could have been highly embarrassing for Samantha Fox — because Foster had spent his time in jail penning his 'prison diaries'.

In this racy version of his life story, he claimed that he had reformed and was now a man of honour. But the diaries went on to describe in intimate detail many of the sexual delights in which he and Fox had indulged. The diaries had to be salacious because he planned to sell them, but he failed to complete them before going on the run, first to Ireland and then to Australia, where he was jailed for five months for entering the country on a false passport and inducing witnesses to give false evidence. The judge in the case, heard at Southport District Court on the Gold Coast, appeared to sympathise with the conman, as ever in contrite and charming mood. Judge John Newton praised his initiative and said: 'As an entrepreneur you have attempted to develop a number of business projects which seem to offer a great deal of scope for success.' He even offered his 'best wishes' for the jailbird's next supposed venture, Outreach Australia, a project to teach children the dangers of drugs and keep them from a life of crime – an idea he had conveniently borrowed from the warders he had conned at Sudbury. For his part, Foster promised, tongue presumably firmly in cheek, that he would 'endeavour to use my period of incarceration constructively and for the benefit of the community as a whole'.

Of course, as soon as he was released he went back to his old tricks. But why did he bother? Why not settle for an honest life as a legitimate businessman, as Judge Newton had suggested? The answer is supplied by Foster himself, who once told a buddy: 'The money's great but the buzz comes with knowing you've pulled off the sting. It's better than sex.' That motivation is in the character of many of the great confidence tricksters of history. For it is the thrill of the sting that drives them, even more than the ill-gotten rewards. It is the mastery of mind games that makes a conman tick. And, on the evidence of former friends, acquaintances, business partners and lovers, Foster is the most persuasive conman they have ever met.

A lawyer who once had dealings with him says that before a visit by Foster he would arrange for a secretary to call him out of his office on a pretext. 'I had to leave the room and shake my head,' he says. 'I reckon I'm a fairly cynical man and experience has made me a good judge of character but if I listened to Foster for too long, even I started to believe him.'

A former business partner says: 'He has a hypnotic effect on people he's trying to sell himself to. He never has any trouble getting the promise of backing from normally hard-headed businessmen. His effect on more trusting people can be devastating. He'll take their money, cheat them and ruin their lives without a qualm. He doesn't stab them in the back, he smiles them in the back.'

Another ex-partner who got to know how the conman worked says that he will always bounce back. 'Peter is a great collector of information and always plans for the future. His schemes have turned to dust so often in the past that he has learned always to have a contingency plan. For instance, while living with Sam Fox he got hold of all the details of her father Pat's secret Channel Islands bank account, where, as her manager, he had squirrelled away much of Sam's earnings from modelling and from her later singing career. He will have somehow used that to his own advantage, that's for sure.'

All of which makes it beyond belief that when Foster next arrived in Britain, he was allowed to get close to the highest seat of power in the land, to trick his way into the confidence of Number 10 Downing Street and to be on first-name terms with the Prime Minister's family. It was the peak of his career as a conman.

The fraudster made front-page news day after day in late 2002 after he embroiled Tony Blair and his wife Cherie, a leading barrister, in serious allegations of political sleaze. It emerged that Foster had become the lover of Cherie's closest confidante, her indispensable fashion and lifestyle guru Carole Caplin, and had taken on the role of Mrs Blair's part-time financial adviser. He had used his negotiating skills to purchase two apartments for the Blairs, at a bargain price, in an upmarket development in Bristol.

At first, few could believe that the Prime Minister and his wife could have allowed a conman such control over their private affairs, but strenuous denials from Downing

Street were soon seen to be a smokescreen as documents proved the closeness of Foster's relationship with the couple at the same time as he was using this prestigious connection to entice investors to sink money into his latest dubious slimming venture.

The scam was devilishly clever. Foster had known of Caplin's link to the Prime Minister before even meeting her. She was a regular visitor to Downing Street and had even holidayed with the Blairs abroad. She conducted Cherie in fitness workouts and alternative therapy sessions and even chose her clothes. Within three days of Foster engineering an introduction to Caplin at a trendy Chelsea coffee bar in July 2002, the 39-year-old conman and the 42-year-old former topless model were lovers. 'She's quite a babe,' Foster told a pal, 'but, more importantly, she knows the Blairs.'

Soon he was boasting to new British investors in his company Renuelle that he was on target to secure the Prime Minister's support for a healthy lifestyle programme aimed at schools. The Children's Education Programme was to be a national tour organised by Renuelle to warn youngsters about the dangers of obesity. With government backing, Foster knew it would win Renuelle instant credibility – enabling him to market his latest quack diet pill, Trimit, through a network of franchises. He sent this email to ex-soccer star Paul Walsh, 40, who had invested £75,000 in Renuelle: 'Carole spoke to Cherie Blair on Wednesday and told her exactly what we want Tony to do with you and the Children's Education Programme. She thinks it's great. Cherie has a lot of influence over him. Carole and I are proposing to discuss it with his eldest son Euan on Monday. We want him and Cherie to get behind it so it is the whole family who tell him what a great idea it is.'

Foster was also exchanging emails of a far more damaging nature – with Cherie Blair herself. Just three months after meeting Carole Caplin, he had so ingratiated himself with the Prime Minister's wife that he was handling the purchase of two £297,000 apartments for her, one for the use of her 18-year-old student son Euan and the other as an investment. The wheeler-dealer invoked the Blairs' name to haggle down the price of the properties by £69,000 and arranged to pick up the legal bill for the purchases.

When news of these negotiations broke, Downing Street spin doctors went into overdrive to play down the connection between the convicted conman and the leading barrister who just happened to be the Prime Minister's wife. But protestations from Number 10 were silenced by the record of a string of emails that had already passed between Foster and Mrs Blair at the time of the negotiations in October. Conveniently released to a newspaper 'from a source in Australia', they made dynamite reading. 'We weren't looking to buy the property but steal it,' Foster told Cherie. Another email read: 'I have spoken to [a property manager] and he will jump through hoops for you. I have reduced his fee. I will keep the pressure on him to perform in double-quick time.' And cosily: 'Let me know if I can be of service. Your pleasure is my purpose – Peter.'

Signing herself 'Cherie', the PM's wife replied: 'I cannot thank you enough, Peter, for taking over these negotiations for me. I really appreciate it.' Other emails assured him that 'we certainly are on the same wavelength' and 'you're a star'.

The emails did not surface until December, by which time many of the investors in Trimit pills were becoming impatient and demanding the repayment of their stakes of

£25,000 upwards. By now Foster was fighting a legal battle against his deportation – which he claimed Cherie Blair was helping him overturn. Indeed, his case papers were faxed to Downing Street for her perusal.

The allegations were seen as so dangerous by the British government that, in an unprecedented move, Cherie Blair was forced to take the stage for a televised address to the nation in which, her voice breaking with emotion, she attempted to win sympathy by portraying herself as a normal working mother trying to cope with a busy life. 'I'm not superwoman,' she declared. 'The reality of my daily life is that I'm juggling a lot of balls in the air: trying to be a good wife and mother, trying to be the Prime Minister's consort at home and abroad, a barrister and a charity worker – and sometimes some of the balls get dropped.' At one point she wept as she explained that she was somehow trying to protect her son by negotiating for the apartments but the verdict of most newspapers the following day was that hers was a sob story rather than the proper explanation expected of a tough £300,000-a-year legal eagle.

In the midst of all this, Carole Caplin, having revealed that she was pregnant by Foster, lost the baby. She nevertheless bravely (or foolishly) invited TV cameras into her home to film what turned out to be her boyfriend's last days in Britain. In the resulting documentary, *The Conman, His Lover and the Prime Minister's Wife*, Foster spoke about the furore over the Blairs' apartments, saying: 'I think Cherie has handled a bad situation atrociously and she let it get out of hand.' Asked if she had lied, he added: 'Yeah, yeah, she has.' An even more uncomfortable piece of viewing for Downing Street was when Tony Blair left a midnight message on Miss Caplin's answer machine, beginning: 'Hi, it's Tony calling ...'

There were other interesting phone calls at around this time, between Foster and his mother, who was renting an apartment in Ireland. Somehow the calls were bugged, transcribed and passed to a newspaper. In them, a petulant Foster tells Polleti he wants to dish the dirt on the Blairs for £100,000, saying: 'I should try to get some money out of this, shouldn't I? I'll do a story but I'll do it only for money. I'm wanting to get paid. I've lost, I've got lawyers' fees, I've got PR nightmares, I'm an absolute f****** pariah. I've suffered losses and I've suffered damages. I may as well get something out of this. I'm f*****, my reputation is f*****.'

Shortly after the revealing phone calls, Foster left Britain for Dublin to join his mother briefly before being deported to Australia. His parting shot to the Blairs was: 'Some say power corrupts and maybe power changes people.' But the person who changed most was Peter Foster. Having quit Britain in a fit of self-pity, he brightened up when he hit the Gold Coast and threw himself into a round of carousing with his old mates. His vows of undying love for Carole Caplin were soon forgotten as he romped with two shapely new girlfriends. In a Surfers Paradise bar in March 2003 he was heard taking a call from Carole on his mobile phone. He spoke earnestly to her for a few minutes before ending the conversation with the words 'Trust me, Carole' – then turning back to the semi-clad blonde in his lap.

In 2004, Foster began hyping an autobiography he said he was writing, 'telling the truth' about his relationship with Miss Caplin and the Prime Minister's family. 'The Blairs should be worried,' he said. Boastful bombast? Not necessarily, say friends who know how the conman's mind works. As a former close associate warns: 'He repaid Sam Fox's loyalty by writing secret diaries giving graphic details of their sex life together. He is quite capable of peddling his story of his sex life with Carole Caplin in the same way. He may even have video records of their love making. He had secret videos which he took of himself and Sam Fox on many occasions. When Sam discovered the tapes, she went ballistic. He promised to destroy them. I doubt he ever did. He is most likely to have kept them to show off to his Aussie mates.'

Miss Caplin must have wondered whether, as a result of trusting her glib-tongued lover, history could repeat itself. And what of the Blairs? The scene in No 10 Downing Street must at times have been one of panic following Foster's involvement in their affairs. Tony and Cherie Blair would have been well advised to check their bank accounts, cut up their credit cards and change their email addresses. For they could not begin to guess what valuable and sensitive information about themselves might have been gleaned by the man Cherie termed her 'star' via his affair with her most trusted soulmate.

'Foster wheedles information out of people and files it away for the right moment,' says the ex-associate. 'He has a computer-like memory and will quietly calculate how he can make use of it all. He knew of Caplin's Downing Street connections before he even met her, so, from the moment they began their affair, he would have been poring over any diaries, correspondence, even itemised telephone bills she might have left lying around. Anything involving the Blairs would be filed away in his mind for future use. Just look at the way he subsequently used their names as part of his Trimit diet scam.'

Foster will be keeping all his information on Cherie Blair on a 'killer CD', adds the ex-associate. 'That's what he always does. The CD will contain a dossier of highly sensitive material. It will be much more than the Blairs or Caplin ever imagined.

'He will do anything to advance himself and will sacrifice anyone else along the way. Every time something goes wrong, Peter believes he is the victim. But he is convinced that eventually his destiny is to be a leader on the world stage. He told me his long-term aim was to find a small country, probably among the Pacific islands, and offer his expertise to its leader to boost that country's economy. He would do this for nothing in return for being granted ambassadorial status, so that he could hobnob with world politicians and travel the globe with diplomatic immunity.

'Peter expected to achieve these aims with the leader of some banana republic. Even in his wildest dreams, he could not have believed that it would be so easy to gain such an influence over the Blairs. It is Britain he has treated like a banana republic.'

CHARLES VAN DOREN
QUIZ SHOW CHEAT

For a brief period in the late 1950s, a respectable, clean-cut, all-American TV quiz show host called Charles Van Doren was the most popular star in the United States. 'Charles who?' would be the question today. Yet for 10 months in 1957, Mr Van Doren got higher ratings than even the King of Rock, Elvis Presley.

Van Doren certainly had the brains to be successful. He was the son of poet Mark Van Doren and mother Dorothy, a novelist and editor of a political magazine. His uncle, Carl, was a Pulitzer Prize-winning biographer. Young Charles did them all proud. At the age of 30 he was a respected lecturer at New York's Columbia University. But that was not enough for the ambitious egghead who got hooked on fame and fortune. Van Doren's brilliant mind gained him an invitation to become a contestant on a popular television quiz show of the time, *Twenty-One*. In a formula that has been often emulated, contestants on the programme would be placed in a soundproof box to isolate them from the studio audience. The hopeful entrants would then be bombarded with quiz questions, the answers to which became increasingly difficult.

To start with, Van Doren seemed like just another

contestant, most of whom lasted only a few weeks before flunking too many of the questions. But, week after week, he came up trumps. His reign seemed to go on and on, as he accumulated an ever-growing mountain of cash. More importantly to the TV company bosses, he also accumulated a vast following of fans. A weekly audience of millions were hooked on *Twenty-One*. Van Doren's happy smile shone out from the cover of every magazine, from fanzines to the influential *Time*. His phenomenal power of recall was studied by psychologists. His brilliant intellect was the envy of educators and the bane of college dunces.

Van Doren did not make his role look easy, however. After quizmaster Jack Barry had asked him a particularly difficult question, his brow would furrow. Beads of sweat would build on his temple as he stared intently at the floor, trying to pluck the answer from his whirling brain cells. Seconds would pass and seem like minutes. These moments of apparent mental torture made the show the astounding success that it became. Every week the same team of Jack Barry and Charles Van Doren would have the audience at home and in the studio perched on the edge of their seats as the tension built to its inexorable climax. Every week, as the last crucial question was correctly answered, the quizmaster would shout 'Correct' and the audience would howl with delight. Every show would end with Van Doren victorious.

After an incredible 15-week run, Charles Van Doren had won more than $75,000 worth of prizes, a small fortune in those days. But it was not such a feat after all – because before he went on air he had been supplied with every answer. Even his nail-bitingly slow responses had all been carefully rehearsed. Charles Van Doren, the all-American hero, was a cheat and a fraud.

It had not always been so. When he was first invited on to the show, Van Doren greeted with disdain the suggestion that he be given clues to the answers. The producer was persuasive, however. He pandered to Van Doren's vanity and told him that, by 'helping glamorise intellectualism', he could do a great service to the youth of America. Like a drug addict, once he had begun to cheat, Van Doren found that there was no turning back. After all, it was a scam in which no one was getting hurt. Everyone made money and the public were ecstatic.

Van Doren's synthetic reactions to the questions put to him were so well acted that he almost got away with the fraud. It wasn't a television watchdog who caught him out, however; it was one of his fellow contestants. Joseph Stempel had been invited on to the show before Van Doren's first appearance and had been equally successful. That was because Stempel, a 30-year-old New Yorker, had also been supplied with the answers. When Van Doren joined him on the show, the producers and advertisers found that the university lecturer's clean-cut image was more popular with the audience.

Stempel was told his time was up and that he would have to give a wrong answer and bow out. Astonishingly, he agreed. But, as he watched his former rival stashing away a small fortune week after week, he changed his mind. He reported the quiz show's shameful secret. Stempel said: 'I was so depressed and disgusted. I just didn't want to have anything to do with the show. I got tired of being in the shadows. Once I saw Van Doren I knew my days on the show were numbered. He was tall, thin and "waspy". I was this Bronx Jewish kid. It was as simple as that.'

The press, the public and, of course, rival television stations were outraged. Even President Dwight D.

Eisenhower publicly condemned the cynical deception. He ordered an investigation by the Justice Department and Van Doren was interrogated by a grand jury. At first he lied through his gleaming teeth. But when faced with the might of a Congressional subcommittee, he broke down and confessed all, saying: 'I would give almost everything to reverse the course of my life. I have deceived my friends – and I had millions of them. The producer, Albert Freedman, told me that giving help to contestants was part of showbusiness. I was deeply troubled by the arrangement. As time went on, the show ballooned beyond my wildest dreams. To a certain extent, this went to my head.'

Charles Van Doren's reputation was utterly ruined. Congress passed the so-called 'Stempel Laws', making fraud by television a criminal offence. Van Doren escaped a prison sentence but he lost his post with Columbia University and found himself snubbed by other leading institutions. He got a job as a researcher-writer for *Encyclopaedia Britannica*, where he remained for 28 years. As a reclusive author, he never again spoke of the *Twenty-One* scam.

One man who tried to make him talk was movie actor and director Robert Redford. As a 20-year-old student at the American Academy of Dramatic Art in New York, Redford had been one of the TV show's enthralled millions – not because he enjoyed quiz shows but because he was convinced Van Doren was a second-rate actor.

In a telling reflection of what the Van Doren story meant to him, Redford said: 'As I watched him come up with these incredible answers, the actor in me said: "I don't buy it." But what is weird is that I never doubted the integrity of the show. I merely accepted that Van Doren was guilty of a poor performance. That's no crime. I did not ask myself why he was doing it. He might have been hamming it up but he was giving education a good name, setting a fine example to the nation's youth. Elvis Presley was the dark-haired nightmare that every respectable parent prayed their daughter would not bring home. Charles Van Doren was the fair-haired and clean-cut man of their dreams. It did not occur to any of us that this paragon was cheating. The producers were feeding him the answers and rehearsing his tortured appearances. That scandal marks the moment when America began its slow journey towards scepticism and distrust, especially of politicians and the media. As long as we kept being entertained, who cared about decency and morality? Van Doren suffered public humiliation while everyone else connected with the show moved merrily on to their next project. He was only as bad as the people feeding him the answers.'

Twenty-five years after watching *Twenty-One* on his black-and-white TV set, Redford decided to make a movie about the scam. It was to be titled *Quiz Show*, with English actor Ralph Fiennes being given the leading part and Charles Van Doren being offered a role as consultant. The aged academic turned the proposal down flat. Frustrated that he could not study the character he was to portray, Fiennes travelled to Cornwall, Connecticut, and knocked on the door of the retirement home of Charles Van Doren. Posing as a lost tourist, he managed to have a five-minute chat with the reclusive ex-contestant.

Charles Van Doren was still the charming, smiling intellectual with the Ivy League accent. Despite his disgrace, he did not seem to have suffered financially from his 25 years in the wilderness. For, after his brief but celebrated career as a television star, no one had ever asked the flawed quiz king to hand back his prize money.

CHARLES INGRAM
'MILLIONAIRE' MAJOR

Fortunes have been won and lost with alacrity in the murky world of crime, but none so fleetingly as that bestowed upon British Army officer Charles Ingram. To the riotous applause of a TV studio audience, Major Ingram was handed a cheque for £1 million by quiz show host Chris Tarrant, only to have it snatched back moments later. The major's fame and fortune were replaced by ignominy and ruin because of another, more annoying sound from the audience – a series of coughs.

The coughs had been persistent throughout the climax of Tarrant's hit show *Who Wants To Be A Millionaire?*, the success of which had seen its format exported all over the world. Like all contestants who had got that far, Ingram had had to answer 15 multiple-choice questions to reach the magic million and a wrong answer along the way would have cost him dear. The major did not fail on any of them, even when they became incredibly difficult.

He correctly attributed the painting *The Ambassadors* to Holbein and won himself £125,000. To double it, he had to answer the question: 'What type of garment is an Anthony Eden?' and did so correctly, identifying it as 'a hat'. For £500,000, Tarrant asked him: 'Baron Haussmann is best known for the planning of which city?', to which Ingram answered: 'Paris.' Which brought him to the magic million-pound question: 'A number 1 followed by 100 zeros is known by what name?' The four alternative answers offered were: (a) Googol, (b) Megatron, (c) Gigabit and (d) Nanomol. The major took his time as the audience held its breath. He could stop right there and safely walk away with £500,000. Or he could risk a wrong response which would lose him all but £32,000 of his gains so far. Ingram puzzled aloud, evaluating each possible answer. Finally he plumped for '(a) Googol'.

Chris Tarrant delayed confirming whether he was right or wrong, to build up the tension for the millions of viewers whom he assumed would shortly be watching the pre-recorded show. Then he stood up, hugged Ingram and handed him his seven-figure cheque. Unbeknown to the show's host, however, suspicions had already been raised that the coughs from the audience were a series of secret codes which had been prompts to help Ingram reach his goal. The major was asked to hand back his cheque – and that was the last he saw of it.

The man who was a millionaire for only a few minutes had never looked destined for the limelight. The son of an RAF wing commander and a successful theatre designer, he had watched his elder brother become a commander in the Royal Navy and his sister a high-flying accountant, but he himself had shown only moderate academic ability. He followed his father and brother into the armed forces, joining the Royal Engineers, then married a former college girlfriend, Diana Pollock, in 1989. Diana gave her husband the resolve that the affable but fairly directionless Charles seemed to have lacked. She was ambitious for his career but army pay gave them little chance to better their circumstances and, after having three daughters, the couple found themselves £50,000 in debt and without a home of their own, since they had always been housed in service quarters. The ambitious Diana decided that, if they couldn't earn their way to a grander lifestyle, they would simply have to win one.

Along with her brother Adrian, Diana Ingram became obsessed with becoming a contestant on the current hit TV quiz show *Who Wants To Be A Millionaire?*. They bombarded the TV company's premium-rate phone lines to gain a place on the show and even practised on a mock keyboard to maximise their chances of getting through the preliminary 'fastest finger first' round. Their perseverance paid off and in 2001 Adrian and then Diana appeared as contestants, each winning £32,000.

It was not enough to pay the Ingrams' debts or satisfy their greed. Diana came up with the idea of writing a book called *Win A Million*, containing tips for getting on to the show, strategies for boosting the chances of winning and typical quiz questions to learn by heart. She approached London publisher John Blake, who described her as 'fanatical about the show' and agreed to publish the guide. Before that could happen, however, Diana's husband got himself a place on the show – and the most public fraud of the century was under way.

Major Ingram was in many ways a perfect contestant when in September 2001 he won the chance to sit in the same seat that his wife had occupied earlier in the year. Chatty and ebullient, he laughed and joked with quizmaster Tarrant as he correctly answered the early, simpler questions, doubling his money from £100 to £200 and ever upwards. By the time he got to the £8,000 question, however, floor managers working for the programme makers, Celador, were already warning senior executives that 'something strange was going on'. A camera was kept trained on Diana Ingram, sitting high up in the audience. By the £32,000 question, unaware that her every move was being recorded on videotape, she coughed twice to signal the answer to the £32,000 question: 'Who had a hit with "Born To Do It"?' The major had initially indicated his belief that it was boy band A1 before changing his mind when his wife coughed twice at the correct answer: 'Craig David'.

The next bout of coughing came from a different quarter, however. A fellow contestant, bespectacled college lecturer named Tecwen Whittock, sitting in the front row awaiting his turn in the hot seat just 10 feet away, seemed to be prompting Ingram with his bouts of coughing when the correct answers to the £64,000 and £125,000 questions were mentioned. When the answers to the £250,000 question came up, Whittock coughed three times to signal that an 'Anthony Eden' was a type of hat.

Extraordinary reactions were also being observed by the camera watching Diana Ingram at this time. She appeared to be fuming that her husband was overplaying his hand and that he had gone on beyond the £125,000 question. And she was heard muttering, 'Oh God, don't start', as he launched himself into the £1-million question.

Chris Tarrant was so intent on doing his job that he was wholly unaware of the drama being played out around him. When Ingram correctly answered 'Googol' and cheated his way to the top prize, the TV host hugged the major and beamed: 'You are the most amazing contestant we have ever, ever had. I have no idea how you got there.' Urging the audience into rapturous applause, he added: 'I have no idea what your strategy was; you were so brave. I am so proud to have met you. You are just an amazing human being.'

Tarrant's effusive praise was played back to a court in March 2003 when Ingram, 39, his 38-year-old wife and Tecwen Whittock, 53, all denied that they had 'procured a valuable security by deception' by dishonestly getting Tarrant to sign the £1-million cheque on 10 September 2001. The winning cheque is a genuine one, the court was told, because Tarrant is a signatory to the show's bank account.

Prosecutor Nicholas Hilliard told the jury: 'You may think it inevitable, human nature being what it is, that where a million pounds is regularly on offer someone, somewhere might have thought about how it might be possible to improve their chances of getting their hands on money by cheating. There is a saying that two heads are better than one and two people's general knowledge is likely to be better than one person's. After all, they won't know exactly the same things.'

Mr Hilliard said there was a clear connection between Tecwen Whittock and the Ingram family in the run-up to the major's TV appearance. The lecturer, who pleaded not guilty, insisted that his only contact had been a few telephone calls to Diana seeking tips on how to secure a place on the show, but the court was told that no fewer than 38 calls had been made between Whittock and the Ingrams, the last being just hours before the second part of the programme was recorded, when Whittock was already at the studios awaiting his own turn on the programme.

During that dramatic studio session, Whittock was heard to cough 19 times, many of them just after Ingram, musing aloud about the four suggested options, had repeated the correct answer to the questions. The plan, said Mr Hilliard, was: 'If you know the answer, cough after I say the right option. It's as simple as that.' Whittock later told the production crew that he had a cough before the show started yet, when he got his own turn in the hot seat immediately after the major, his cough disappeared. So, it seems, did his skill at answering the questions – for, humiliatingly, after risking all for Ingram, he himself walked away with only £1,000.

The jury's attention was also drawn to the timely coughing of Diana Ingram when, as in the case of the £32,000 question on pop music, she apparently knew the answer whereas Whittock did not. But the prosecution suggested that the coughing ploy was a back-up to another, more sophisticated plot that had gone wrong. The Ingrams, it was alleged, had practised a high-tech scam in which the correct answers would be sent to the major via four vibrating pagers hidden about his person. The prosecution suggested that the Ingrams' intended deception involved planting a stooge in the audience who would have a mobile phone with the line permanently open to another accomplice outside the studio. This fourth person could hear the questions, look up the answers and send the right responses to the pagers: one bleeper for each of the four multiple-choice answers. Just hours before Ingram went into the hot seat, messages were being sent from the major's mobile to the four pagers, but by the time he appeared on the show the plan had been abandoned as being too risky.

After 22 days in court and still protesting their innocence, Charles and Diana Ingram and Tecwen Whittock were all found guilty but were spared the ignominy of being sent to prison. Whittock was given a suspended jail sentence of one year and was fined £10,000 with £7,500 costs. He subsequently resigned from his job as head of business studies at Pontypridd College in South Wales. The

Ingrams each received an 18-month suspended jail sentence and were fined a total of £30,000 with £20,000 costs.

Passing sentence, Judge Geoffrey Rivlin described the pair as quiz-show addicts and said it was this obsession that had caused them to be overcome with the idea of cheating the system. 'You, Tecwen Whittock, were only too prepared to go along with it,' said the judge. 'As to the shabby schoolboy trick you two men ultimately played, you certainly had no notion that it would result in you, Charles Ingram, going on to win £1 million. But somehow, more by good luck than good management, it did.' Turning to Diana, he added: 'You might be well advised to thank your lucky stars you are not going to prison today, and put aside any childish wishes of bravado that you are entitled to this money.'

The judge's entreaty went unheeded, however. Immediately after their court ordeal, the major and his wife made a further string of television appearances – this time legitimate – to proclaim the unfairness of the verdict. Diana Ingram countered press portrayals of her as a 'Lady Macbeth' character, saying she was no evil schemer leading her husband on but, as a lifelong fan of Chris Tarrant, was simply someone who had seen an opportunity to get her family out of financial difficulties. Her husband told a newspaper that he had considered suicide after the court verdict, knowing that it would mean the end of his army career. He accused TV company Celador of 'ruining our lives', adding that they were now so in debt that they would have to leave their rented home in Easterton, Wiltshire, and find more humble lodgings.

However, the news that a movie about the case was being considered seemed briefly to change the outlook for their future fortunes. The subject matter was, after all, well tested. The rigging of the 1950s US quiz show *Twenty-One* became the hit movie *Quiz Show* in 1994, as we saw in the story of Charles Van Doren. The Ingrams, who crossed the Atlantic for talk shows in the wake of the trial, believed they already stood to make a mint from after-dinner speaking and thought that, with their image glamorised by Hollywood, their earning power could be boosted further. When the canned episode of *Who Wants To Be A Millionaire?* was finally shown in the spring of 2003, 17 million viewers tuned in to watch it in Britain alone. Against all the odds, would the cheating Ingrams become a money magnet after all?

It was not to be. In October 2003, Ingram was convicted at Bournemouth Crown Court of another bit of cheating: an insurance fraud. He had duped one company into insuring his house by failing to declare past claims with another firm, and had then claimed £30,000 for a burglary at his home. He narrowly escaped jail and was given a conditional discharge because Judge Samuel Wiggs said he had 'reflected on the punishment you have brought upon yourself and your dire financial state'. It had been revealed during the case that Ingram, the man who had been a millionaire for a moment, was now £400,000 in debt.

DANIEL FARIES
JAIL CELL TYCOON

Daniel Faries was a petty crook and, judging by the number of times he was caught, not even a very clever one. He spent most of his adult life in houses of correction, where not much seems to have been done to correct him. When he wasn't behind bars, he was leaning on them getting drunk. And when he wasn't drunk, he was drying out.

In March 1986 Danny was halfway through a course of treatment at a clinic in Jacksonville, Florida, when he decided to go back on the booze in a big way. A pal of his was having a party down south in the fleshpots of Miami, so Danny broke out of the clinic, stole a van and hightailed it to where the action was. It was some party. After two days' solid drinking, the shindig degenerated into arguments and brawls. Danny said later that someone handed him a gun and, although he couldn't recall why, he shot his old pal three times in the head. Surprisingly, the victim survived but, when police raided the house and found the trappings of drug-taking, the injured man was questioned and taken to hospital. The following evening police were again called to the house, where they found Danny in the backyard, unconscious and reeking of booze, with the gun in the waistband of his trousers. He readily confessed to the shooting and, when his buddy died in hospital two months later, found himself charged with first-degree murder

For the next four years Danny Faries was locked up in Dade County Jail awaiting trial. They turned out to be the most lucrative years of his life as the failed small-time crook proved himself to be an inspirational entrepreneur, running a multi-million-dollar business from within the prison. His cell had cheap furniture, curtainless windows and bare walls, but it became his 'executive office', where, under the eyes of the guards, he made a fortune from fraud.

Danny shared a dormitory-style cell with up to 30 fellow inmates and, because they were all on remand, they had access to a telephone in the cell. As it says in the Florida Administrative Code, section 33-8.009 (9): 'Each inmate shall be provided with reasonable access to a telephone at reasonable times ...' The battered black telephone provided by the state's prison service was the key to Danny's nefarious trade. It was all he needed to let his fingers do the stealing — the only tool he needed to pull off one of the most fantastic, yet little known, frauds in history.

While he was awaiting trial, Danny's phone was seldom silent as he skilfully used it to defraud credit-card owners. With other people's card details, he ordered goods and services for accomplices on the outside, for his fellow jailbirds, for himself, even for his prison guards. His business, which became known among Miami villains as the Jailhouse Shopping Network, boomed to the tune of $3 million. This is how it worked.

First, Danny would phone his pals and tell them to go 'dumpster diving': underworld slang for rummaging around in skips and rubbish bins looking for discarded credit-card slips. Danny knew how careless people could be with their carbon receipts, which contain the name and number of the cardholder. Armed with the numbers from his 'divers', Danny would then phone the credit-card companies pretending to be a retailer checking on a sale. Thinking it was a genuine enquiry, they would give him the address and the credit limit of the cardholder.

Danny would then call, say, an electrical store and order their most expensive hi-fi, paying over the phone with the credit-card details he had just been given. In case the firm checked, he would ask that the hi-fi be delivered to the cardholder's real address at a particular time. Danny would then call his 'diver' with details of the purchase, the time it was to be delivered and the name and address of the cardholder. At the appointed hour, the 'diver' would hang around outside the address. When the delivery van drew up, he would saunter over and say: 'Hey, I'm Mr So-and-so. That's my new hi-fi you've got there. Thanks a lot.' He would sign for the package, wait till the van had driven off, then head straight for the city, where any one of a thousand 'fences' would give him hard cash for the goods.

The downside was that thousands of shocked credit-cardholders would look at their statements every month and discover they had bought a new TV, a slap-up meal at a top restaurant, an airline ticket to South America or a new Armani suit, courtesy of Danny Faries and his amazing jailhouse shopping fraud. But the scam worked like a dream and, from his 'office' in cell 10 B 3, Danny was becoming on paper a very rich man.

Sometimes, if he wasn't sure of an address, he would have goods delivered to the jail itself. The stores and card companies never checked – although the delivery drivers and prison guards must have raised an eyebrow at the high-class merchandise passing through the prison gates. Danny and his fellow inmates soon became the best-dressed convicts in America, wearing designer jogging suits and flash jewellery. 'Oh yes, sir, I had a bumper business,' Faries told a jail visitor. 'It's so easy to find confederates. I never took more than half. I split half with everybody. I got robbed a lot but you just take it on the chin. Heck, it's all free.'

Even when credit-card companies began to abandon the idea of carbon receipts, Danny had an answer. He formed a network of crooked sales assistants at shops, bars and restaurants and paid them $20 for every card number they gave him. He would get his team to ask the cardholders to jot down their addresses and phone numbers so they could 'check the card's authenticity'. Grateful cardholders were happy to oblige, impressed at such security measures which prevented their precious cards falling into the wrong hands. Little did they know that the information they were providing would be relayed by phone to a cell block in Dade County Jail.

Danny was beginning to look upon himself as a Robin Hood character. He reasoned that the smart cardholder, after the initial shock of seeing his outrageous statement at the end of the month, would promptly contact the authorities and have the offending item struck from his bill. It would be the profit-bloated credit-card companies who would ultimately pick up the tab. Danny's Jailhouse Shopping Network even branched out into the world of philanthropy. He used the stolen credit-card numbers to pledge thousands of dollars to charity – starving children, the homeless, the sick and the aged. All from the phone in his prison cell.

More in his own interests, Danny also ordered up presents for his cellmates and their relatives. If a fellow inmate was unable to celebrate his wedding anniversary because he was locked up, Danny would make sure that his wife got a bunch of roses and a gift of jewellery, bought with some unsuspecting victim's credit card.

Faries subsequently claimed that his guards also got their fair share of his ill-gotten largesse. 'All the correctional officers knew what I was doing,' he told a reporter when the story of his prison business reached the Florida newspapers. 'Their families knew what I was doing because they were receiving gifts on every holiday, birthday and anniversary.' Faries told a CBS television newsman: 'The officers are just working stiffs, they're not making much money, and they're seeing all this stuff going on. They're hearing about Dom Perignon champagne and trips to the Caribbean. So I try to send things at Christmas and on holidays.' The interviewer then asked Faries what it cost the guards. He replied: 'Oh no! Perish the thought. No, sir!'

Jail officials naturally denied accusations about gifts from Faries but there was no secret made of his generosity towards charities. Danny's explanation was that, with nothing to do in his cell but watch television, he would see reports of famine and hunger and would immediately get on the phone to pledge a credit-card donation. He reckoned that, if the victims of his frauds had actually seen the television pictures of famine victims themselves, they'd have made the donation anyway.

The first hiccup in this otherwise smooth operation came in September 1987 when Danny, ever generous with other people's money, decided to hold a party for a group of fellow inmates who were all being released at the same time. Using the credit-card number of a Dr Felix Entwhistle, Danny booked a suite at the luxurious Mayfair House Hotel in downtown Miami. From his cell, the unselfish Danny ordered the best champagne and wall-to-wall call girls for his newly freed chums. And all night they toasted Dr Entwhistle, whose gold card was making the evening possible.

By midnight, however, a member of the hotel staff, concerned at the quality of the guests, who hardly looked like a convention of eminent physicians, decided to check on Dr Entwhistle's credit limit. It amounted to $2,500, which by then had been well and truly spent. The hotel employee found a sober member of the raucous party and suggested that credit had run out. A phone call was made and within minutes an indignant 'Dr Entwhistle' was on the telephone to the hotel's night manager, furious at the treatment of his guests. The credit limit was immediately extended by the fawning night manager, who apologised for spoiling the doctor's party.

Some weeks later the real Dr Entwhistle was equally indignant when he phoned his credit-card company. Following his complaint, Detective Raul Ubieta of the Metro-Dade Police visited the Mayfair House to discover that no one, genuinely, could remember who had signed the bill as the party wound up. There was, however, a hotel record of a phone call made from the suite that night. It was a local number: 5454494. Detective Ubieta dialled the number – and got Dade County Jail, cell 10 B 3.

The game appeared to be up for Danny. A special Metro-Dade Police investigation unit, headed by Ubieta and fellow officer Lieutenant Ross Hughes, moved in on the Jailhouse Shopping Network. They bugged the phone in Danny's cell and recorded all numbers dialled. Ubieta was stunned by the result. 'We'd never seen anything like this,' he said. 'He was making orders all over the place for everybody – airline tickets, video equipment, computers, clothes. The hours he worked were outrageous.'

Sometimes police noticed a sharp decrease in the number of calls. They were worried that Danny might have smelled a rat. But an informant would tell them that the 'Managing Director' of the Jailhouse Shopping Network was high on drugs. Danny had simply taken a day off.

Ubieta and his team would try to intercept the goods Danny had just ordered over the phone. 'I'd call the suppliers and point out to them they had just been the victims of a fraud,' said Ubieta. 'Many of them got angry and said that the card was genuine and that they had checked the address and phone number. They were furious that they were losing trade. I never mentioned to them that the number belonged to Dade County Jail. They would never have believed me.'

Within weeks, evidence against Danny was building up nicely when suddenly the police's case collapsed around their ears. The Dade County Department of Corrections, who understandably had not been informed of the police investigation since some of their officers were on uncomfortably close terms with Danny, organised a search of cell 10 B 3. They found 300 stolen credit-card numbers, with names, addresses, phone numbers and credit limits, requests for merchandise and even the scribbled text of messages to go with flowers ordered over the phone.

The police were furious at the cell shakedown. They had hoped to gain enough evidence to nail not only Danny but also his associates working on the outside and, hopefully, any prison officers who might be on the take from Danny's activities. As it was, they had to cut their losses, consoled that at least they had enough evidence to get a conviction against Danny Faries. After the cell raid they confronted him. 'He was no problem,' an officer recalled. 'He showed us how he did everything. He told us he'd order up lobster dinners from the guards and how they allowed him to get laid during visits.'

After handing over all their statements and evidence to the Florida State Attorney's office, the Metro-Dade Police waited for fraud charges to be brought against Danny. But nothing happened. At first they were told that charges would have to wait pending the outcome of Danny's murder trial. Then, months later, the case against the Jailhouse Shopping Network was suddenly dropped. No official reason was given, although an official in the State Attorney's office was reported as saying: 'There is very little deterrent value in bringing a couple of minor felonies to court when a guy is facing the electric chair.'

In 1989, to the annoyance of the police, the State Attorney's office closed the case once and for all. It said that using the evidence of an accused murderer against prison guards could not lead to a successful prosecution.

Meanwhile, Danny Faries was moved from cell 10 B 3 to cell 104 in the nearby Interim Central Detention Center, where, incredibly, he still had access to a phone. On hearing this, shocked police investigators demanded a meeting with the Department of Corrections, only to be told that there was 'no legal basis for imposing prohibitions or restrictions on inmates' access to a telephone'.

Faries was still in business. In fact, he was delighted with his new office. He had cell 104 to himself and shared the phone with only five other inmates in other cells. He said later: 'About the only difference the move made was to give me some more privacy. I didn't have so many people looking over my shoulder all the time.'

His only problem was that his stock of credit-card numbers had dried up, having been seized from his cell by the prison authorities. So, as he later revealed to viewers of the TV show *Sixty Minutes*, he came up with a new corporate strategy. 'After the raid I still had one hidden card number, written on the bottom of my bunk. It was a woman's card. Regina Donovan was the name. It was a good number and I said, well, here we go – we gotta do something!'

Danny took out an advertisement in the national newspaper *USA Today*, calling himself Regina Donovan Cosmetics. It advertised $90 of top-quality women's cosmetics for the bargain price of $19.95, all credit cards accepted. The conman hired an answering service in New York for a week and the calls flooded in. There were no cosmetics, of course, but the callers dutifully left their names, addresses, card numbers, expiry dates – all the information that Danny needed.

As he explained: 'The girls took the orders, saying: "Thank you for calling Regina Donovan, may we help you and what credit card will we be using today?" They wrote down the number and the expiry date, and at the end of the day I'd call them and they'd have this whole new stack of numbers. It was like a goldmine.' Business boomed and, in a fit of generosity, Danny even ordered an expensive set of weights and workout equipment for the detention centre's gym – on a stolen credit-card number, naturally.

By early 1989 Danny had managed to postpone his murder trial date several times simply by firing one defence lawyer after another. Around this time, however, the TELCO telephone company noticed that the number of long-distance calls made on fraudulent credit-card numbers had increased in southern Florida by a staggering 4,000 per cent. Painstakingly, the company went through the figures and was surprised to discover that no fewer than 1,500 of these calls could be traced to the telephone outside cell 104 of the Interim Central Detention Center in

Dade County. TELCO bypassed both the police and the Department of Corrections and called in the US Secret Service. Danny Faries's Jailhouse Shopping Network was about to go into liquidation.

It took 10 months for federal agents to get the evidence on Danny. During that time they established documentary proof that he had stolen $750,000. But they were convinced that the real figure was nearer $4 million. They raided Danny's cell twice and found thousands of credit-card numbers. One senior agent asked the Department of Corrections why, in the light of the previous police investigation, Danny was still allowed near a phone. He was told that there was an administrative rule that 'this particular class of prisoner in this particular cell block was entitled to access to a telephone'. Rules were made not to be broken.

Danny was locked in his cell 24 hours a day while the Secret Service prepared a case against him. During that time he was allowed to use the phone for only 15 minutes, and then under the strictest supervision. But Danny claimed that business went on as usual. He boasted that he managed to run a telephone wire into his cell from the nursing office next door. Someone smuggled him in a telephone and he rigged the whole thing up to his cell light so that, instead of the phone ringing, the light flashed and the guards were not alerted.

Even Danny Faries could postpone his murder trial no longer. On 16 May 1990, four years after the crime, he was convicted of the first-degree murder of his partying pal and was sentenced to 25 years. Federal agents hauled him off to the Metropolitan Correctional Center in Chicago to await trial on fraud charges. Refusing a defence lawyer and choosing to represent himself in court, he pleaded guilty to one charge of fraud and was given a further five years in jail. Faced with serving his time in a federal prison, Danny suddenly complained of paranoiac visions and went conveniently cuckoo. He was promptly dispatched to Charlotte Correctional Institution near peaceful Fort Myers, on Florida's west coast, where, in the much higher-security state 'psychiatric facility', he claimed to have put the credit-card business behind him. Cynics were not so sure.

Pete Collins is the man who knows more about Daniel Faries than perhaps anyone else. A teacher at Jackson High School who became fascinated by the Faries case, he met Danny and began collating material for a book on the amiable conman. In 1991 the row over lack of action taken to curb Danny's excesses became the subject of an investigation in the *Miami Herald*, principally because of the thorough research of Collins, by now a freelance writer based in Miami. Collins told a TV audience: 'When I was interviewing him you could call him up at any time of the day or night and he would be working around the clock. He was operating in as many as 40 states. There were as many as 150 drop sites, dozens of employees, $750,000 documented in stolen goods – perhaps in reality up to two to four million dollars – and that was just during an 11-month window of his captivity.'

So how did Daniel Faries manage to operate his bizarre one-man crime wave for so long? Asked this question, the man in charge, Director of Dade County Corrections, Lonnie Lawrence commented: 'We don't have a perfect system.'

But, for Faries himself, the system was absolutely perfect. As he said: 'If they put you in a room the size of a bathroom for years at a time with only a telephone, you come up with some pretty inventive stuff because, everything you do, you do through the phone. I feel like I constructed a train, and just darn near anybody can drive a train. You don't have to be terribly intelligent and only marginally capable. Heck, it's on a track. All you have to do is put in the fuel – credit-card numbers – and this train'll go! What I did was not really so smart. And there was certainly nothing very secret about it. It was all pretty wide open. On the outside of my cell door I had Master Card and Visa logos.'

JOHN STONEHOUSE
VANISHING POLITICIAN

He was charming, good-looking and extremely polite. And, oh, that English accent! Mrs Helen Fleming, the 65-year-old receptionist on duty at the beachside office of the luxurious Fontainebleau Hotel, was highly impressed. She would long remember the English gentleman who had strolled casually up to her booth on Miami Beach. Which was precisely his plan.

Before bidding Helen Fleming farewell, the stranger passed the time of day with her and the pair enjoyed a long, uninterrupted chat. He mentioned that his name was John Stonehouse and that he was going for a swim. He wished her good day and she watched as he strolled casually down to the thundering surf, seemingly just another Briton soaking up the Florida sun. Hours later his clothes were found in a neat pile on the sand. Of John Stonehouse there was no trace.

So began one of the most audacious deceptions of the twentieth century. Yet it proved much more than an elaborate con trick. Stonehouse was a Labour Member of the British Parliament with personal debts of around £375,000. His business empire lay in tatters and his personal life – he was attempting to keep both a wife and mistress in tow –

was a constant strain. His attempt to drag himself out of the mire by apparently vanishing off the face of the earth was nothing short of a gigantic political scandal.

Yet, when he had taken his seat as an MP in the House of Commons in 1957, Stonehouse had seemed destined for the very top. After serving his apprenticeship on the back benches, he was talent-spotted by Labour leader Harold Wilson and put on the fast track to promotion, rising from Aviation Minister and Technology Minister to Postmaster General. As a Privy Counsellor, he was entitled to be known as the Right Honourable John Stonehouse. And he was so close to the Prime Minister that Wilson loaned him his private holiday home on the Scilly Isles. He was even tipped as the PM's successor.

When Labour lost to the Conservative Party in the 1970 elections, Stonehouse decided he could not accept either the comparative anonymity or the reduced salary of life on the back benches of the Commons. He began pumping money into a web of companies, including a merchant bank, in a bid to make his fortune. Over the next four years not one of them returned a decent profit. Stonehouse resorted to the oldest trick in the book – switching funds between them to satisfy investors and auditors that all was well.

In his heart, he probably knew it couldn't last, and in early 1974 he got wind that Department of Trade investigators were taking an interest in his companies. Even the political 'old boy' network couldn't help him now and he resolved to take desperate measures in a bid to avoid exposure. He disliked the idea of spending the rest of his life on the run, so there was only one thing for it – he would have to 'die'. Stonehouse decided that only one person should share his secret: his divorced mistress and secretary Sheila Buckley, then 28. The aim was for them to move to New Zealand and live off whatever money he could smuggle out from the wreckage of his businesses.

There was only one snag – he had to have a new identity. To get round this, Stonehouse used a technique described by thriller writer Frederick Forsyth in his classic novel *The Day of the Jackal*. He first tricked a hospital in his Walsall, Staffordshire, constituency to release personal details on two men of his own age who had died recently, Donald Mildoon and Joseph Markham. The 48-year-old MP then obtained copies of their birth certificates and, believing Markham's background was closest to his own, applied for a passport in that man's name. He obtained photo-booth shots of himself wearing glasses and smiling and on the back forged the counter-signature of an MP he knew to be dying of cancer, Neil McBride. The application was rubber-stamped at the Passport Office and on 2 August 1974 Stonehouse picked up his new passport. He now had a dual identity and could switch his name whenever necessary.

Then came the second part of his plan. Over the next three months he opened 27 accounts in his own name and a further nine in the name of Markham or Mildoon. A Swiss bank received one huge cheque credited to Mr Markham while further amounts were quietly channelled via a London account to the Bank of New South Wales. Numerous credit cards were set up in Markham's name using an anonymous address at a downmarket London hotel. To help his cover story, he even set up a company in the name of 'J.A. Markham, export-import consultant'. The only exports it handled were cash and the only customer was Stonehouse.

After a dummy run to America, Stonehouse was ready for the real thing. He left London for Miami on 19

November 1974 with Jim Charlton, deputy chairman of one of his companies. When he failed to return from his swimming trip the following day there seemed little doubt that he had drowned. The message flashed from Miami Beach Police Department to New Scotland Yard read: 'John Stonehouse Presumed Dead.' Of course, they were wrong. After dumping his clothes, the MP had raced up the beach to a ramshackle building where he had hidden a suitcase containing new clothes, cash and false identity papers. He took a taxi to the airport, flew to Hawaii via San Francisco and then called Sheila Buckley to tell her their scheme had worked like a dream.

His optimism was premature, however. Stonehouse arrived in Australia and was soon switching cash from a bank account in Melbourne in the name of Mildoon to one in New Zealand belonging to Joseph Markham. The amounts were more than enough to raise the suspicions of bank officials and soon the police were called in. A tail was put on Stonehouse, who, by 10 December, was beavering away daily, transferring funds between a string of banks. The only brief respite came with a flight to Copenhagen for a tryst with Sheila Buckley.

The net seemed to be closing, yet Stonehouse might still have bluffed his way out had it not been for an unfortunate twist of fate. That autumn police across Australia had been briefed to look out for Lord Lucan, the English peer who had disappeared after murdering his family's nanny. When Victoria State Police asked Scotland Yard for more pictures of Lucan they received some of John Stonehouse too. The missing MP bore a remarkable resemblance to Joseph Markham.

Stonehouse was arrested on Christmas Eve 1974. At first he laughed off the questions about his false identity, but a love note from Sheila Buckley found in his jacket ended the pretence. It read: 'Dear Dum Dums [her pet nickname for her lover]. Do miss you. So lonely. Shall wait forever for you.' Both Sheila and Stonehouse's 45-year-old wife Barbara flew to Australia to be at his side. Barbara quickly returned to the UK to file divorce papers but Sheila stayed on until his extradition in July 1975.

After a 68-day trial the disgraced politician was found guilty on 18 counts of theft, forgery and fraud. He was given a seven-year sentence. His mistress got two years, suspended, for aiding and abetting him. The judge's comments at the end of the trial, that Stonehouse was an 'extremely persuasive, deceitful and ambitious man', mattered little to Sheila Buckley. She waited for him for three years – and through two heart attacks he suffered in prison – to take back a bankrupt and seriously ill man.

They married in secret in 1981 and for the next few years the MP tried his hand in the world of publishing by becoming a thriller writer. He didn't make it big as an author. Perhaps his imagination couldn't compete with the astonishing exploits of the real John Stonehouse. He died, aged 62, in 1989. Sheila said of him: 'I've never met a man like him. John was gentle with everybody and, in particular, with me. I'll miss him forever.'

THÉRÈSE HUMBERT
THE LOCKED CHEST

Peasant farmer Gilbert Aurignac neglected his fields to spend idle days in the cafés of the small town of Beauzelle, drinking himself into a stupor on cheap red wine. He would regale his fellow drinkers with unlikely tales of his family's former glory, of how his real name was d'Aurignac and how he had been disowned by his aristocratic father. But, he said, his two sons and two daughters would inherit vast wealth on his death. Aurignac's oldest child was Thérèse, born in 1860, and she too had heard her father's boastful story, so often that she believed it. When he died in 1874, however, she discovered the truth: she, her sister and two brothers had been left paupers and she would have to take in washing to keep the family fed.

Thérèse soon learned one other truth: that the world is full of gullible people who will believe anything if it is repeated often enough. And although she was no beauty – the provincial washerwoman was as podgy as she was penniless – she had a certain magnetism that would win over the rich and famous. Her charismatic attraction would also gain her a trusting husband and ultimately make her a fortune.

Thérèse took her first steps on her path to riches when she went to work in the nearest city, Toulouse, as a laundry maid at the home of the mayor, an ambitious lawyer and politician named Gustave Humbert. There she allowed herself to be seduced by her boss's son, Frédéric, to whom she wove the most astonishing story. As a youngster, she said, she had attracted the attention of a rich spinster named Mademoiselle de Marcotte. Now very old and without any surviving relatives, this venerable lady had written a will bequeathing her entire estate, including its chateau and vineyards, to Thérèse. Frédéric believed every word of her tale, fell madly in love with her and, despite the protestations of his father, secretly married her.

Frédéric took Thérèse to Paris, where he launched a career as an advocate. The fees he earned, however, were wholly insufficient to sustain the extraordinary spending of his ex-washerwoman wife. Thérèse fell in love with 'Gay Paree' and entered into the social whirl. On the back of her 'inheritance' the couple borrowed more and more money – until one day their creditors checked on the identity of her benefactor and found there was no such person as Mademoiselle de Marcotte. There were several things that Thérèse could have done. She could have fled the city. She could have stuck to her original story. She could have owned up to her fraud. Or she could simply pile fresh lies upon the old ones. Thérèse chose the latter course.

Her story about Mademoiselle de Marcotte had indeed been untrue, she said, but she had fabricated the tale only to disguise the true identity of her benefactor. He was one Robert Henry Crawford, a millionaire American from Chicago, whom she had met on a train two years earlier. They had become friends and, when he subsequently suffered a heart attack, she had nursed him back to health.

Mr Crawford had since died, however, and had left his fortune to be shared between his two nephews in the United States and Thérèse's younger sister, Marie. Marie, then still a schoolgirl, would not receive her inheritance until she was 21 years of age but in the meantime Thérèse was to receive an annual income of just under $100,000.

One of the people to whom Thérèse told this fresh pack of lies was her father-in-law, Gustave Humbert. The Toulouse mayor had risen rapidly in the world of politics and was now Minister of Justice in the national government. Whether or not he believed Thérèse's tale, she nevertheless persuaded him to pay all her and Frédéric's Paris creditors to avoid a family scandal. In turn, she 'repaid' old Monsieur Humbert by announcing that the documents containing her inheritance had been placed by American lawyers in a locked safe, the administration and secure keeping of which had been guaranteed by the Humbert family until her sister Marie came of age.

As Paris buzzed with the story of the 'Crawford Inheritance', Thérèse boldly turned up at the bank to which she had previously owed the most money. Warmly welcomed by the manager, she told him: 'Sadly, Monsieur, I am not permitted to open the safe and exercise the bonds and securities therein until Marie comes of age. Otherwise, I am in danger of forfeiting all claim upon the Crawford millions.'

Predictably, she then asked for a loan. It was readily given. Thérèse repeated the trick at banks throughout Paris and elsewhere. One Toulouse bank alone advanced her seven million francs. Much of the money was used to purchase a lavish mansion in the capital, where, in her bedroom, she installed a safe supposedly containing the secrets of her and her little sister's fortune.

The door of this massive, fireproof steel structure was opened only once – when she invited an overawed provincial notary to examine a number of bundles of paper and to itemise the wrappers that supposedly indicated their contents. Then the safe was locked and thick wax seals were applied to the doors and handles. The imposing safe was not to be opened again until Marie's twenty-first birthday.

Meanwhile, Thérèse and Frédéric embarked on a huge spending spree. Thérèse also invited Marie and their two brothers, Émile and Romain, to join her in an orgy of extravagance. The human cash-dispenser became known in Paris society as 'La Grande Thérèse' as the amplebosomed lady swept in and out of restaurants and fashion salons and opera boxes.

Only one mishap threatened their idyll. A banker from Lyons named Delatte visited Thérèse at her Paris mansion to arrange the advance of a further loan secured on the inheritance. Idly, he enquired of her where in America her late benefactor had lived. Off the top of her head, Thérèse replied: 'Somerville, a suburb of Boston.' Unbeknown to Thérèse, the banker was about to sail to the United States and, while in Boston, made enquiries about the fictitious millionaire James Henry Crawford. Realising that no one had ever heard of such a person, Delatte wrote to a fellow banker in France telling him of his suspicions. But, before further investigations could be made in the United States, Delatte mysteriously vanished. After a few days his body was fished out of the East River, New York. He had been murdered.

The killer was never uncovered but it has always been assumed that Delatte's untimely death was what would now be known as a 'contract killing', ordered by Thérèse or her brothers. It took only the glib tongue of La Grande

Thérèse to calm the fears of the French banker to whom Delatte had written. The threat of exposure evaporated, as did the money that the Humbert clan continued to borrow – which had now reached an estimated 65 million francs.

There was one event that Thérèse Humbert could not influence, however: the twenty-first birthday of sister Marie. The day was looming like a time bomb ticking away inside the great safe. Thérèse countered with two plans. The first was to distract attention from the vital birthday by inventing a dispute between herself and the non-existent American nephews over where the securities should be stored. Her second ploy was for her brothers to establish a finance house in a rented building in fashionable Boulevard des Capucines and to seek investment business through a chain of salesmen. Early investors found their returns swift and satisfactorily high, and the money flowed in. None of it was invested, of course. Apart from the small sums paid out in high 'interest', the rest was put aside to repay some of the more pressing creditors, who wanted their loans repaid the moment Marie came of age.

The whole corrupt edifice began to collapse when a Bank of France official, Jules Bizat, investigated the invested funds of the Humbert brothers' finance house and found that there were none. He went straight to the Prime Minister, Pierre-Marie Waldeck-Rousseau. Fearing that official involvement would precipitate yet another governmental scandal (there had already been several at the close of the nineteenth century) the premier decided to leak the story to the Paris newspaper *Le Matin*. Thérèse had no alternative but to protest her innocence while fending off the demands of creditors.

Now began an extraordinary chain of events. The Humberts' lawyer, Maître du Buit, believed so fervently in the truth of the Crawford Inheritance that he threatened to sue the newspaper for libel and offered to open the safe to clear Thérèse's name. This was the very last thing that she wanted, of course, and she panicked. On 8 May 1902, two days before the safe was due to be opened by du Buit, Thérèse or one of her accomplices set fire to the upper floor of her home. Everything in her bedroom was gutted, apart from the safe, which was indeed totally fireproof.

Thérèse, now enmeshed in a web of her own lies, assembled her sister, her brothers and husband Frédéric, and took a train to an unknown destination. So she was nowhere to be found when, on the appointed day, lawyer du Buit led an anxious band of businessmen and bankers into her bedroom. The wax seals were broken, the doors were unlocked and eager hands swung them back – to reveal a single house brick.

Many years earlier, on the death of Thérèse's boastful father Gilbert Aurignac, his children had stood around as Madame Aurignac turned the key in an old oak chest which, he had long boasted, contained papers documenting the family's secret fortune. It too had contained nothing but a brick. Now Thérèse was repeating history, though for a much more august company. The aftermath of the discovery in her bedroom safe in 1902 reverberated around the social and financial circles of France. Ten suicides were attributed to her fraudulent machinations, one of them that of a leading banker. But of the lady herself there was no sign.

Thérèse and her family remained undetected for seven months until Spanish police traced them to a lodging house in Madrid. They were extradited and in February 1903 she, Frédéric, Émile and Romain were sent for trial on no fewer than 257 charges of forgery and fraud. On 8

August they stood in the dock at the Palais de Justice while outside the court queues formed of thousands of spectators from all over France. Special trains had even been laid on, such was the fascination with this 'trial of the century'. The crowds were disappointed, however, to see that the arch trickster La Grande Thérèse was by now just a plump, sallow old woman whose once-magnetic personality had seemingly deserted her. A foreign newsman disparagingly called her 'a typical French cook'.

Both Thérèse and Frédéric were sentenced to five years in prison. Romain got three years and Émile two. The famous brick, along with the charred metal safe surrounding it, went on display in a Paris shop window, where it became something of a tourist attraction. Thérèse herself was released after three and a half years because of her good conduct in jail. She hid herself away in the countryside and died in 1917, her deeds largely forgotten and her passing unreported during the horrors of the First World War.

D.B. COOPER
MYSTERY SKYJACKER

It was 24 November 1971, Thanksgiving Day, and the man clutching a canvas bag close to his chest in the departure lounge at the airport in Portland, Oregon, attracted little attention. The place was crammed with travellers anxious to get home to spend the holiday with their families. The quiet little man was among 150 passengers waiting patiently to take the 400-mile flight to Seattle. After acquiring a ticket under the name of D.B. Cooper, he had entered the departure lounge and waited patiently, his eyes hidden behind dark tinted glasses. Fifty minutes later he filed aboard the Boeing 727, still clutching the canvas bag. He placed no luggage in the hold, requested an aisle seat from the stewardess and settled down with the bag on his lap, apparently to enjoy the one-hour journey.

About halfway through the Northwest Airlines flight he pushed the overhead button to summon a stewardess. Tina Mucklow walked down the aisle ready to take his order for a drink, when the drama began. Instead of giving her an order, Cooper thrust into her hand a note that read: 'I have a bomb with me. If I don't get $200,000 I will blow us all to bits.' As the startled stewardess hurriedly digested the dire warning, he opened the bag to show her a bomb; she could clearly identify the dynamite sticks, wiring and detonator. Cooper never took his eyes off her as he closed the bag, watched her walk up to the flight deck and sat back, awaiting the response.

So began the amazing saga of a 'perfect crime' which, because of its unique conclusion, captured the imagination of an entire nation. It switched public sympathy away from the forces of law and order and onto the side of the culprit, the man known as D.B. Cooper who passed not into infamy but folklore. In smoky bars they would sing songs about him as if he were a modern-day Robin Hood. Poems were penned to his memory, T-shirts bore his name and newspaper editors were sent letters from admiring girls pledging to be his bride. The object of all this adoring attention was a man who carried out one of the most heinous of crimes, skyjacking. But, although he threatened to kill men, women and children, he ultimately caused harm to no one, finally leaping into sub-zero temperatures – and into enduring mystery.

Within seconds of Cooper handing his demand for $200,000 to Tina Mucklow, the pilot of Boeing N467 had flicked a switch on a special device that broadcast a message over several frequencies that an emergency was under way. Within two minutes the alert had been picked up by ground control at Seattle, where a team of FBI agents, police marksmen and units of the National Guard were mobilised and placed at strategic positions.

The plane landed uneventfully at the airport, where a message from the captain announced that disembarkation would be delayed. Amid the commotion of disgruntled passengers, Cooper left his seat. Still clutching his canvas bag, he walked through the bulkhead door into the flight deck, where he confronted the pilot, co-pilot and flight engineer. 'Now, gentlemen,' he said coolly, 'don't bother to look round.' There followed a tense, 20-minute dialogue with air traffic control staff and then a police chief, who asked for the release of the passengers before any bargains were struck. The man was unequivocal in his demands. The passengers would be released only after $200,000 in used dollar bills had been handed over to him.

Cooper got his way, and two FBI agents dressed as maintenance men wheeled a trolley aboard. Inside it was a white sack sealed with wire. Cooper ripped it open and found to his delight the money, together with the four parachutes he had demanded. He then relented and allowed the passengers to leave. As they filed out to buses waiting to take them to the main terminal building, they were still completely unaware that a man had played a ruthless game with their lives. They thought a simple delay in transportation had held them up.

Once the passengers were all safely off the plane and in the terminal, Cooper moved into phase two of his bold plan. Now captor of only the flight crew, he began making further demands of the police and airport authorities. He asked that the plane be refuelled and he warned that he wanted flight plans to take the aircraft to Mexico. In his exchanges with the ground staff, Cooper displayed a depth of knowledge about aircraft which indicated he was neither a crank nor a lucky amateur. This escapade had been plotted to keep it simple – brilliantly simple.

When the aircraft took off again, it was shadowed by a US Air Force fighter scrambled to track the plane to its final destination. Cooper seemed to sense the precautions that the authorities down below would take and, when airborne, he told Captain Bill Scott that they were to alter course. He was not to head for Mexico but to veer south-east. He issued specific instructions to Scott, again indicating an astute knowledge of flying. He said: 'Fly with the flaps lowered, 15 per cent, keep the landing gear down, keep the speed below 90 metres per second, do not climb above 7,000 feet ... and open the rear door.'

The captain did some quick mental arithmetic before telling Cooper that his instructions would mean a massive leap in fuel consumption. The skyjacker replied that he could, if he wished, land in Reno, Nevada. Then he moved through the bulkhead door from the cockpit to the body of the aircraft, turning only to order the crew to keep the door locked. As Cooper stood in the belly of the plane, there was a huge rush of air and a deafening roar as Captain Scott activated the mechanism opening the rear door, as demanded by his sole unwanted passenger.

Scott was not to know it until he landed at Reno nearly four hours later but, in the freezing night sky, shrouded by cloud and out of sight of the shadowing plane, Cooper made his leap into the thin air. He left behind two parachutes, one intact, one in shreds. Investigators theorised later that he had ripped one apart to make a pouch for his loot and strapped it to his body. Examination of the flight's black-box recorder showed a slight increase in altitude at the moment he jumped, as the aircraft compensated for his weight and that of his ransom. This indicated that Cooper had jumped at 8.13 p.m., just 32 minutes after leaving Seattle.

When the aircraft landed, the authorities became painfully aware that they had been duped. An FBI contingency plan to storm the aircraft was rendered worthless but they consoled themselves with the thought that the parachute jump was the one weak point in Cooper's expert plan. He had no winter clothes and no food, and wore just lightweight shoes and a raincoat for protection. Investigators took solace in the fact that Cooper had baled out over rocky, mountainous, deeply wooded terrain into sub-zero temperatures and dangerous wildlife and judged there was little point in attempting an instant ground search over such a hostile environment. Aviation experts calculated that, in any case, the odds of Cooper even surviving his leap in the dark were heavily stacked against him.

For two weeks after his vanishing act, exhaustive aerial searches covering vast tracts of land went on unabated. Planes with heat-seeking sensors and cameras criss-crossed the skyways over Oregon and Washington State. There was no sign of Cooper. Army and air force personnel joined in the ground searches, but they found nothing of the man or his loot. Then, three weeks after the hijacking, the following letter arrived unexpectedly at the office of the *Los Angeles Times*:

'I am no modern-day Robin Hood. Unfortunately I have only fourteen months left to live. The hijacking was the fastest and most profitable way of gaining a few last grains of peace. I didn't rob Northwest because I thought it would be romantic or heroic or any of the other euphemisms that seem to attach themselves to situations of high risk. I don't blame people for hating me for what I've done, nor do I blame anybody for wanting me caught and punished, though this can never happen. I knew from the start I would not be caught. I have come and gone on several airline flights since and I'm not holed up in some obscure backwoods town. Neither am I a psychopath. I have never received a speeding ticket.'

The note, probably more than anything, helped lift the status of D.B. Cooper from that of villain to that of folk hero. Letters poured in to newspapers and radio stations across the USA praising the man who had 'beaten the system'. He might not have regarded himself as a modern-day Robin Hood but the public certainly did. A university professor was engaged by FBI agents to build up a mental profile of Cooper. His findings were never published; it is believed they would only have enhanced the glamour and mystique of the man in the eyes of the public.

Many of the 'mountain men' living in the region where Cooper jumped disregarded the letter, preferring to believe it was a spoof. Instead they embarked on wild treasure hunts amid the peaks and valleys. Clubs organised 'Cooper Loot' hunt weekends, and it became fashionable for families to spend the weekends barbecuing in the mountains – with a little light treasure hunting thrown in.

The authorities harnessed the latest technology to try to trace the money or at least locate Cooper's remains. Despite the letter, many high-ranking federal agents, accepting the evidence of the experts, could not believe that he survived the leap. One year after the skyjack, the FBI publicly announced that they thought Cooper was dead. Five years after the crime, on 24 November 1976, the file was closed on him and the Statute of Limitations meant that, even if he were alive, he would be a free man. The only crime he could possibly be convicted for after that was tax evasion.

In 1979 a deer hunter out on a dawn walk discovered the plastic warning sign from a Boeing 727 rear door. It read: 'This hatch must remain firmly locked in flight.' The discovery was akin to gold being struck in the Klondike. Treasure-seekers from all over America flooded into the village nearest to the Kelso forest, where the sign was found. In their wake came map-makers, astrologers and souvenir sellers, who certainly got far richer than the luckless prospectors who scoured the forests and mountains in vain for the Cooper Loot.

It was not until seven years after the crime that painter Harold Ingram and his eight-year-old son Brian made a discovery which many believe proves conclusively that Cooper died in his spectacular jump. They found $3,000 near a river bank and experts calculated that it had probably been washed down to the tranquil picnic spot by a mountain stream. The money was conclusively identified by the serial numbers as being Cooper's haul. The Ingrams' discovery sparked a new wave of treasure fever. This time a group calling itself the Ransom Rangers set out to try to find the rest of the skyjacked booty. But no more money was found, nor the remains of D.B. Cooper. 'That's the closest we ever got to him,' an FBI agent remarked of the mystery man who pulled off one of the greatest vanishing tricks in history.

ANTHONY WILLIAMS
LAIRD OF TOMINTOUL

Fraud Squad detectives would normally be celebrating the arrest of an embezzler on the scale of Anthony Williams. Had the criminal been anyone else, they would have heartily welcomed the attention, the glory, the headlines. In this high-profile case, however, the fraudbusters of London's Metropolitan Police could only bury their heads in their hands in shocked disbelief. For the villain they had nabbed was one of their own: Scotland Yard's deputy director of finance, Anthony Williams.

Over 12 years of lies, deception and downright theft, Williams had siphoned off £5 million of funds that should have been spent on the Yard's undercover operations. He had used it to finance a secret life – a life which had him opening bank accounts around the world, living as a nobleman, owning virtually an entire village in Scotland and recognised as a man of considerable substance and property just about everywhere else.

There may have been some who envied or even admired one of the twentieth century's cheekiest conmen, but others, like Sir Paul Condon, the Commissioner of the Metropolitan Police, were left to pick up the pieces of the biggest, most humiliating inside job ever. At a press conference, Sir Paul offered the people of London an 'unreserved apology', admitting he was 'angry and embarrassed that the courageous work of police officers had been betrayed'. The unprecedented apology followed an incredible and intriguing trail of corruption that had led to 55-year-old Williams being sentenced to seven and a half years' imprisonment on 19 May 1995.

The astonishing catalogue of deceit had begun with one small theft of £200 in 1981. The cash was earmarked as payment for an officer to take his seriously ill wife on holiday but the excuse was fictitious and the £200 was pocketed by Williams. Having succeeded so easily in his first attempt at crime, the mild-mannered accountant stole again and again – and kept on stealing, right under the noses of Britain's nucleus of top crime-busters. He was in a convenient position to make his thefts easy for he was overseer of the Met's staff welfare fund, from which he began to make regular 'withdrawals'.

Just once, Williams got close to being caught. A colleague noticed that one sum didn't quite add up. Williams quickly paid in a cheque to cover the discrepancy. In total, the bespectacled, respected handler of police welfare funds diverted £7,000, money which should have gone to the hard-up and the ill. Much of the loot was used to ease Williams's own money problems caused by the ending of his first marriage: £500-a-month maintenance payments for his two daughters and a hefty overdraft.

Over the years, Williams became proud of his deception. His bravado grew as an accountant who could not just cook the books but make them boil. Without really knowing where he could get his hands on unlimited money, Williams opened an account at Coutts, bankers to the Queen and the upper crust. His creation of an 'uncle in

Norway' who was set to leave him a healthy inheritance not only smoothed the way with Coutts – the bank authorised a £30,000 overdraft – but was also to later prove invaluable when questions were raised about the high life he was leading.

In 1986 Williams was to strike gold. When a matter of a highly confidential and sensitive nature arose, Scotland Yard could find no one better to handle it than the deputy finance director. Williams was put in charge of a 'secret fund' to fight organised crime. The fund was supposed to pay police informers and for general undercover work but only part of it was allocated for this purpose. In fact, for over eight years Williams administered two companies operating an anti-terrorist surveillance aircraft based at a Surrey airfield. Throughout the period when he was financing the running of the plane, IRA bombing in mainland Britain was at its peak and police needed an aircraft to keep watch on suspected arms caches and safe houses. So secret was the project that just a handful of people within Scotland Yard knew of the operation and Williams's involvement in it. Enquiries by any curious outsider would reveal only the existence of two firms, one apparently owned by the other, running a small, fixed-wing Cessna.

Such was the determination by anti-terrorist squads to control the IRA's activities that the aircraft was in constant use. For instance, in 1989 it was used in a successful operation that led to the capture of two IRA activists, Damien Comb and Liam O'Dhuibhir, at an arms dump on a desolate beach on the Pembrokeshire coast of South Wales. They were caught after a seven-week stake-out codenamed Operation Pebble. It suited Williams greatly that the Cessna was so heavily used. Such victories against IRA terrorists meant few worries were raised over its costs – £250,000 in the first year alone – and this allowed Williams to rob the fund blind.

Whatever the aerial surveillance operation required, Williams immediately paid. No complaints were made about his speedy requisitioning of anything from aviation fuel to paperclips. What was to come to light when he eventually stood trial, however, was that over eight years he requisitioned £7 million but only around £2 million had actually been spent. The Old Bailey court was told: 'The defendant was allowed unlimited private access on his own discretion to the funds of the Receiver [the Yard's financial controller]. It was placed in a specified account. He did not have to answer to anyone ... he controlled the payments in and the payments out.'

As the money rolled in, Williams was glad that he had his 'uncle' in Norway to explain away such untold wealth. The inheritance story fended off enquiries about his grand homes and grand lifestyle. And Williams certainly knew how to splash the cash around. The money was spread across banks and building societies in Scotland, London and the Channel Islands. He even paid cash for some of the many properties he acquired, an apartment being bought directly from the secret Scotland Yard fund. In 1989 alone, he stole more than £1 million.

It was remarkable that Williams's wife, Kay, happily accepted the 'Norwegian uncle' story to explain the couple's elevation into a style of living most people can only dream of. It was even more remarkable that no one at Scotland Yard got wind of the millionaire lifestyle of the £42,000-a-year accountant. He bought homes in Leatherhead and Haslemere in Surrey and a flat in Westminster, central London. Not far away, in Mayfair, he rented another flat which cost him £2,000 a month. Friends he entertained there lavishly marvelled at Williams's good fortune in having a foreign relative who had left him such wealth. Yet another house in New Malden, Surrey, was purchased for £178,000 cash. A holiday villa on Spain's Costa del Sol was added to the property empire. As well as Coutts, where he was given a gold bank card, Williams opened accounts at three other banks, the National Westminster, Standard Chartered and Clydesdale, and two building societies, the Leeds and the Bradford & Bingley.

But it was in Scotland that Williams's stolen wealth allowed him to feel as if he owned the world. He had fallen in love with the Highland village of Tomintoul, where he had spent several happy holidays, so in 1989 he decided to buy a large chunk of it. First there was a £6,000 cottage in The Square, on which Williams carried out £40,000 of renovations. Then there was the £120,000 Gordon Arms Hotel, which underwent a £1.5-million restoration, the old fire station (£21,000) and the Manse in Glenlivet (£192,000). Williams even had the cheek to apply for a Business Expansion Scheme grant from the Moray Enterprise Board for one of his companies, Tomintoul Enterprises, which in turn provided £3 million towards his regeneration of the little village.

The good people of Tomintoul hailed Williams as a saviour and indeed to them he was. He created dozens of jobs at his hotel, pub and restaurant, which at one time employed seven chefs, and he sponsored local events, including the Tomintoul Highland Games. The villagers had even more reason to believe the Lord had provided. For Williams invested £70,000 on acquiring the title Laird before taking over Tomintoul. Not content with one feudal title, he bought himself another eight at a cost of £144,000.

When the Laird of Tomintoul was finally arrested, the villagers could only speak well of him. 'I know what he did was wrong but it wasn't that bad,' remarked George McAllister, 60, in charge of the local museum. 'Most of these fraud types spirit the money away into foreign bank accounts or investments abroad but he didn't. He put most of it back here into our wee place. It really made Tomintoul a better place. Just look around you.'

Iain Birnie, who was running the village shop in those days, said: 'So it was money from London? Big deal. They've got enough of the stuff down there anyway. It should be coming north. Tony Williams did a damn sight more good with it up here than it would ever have done down south.'

Williams's eventual downfall came when banks grew suspicious about the large and endless amounts of cash he was depositing. It was believed something more sinister than downright fraud was afoot. So, as obliged to under the Drugs Trafficking Offences Act, they disclosed their worries to the police. Williams's arrest came in July 1994. Two months later he was dismissed from his job.

At his trial, Williams pleaded guilty to 17 charges of theft from the Receiver of Scotland Yard and two charges of theft from the civilian staff's welfare fund. Initially he denied any charges relating to the welfare fund – simply, said his barrister, James Sturman, because he had forgotten all about the crime. Williams asked for 535 other charges to be taken into consideration. In all, he had stolen £5,320,737 of the £7,413,761 entrusted to him over the years.

Mr Sturman told the court that it had been a relief to Williams when he was finally caught. Apart from uttering a few panic-stricken lies and half-truths when first arrested, Williams had fully co-operated with the police. Around

£529,000 of the stolen funds had been recovered and there were hopes of seizing a further £200,000 to £300,000, the court heard. Mr Sturman added that Williams felt terrible remorse for his sins and had expressed as much to priests. 'He has lied to his wife, he has lied to his friends, he has lived a lie,' he said. Referring to Williams's double life in Scotland, prosecuting counsel Brian Barker QC summed up the disgraced accountant's influence on the Highland village he had changed out of all recognition. He said: 'The suburban civil servant became, when he crossed the border, a nobleman and benefactor of Tomintoul.'

Williams did not call any character witnesses. The defendant told the court: 'I don't want to put my good friends in the box to say I was honest. Obviously, I haven't been for years.'

Sentencing him to six and a half years for the thefts from his employers and one year for stealing from the welfare fund, the Recorder of London, Sir Lawrence Verney, told him: 'Such crimes are inexcusable. No one minded to follow your example must be left in any doubt as to the consequences.'

Still bearing a healthy tan from his travels and clutching a carrier bag which contained what seemed now to be his only worldly goods, Williams left the dock to begin his sentence. His 47-year-old wife vowed to stand by him. She did so and, a mere three years later, the couple were seen strolling hand in hand near the open prison from where he was shortly to be allowed early release after serving only half his sentence – and with only a fraction of the missing £5 million recovered.

Two investigations were launched into just how Williams got away with his criminal activities for so long, one concentrating on the civil welfare fund, the other on the secret fund. They did not make happy reading for the red-faced top brass at Scotland Yard.

Meanwhile, the folk of Tomintoul were left to pick up the pieces of a property explosion which no longer had funds available to sustain it. Jobs were lost and fewer lavish shindigs graced the £25,000 carpet of the bar of the Gordon Hotel. But the village devised one final reminder of the high-living fraudster: a new brand of ale cheekily named 'Laird of Tomintoul Beer' and bearing a label in the shape of a Metropolitan Police helmet.

HARRY BENSON
RACING 'CERTAINTIES'

Harry Benson was a man whose eye for the main chance and confidence in his own smooth-talking ability marked him out as a prince of conmen. Benson, son of a respectable Jewish merchant, portrayed himself as a member of the European nobility. His ability to speak several languages fluently impressed his acquaintances and he carried off his image as an educated English gentleman with panache.

Benson's arrival on the London social scene coincided with the era of a sudden and inexplicable upsurge in fraud cases. In the 1870s Scotland Yard found itself under intense pressure to catch the scoundrels responsible, not least because their gullible victims tended to be the rich and influential. Fleecing the wealthy was easy money for a skilled operator, and they didn't come any more skilful than Harry Benson.

That is not to say he didn't make mistakes. At the end of the Franco-Prussian War of 1870–71 he turned up in London calling himself the Comte de Montague, Mayor of Châteaudun, and persuaded the Lord Mayor to hand him £1,000 towards the relief of war refugees. Hardly had he pocketed the cash than his forged receipt was spotted and he went on to spend an uncomfortable year in prison. It was an experience so loathsome to him that he tried to commit suicide in the most horrific manner, attempting to incinerate himself on his prison mattress. The flames left him half-crippled and able to walk only with the aid of crutches.

On leaving prison, Benson advertised his services as a multilingual secretary and was approached by a man called William Kurr, who made his living through gambling swindles. Kurr's usual method was to place bets for clients at a race meeting and then vanish with the proceeds of any big win. It was a primitive technique but effective enough. The two men quickly got the measure of each other and soon Benson was persuading Kurr to try more sophisticated scams. They began publishing a newspaper called *Le Sport*, which comprised mainly British racing articles translated into French. It was delivered free to selected French aristocrats with a keen interest in the turf.

Those who bothered to scan its pages read how a professional British punter called Mr G.H. Yonge had such an incredibly successful track record that many bookies cut the odds whenever they did business with him. Soon some of the aristocrats began receiving letters from Mr Yonge which asked them to act as his agent in laying bets. He could not, he explained, trade using his real name because bookmakers wouldn't give him decent odds. All his agents had to do was receive a cheque, forward it to a certain bookmaker in their own name and return the winnings to Mr Yonge. In return the agent would receive a five per cent commission.

One wealthy Frenchwoman, the Comtesse de Goncourt, found this a particularly agreeable arrangement. She would mail Mr Yonge's cheque for several hundred pounds, receive back thousands in winnings and pocket £50 or so commission for herself. After a few trial runs she became so convinced that Yonge was a gambling genius that she asked him if he would mind very much investing £10,000 of her own money as he saw fit. Unfortunately the Comtesse did not cotton on to the simple truth that Yonge's 'bookmaker' was, like Yonge himself, just another of Benson's aliases. She never saw her £10,000 again.

Into this cauldron of deceit and double dealing stepped a handful of detectives from Scotland Yard. Their stock-in-trade was to hobnob with 'narks', usually petty criminals who kept themselves out of jail by passing on useful criminal intelligence. The use of informers was, and remains, a vital part of police work but, as any detective knows, there is a fine line between professional agreements and corruption. The taking of bribes was much more of a temptation to an officer in Victorian England (who, at the time of this scam, earned a meagre £5 6s. 2d. a year) than to his present-day colleagues. So when a Chief Inspector, John Meiklejohn, was offered gifts of cash by William Kurr in return for dropping investigations into Kurr's criminal dealings, he readily accepted.

The web of corruption soon widened. A police friend of Meiklejohn, Chief Inspector Nathaniel Druscovich, privately admitted that he had money worries. Meiklejohn introduced him to a 'businessman' who would help, and soon Harry Benson was cheerfully handing over a £60 'loan' to Druscovich. All he wanted in return, he said, was to be alerted to any plan Scotland Yard might have to arrest him. The deal was struck and soon a third detective, Chief Inspector William Palmer, was brought on to Benson's payroll. Not long after the corrupt circle was in place, Meiklejohn warned Benson that detectives were snapping at his heels. A Chief Inspector Clarke had been assigned to close down bogus bookmakers and he was very interested in the firm of Gardner & Co, the front company used by Kurr, Benson and their circle.

One of these associates was a swindler called Walters, whom Clarke had encountered while he was in the process of smashing another gang. With impressive nerve, Benson (using his Yonge alias) wrote to the officer inviting him to visit his palatial country home at Shanklin on the Isle of Wight. He explained that he had some useful criminal intelligence but that he couldn't get up to London because he was crippled. Intrigued, and keen for a chance to mix with the upper classes, Clarke agreed. At the meeting, Clarke was informed by Mr Yonge that Walters had been boasting of success in bribing him and, worse, that Walters still had a letter penned by the Chief Inspector which proved the allegation. Clarke had indeed once written to Walters and he now acknowledged that his words were open to misinterpretation. It seems this whole episode was cooked up by Benson to try to warn off Clarke. If so, it failed. The officer reported to his superiors that Yonge was probably a crook and Benson's next move signalled the beginning of the end of his swindling career.

Benson contacted the Comtesse de Goncourt with the offer of a unique investment opportunity. She swallowed his line and instructed her solicitor to convert a number of assets into ready cash. But the solicitor was suspicious and contacted Scotland Yard to make sure Yonge had no criminal record. The message was intercepted by Druscovich, who immediately warned Benson of his imminent peril.

Benson, Kurr and the rest of the gang pulled £16,000 in cash out of a Bank of England account and headed for Scotland in the hope their trail would go cold. It didn't.

Druscovich was dispatched to arrest them but, before he did, he sent a telegram warning Benson that he was on his way. Soon after this, he and the other two 'bent' officers received £500 apiece for their trouble. Senior detectives at Scotland Yard were by now growing frustrated and puzzled at their inability to nail the Benson gang. At first the thought that men within their own ranks had been 'nobbled' did not occur to them. Even when Meiklejohn was spotted hobnobbing with the crooks at their hideaway in Bridge of Allan, Scotland, he talked himself out of trouble by claiming he didn't realise they were scoundrels.

As the heat increased, Benson fled to the Netherlands. There he tried to pass a Bank of Clydesdale £100 note, which Scotland Yard knew was one of a batch he had withdrawn some weeks earlier. They had already alerted Dutch police to the possibility that Benson, perhaps travelling under one of his aliases, would turn up on their doorstep, and now the Dutch moved in to make an arrest. Druscovich was briefed to bring the suspect home and he realised he could do his crooked benefactors no more favours.

The rest of the gang were duly rounded up, tried and sentenced. Benson got 15 years in jail and Kurr 10. Within hours of their reception at London's Millbank Prison, they demanded to see the governor and spilled the beans on the network of corruption they had established within the very heart of Scotland Yard. Druscovich, Meiklejohn and Palmer were later convicted of conspiring to pervert the course of justice and all were sentenced to the maximum two years' hard labour. Clarke was acquitted and, although compulsorily retired, was permitted to keep his police pension.

When the jailed officers were released, Meiklejohn set himself up in business as a private eye, while Palmer used his life savings to open a pub. What became of Druscovich is not known.

Benson and Kurr both got time off their sentences for good behaviour. They teamed up again, this time as mining company consultants in America, and soon the hapless European public were being offered shares in mines that didn't exist. Benson was again arrested and served two years in a Swiss prison. His last great con was in Mexico, selling bogus tickets for concerts by the celebrated soprano Adelina Patti. On his return to America, he received yet another prison sentence, this time in the infamous Tombs. He couldn't face the prospect and committed suicide by breaking his back in a 40-foot leap off a prison balcony.

HORATIO BOTTOMLEY
FLAMBOYANT FELON

Horatio Bottomley was a swindler without rival in his day. In a roller-coaster career of fraud, he went from rags to riches and then back to rags again. During a lifetime of financial villainy, he charmed people into parting with their money and usually smooth-talked his way out of trouble afterwards. The phrase 'gift of the gab' seemed to have been coined just for him.

Bottomley was born in poverty in London's East End in 1860 and raised in an orphanage. His first introduction to the laws he was to flout all his life came when he got a job as a solicitor's clerk. Next came a post as shorthand writer at the Law Courts. While faithfully transcribing the devious deeds of those hauled before the bewigged judges of Victorian England, Bottomley realised where his true talents lay and determined to embark on the pursuit of money, women, fame and political power.

His first foray was into the publishing business, the natural habitat of hundreds of rogues before and since. He persuaded a group of 'friends' to invest in the business and to agree to buy a number of properties, including a printing works in Devon, for the handsome sum of £325,000. His fellow directors were less than delighted when, having parted with the money, they discovered that the properties were all owned by Bottomley himself and were virtually worthless.

Bottomley suddenly found himself back in a courtroom, this time in the dock. The judge listened to the damning evidence heaped against the accused, then invited him to speak in his own defence. This was Bottomley's chance to reveal his magical talent for twisting the truth. The court was dazzled by his oratory and, after half an hour, the judge became convinced that it was Bottomley, rather than his fellow directors, who had been wronged. Clearing him of all charges, the judge even suggested that Bottomley should enter the legal profession.

This then became the modus operandi of fraudster Horatio Bottomley. He would set up companies and sell them at inflated prices to other companies under his control, which then went bankrupt.

His method was simple, and it was a tribute to his silver-tongued sales spiel that so many eager punters fell for it. He would start a company, declare especially high dividends and watch as the share price rocketed. He would then sell his own shares at an inflated price. In the days before strict stock-market controls, this would usually go undetected. Under the pressure of his own unloading of shares, the prices would invariably plummet. At this stage Bottomley would 'come to the rescue' of investors by offering to take over the failing firm. All he asked for was a fresh injection of funds from the poor shareholders.

During the Australian Gold Rush, Bottomley financed mining operations and made a fortune by juggling funds between his many companies, despite being served with 67 writs of bankruptcy. By 1897 he had made more than £3 million from his Australian ventures alone. The East Ender born into poverty now lived like a lord, mixing with the highest in the land, he and his respectable wife accepted at the dinner tables of the aristocracy. Unbeknown to his hosts and his spouse, however, he kept a succession of young mistresses in love nests throughout the country.

Bottomley had money, women and fame. What he lacked was political power. This he remedied by a string of much-publicised charitable ventures, by which he 'bought' his way into Parliament. Elected to represent the poverty-stricken London constituency of Hackney South, Bottomley spent most of his time living the life of a country squire at his stately residence in Upper Dicker, near Eastbourne, Sussex.

In further pursuit of power and respectability, Bottomley returned to the world of publishing, through which he had first made his ill-gotten gains. He was instrumental in founding the *Financial Times*, which was to grow into one of the most authoritative journals of the twentieth century. He also started the fiercely patriotic magazine *John Bull*, which offered its readers huge competition prizes.

There were setbacks, of course, the most dramatic of which arose from the fraudster's inveterate love of gambling. Bottomley, a racehorse owner himself, knew that the only way to be sure to win a race was to own every horse in it. And that is exactly what he decided he would do.

Bottomley scoured the Continent for a racecourse that would suit his purpose in a country where racing regulations were suitably lax. The Belgian seaside resort of Blankenberge fitted the bill precisely because the racecourse there wound its way through sand dunes and the horses were often hidden from the view of spectators and officials. On the appointed day, six horses were entered for an afternoon race – and all were owned by Bottomley.

As the time of the race approached, dozens of the

schemer's accomplices placed bets on his behalf. Some of the bets were on the winner, some on the precise order in which the six horses would pass the finishing post. The six jockeys, also in the pay of Bottomley, were under strict instructions as to how to perform over every yard of the course. Then disaster struck. Just before the start, a thick sea mist blew in and obscured the entire course. The jockeys could not even see the other horses, and their shouts to one another were swallowed up in the mist. All six horses galloped to the finishing post in entirely the wrong order, losing the frantic fraudster a small fortune.

Further disaster beset Bottomley in 1912 when he was forced to resign from Parliament after a particularly scandalous bankruptcy. The suspicion was also voiced that some of the amazingly generous prizes he was offering in the pages of *John Bull* were going straight into his own pocket. The outbreak of the First World War rescued him from political oblivion. No journal was more jingoistic than *John Bull* in supporting the war effort. Bottomley himself toured the country using his oratorical gifts to boost recruiting – always charging a healthy fee for his services, of course. At the cessation of hostilities in 1918, Bottomley was re-elected as Member of Parliament for his old constituency of Hackney South. Flushed with pride and fresh ambition, the crafty crook embarked on a fresh string of fraudulent ventures. His past, however, was about to catch up with him.

During the war, Bottomley had instigated his biggest scam ever. The government had launched war-loan stock under the title Victory Bonds. Each bond, with a redemption value of £5, cost £4 15s. – a high sum at the time for the working man and woman. To 'help' them, Bottomley launched a Victory Bond Club into which the poor could pay as little as they could afford, their pennies then being invested in the £5 bonds. Bottomley was hailed as the 'friend of the little man' as an estimated half a million pounds flowed into the Victory Bond Club. In reality, however, the crook was siphoning off about £150,000 of the paupers' cash. He used £10,000 to pay off debts, invested £15,000 on a risky business venture of his own and squandered another £15,000 gambling on the horses.

When one of his former partners, Reuben Bigland, accused him of fraud, Bottomley foolishly sued for criminal libel before dropping the case. The alarm was raised and in 1922 he faced an Old Bailey jury on a charge of fraudulent conversion of Victory Bond Club funds. This time the gift of the gab failed to sway the jurors, who took just 30 minutes to find him guilty on all counts. The judge sentenced him to seven years' penal servitude.

Released on licence in 1926, the flamboyant crook vainly attempted to restore himself to public esteem. But his fortune and his credit had long evaporated. From being one of the most respected men in Britain, he was now the most despised. In 1933 he started a new career as a concert-hall comedian but after only a few nights he collapsed from a heart attack. He died a broke and broken man.

BERNIE CORNFELD
SERIOUSLY RICH

When a small, tubby, wrinkled ex-jailbird called Bernie Cornfeld died in March 1995, all the newspaper photographs accompanying his obituary showed him with a beaming smile and surrounded by beautiful young women. Why was the old crook always so happy? On the face of it, Bernie Cornfeld had little to smile about. He had perpetrated one of the most extraordinarily audacious frauds in history, had been uncovered, disgraced, severely censured and locked up in prison. He had once owned a private jet, a mansion in Beverly Hills, a house in London's Belgravia and chateaux in France and Switzerland, all bought with other people's money. He had never seemed to care a damn about those he defrauded, although he must have felt the loss when the courts removed most of his wealth.

Nor was he very gallant about the women in his life. He once said: 'A beautiful woman with a brain is like a beautiful woman with a club foot.' Yet, until his dying day, at the age of 67, Bernie Cornfeld shared his Californian home with eight beautiful women, with two more waiting for his call in London. What was the secret that kept the ugly old fraud smiling to the very end?

Bernie Cornfeld was a former American schoolteacher

who became one of the smoothest, brightest and most successful salesmen the world has ever known. As head of his own company, Investors Overseas Services (IOS), which he founded in Switzerland in 1965, he recruited an army of salespeople by promising them untold riches. As an incentive, he would invite them to his palace on Lake Geneva, his French chateau or his Beverly Hills mansion, where they could witness the trappings of the fabulous wealth that could be theirs too.

Cornfeld also liked to show off his 'harem' of 20 or so beautiful girlfriends who lived in his exotic homes and to display his stables of racehorses and expensive cars. He boasted of his romantic friendships with international glamour girls. The message to his staff was clear. Few could resist the blunt question he always asked them and for which he became famous: 'Do you sincerely want to be rich?' As far as 10,000 salespeople and 100,000 investors in 95 countries were concerned, the answer had to be a resounding 'yes'.

As punters rushed to part with their savings, IOS grew into a mammoth insurance and investment fund which controlled more than £1 billion in stocks and shares. Within five years the assets of IOS were spread among investments which included oil prospecting, electronics, insurance and gold fields. Some were profitable, some lost money. Many of the sales force did indeed become wealthy, earning colossal fees in commissions for enrolling more subscribers. But most of the unfortunate investors made little or nothing – and many lost the lot as their funds were squandered to sustain the unashamed luxury of the wildly spending IOS boss. Cornfeld's personal stake in the company grew to £100 million.

The bubble had to burst. IOS needed to expand at an impossible rate to keep paying its sales commissions, quite apart from the boss's perks. Indeed, Cornfeld's publicly excessive lifestyle scandalised the conservative Swiss financial authorities and they announced that they were investigating his entire set-up. There were worries that IOS's assets were being mismanaged and that much of its wealth existed only on paper.

By 1970 nervous investors shared the alarm of international bankers. Many IOS punters could do no more than suffer in silence, for they had broken the currency laws of their own countries by investing in overseas stock. Others refused to take their losses lying down. At an angry shareholders' meeting, Cornfeld was removed from control of IOS, squealing in protest at the loss of power over the company he had single-handedly created. He was even more upset as his own personal share of the firm dwindled in value to £4 million.

The Swiss authorities launched a fraud investigation into the conduct of IOS, and Bernie Cornfeld was ordered not to leave the country. In 1973, in stark contrast to his former lifestyle, the glib-tongued trickster was leading the humble life of an inmate in a Swiss jail, facing fraud charges. The investigation petered out, however, and Cornfeld was finally released from jail without any of the charges being pressed – thanks to an entirely new scandal surrounding IOS's funds.

While Bernie Cornfeld was languishing in a Swiss cell, unable to control the fortunes of his old company, another American financial expert took over IOS as president. His name was Robert Vesco. The fact that the dour, poker-faced Vesco was as far removed from flamboyant Cornfeld as chalk from Swiss cheese encouraged shareholders to trust the newcomer as their financial saviour. They could not have been more wrong.

Vesco, who lived an almost spartan life far from the spotlight of publicity that Cornfeld had bathed in, began a ruthless policy of translating the far-flung assets of IOS into hard cash. He managed to salvage some £150 million. The gratitude of the shareholders was short-lived, however, for Vesco vanished – and so did most of the money. American authorities issued a warrant for his arrest in 1974 but the combined resources of the FBI and the CIA could not catch him as he island-hopped around the Caribbean, increasing his ill-gotten gains by investments in the Bahamas, Costa Rica, Cuba and Panama.

But in May 1974 Vesco suffered one dramatic setback when pilot Alwyn Eisenhauer flew to Panama on behalf of a group of IOS creditors. Eisenhauer marched on to an airfield where Vesco's private Boeing 707 airliner was parked and told the startled ground crew that he was taking his 'boss' on a sudden business trip. Vesco could only watch in anguish from the balcony of his heavily guarded villa near the airfield as his plane roared into the air and vanished in the direction of the United States. The plucky pilot claimed his bounty when the jet was sold by IOS creditors for $10 million.

Meanwhile Cornfeld, freed from his Swiss jail cell, retired on the money that he had managed to salt away before the final crash of Investors Overseas Services. He continued to live in style in Europe, always enjoying the finest of wines and surrounding himself with the most beautiful of women. He finally moved to California – the final, happy homecoming of the crook who died laughing.

ROSEMARY ABERDOUR
SHE WAS NO LADY

Rosemary Aberdour, the plump only child of a comfortably off middle-class English family, always knew she was destined for better things. That inner confidence, plus a winning smile, were to see her through three years of lies, fraud and fantasy as she lived the life of an aristocrat – becoming rich off the generosity of others.

There were lavish parties, expensive cars, made-to-order jewellery, luxury homes, vintage champagne and all the other trappings of a millionaire lifestyle. And that's just what Rosemary led, under the assumed title of Lady Rosemary Aberdour. In a period of just three months, she spent nearly £1.5 million. And, all the while, she spoke of an inheritance which existed only in her mind ...

Rosemary had decided at an early age that she was good at handling other people's money. While living at home with her parents, a doctor and a medical secretary, in the village of Wickham Bishops, Essex, she had helped raise funds for her local parish church. But already she was dreaming and scheming about unlimited funds of her very own. Rosemary was telling friends she was due to come into money. Even she could not have imagined how much, or indeed just how it was going to come her way but, as always, she wore her secret smile and knew fate would treat her kindly.

It was when she arrived in London that Rosemary set in train her master plan of having at her disposal as much money as she could lay her stubby little fingers on. She took a course in bookkeeping, a skill which was to come in exceptionally useful when she was in a position to make the books balance greatly in her favour. That opportunity came in November 1986 when she successfully applied for a £20,000-a-year bookkeeping job at the National Hospital in Queen's Square, London. The hospital had a development fund, a charity launched to raise £10 million to build a new wing, and Rosemary knew she was just the person to use any donations wisely – on herself. After organising a charity ball at London's Guildhall, attended by the Princess of Wales, she realised that this was the glittering life she wanted to lead and earnestly set about achieving it.

In July 1987 Rosemary's months of devotion to duty paid off. She was promoted to the post of the charity's deputy director. It was a position of great trust: she was to bank all the cheques that came into the National Hospital Development Fund and look after the accounts. At first she stole a mere £500 to take herself on holiday but, once she realised she had got away with the theft, there was no stopping her. It was easy. Hundreds of thousands of pounds passed through her hands and she simply took the cheques for herself and fiddled the books.

Rosemary's golden opportunity came when she was asked to become chairman of the Queen's Square Ball, a separate fundraising committee. The contents of its bank account were perused only when the date of the annual ball came around; the rest of the year, the account came under no scrutiny. Rosemary had all the time in the world to deposit money stolen from the National Hospital Development Fund into the Queen's Square Ball account and to use it as her very own nest egg. She regularly stole cheques received in the post, amounting to anything between £20,000 and £100,000 at one time. Not content with having one source of illicit income, Rosemary started forging the signature of the charity's director, Richard Stevens. She now had fraudulent cheques to increase her spending power. At last, money was no object.

When Rosemary wanted a new car, she bought one: a £70,000 Bentley. And as always, she had an answer when asked about her purchase, made on the Queen's Square Ball account, telling top-notch car dealers H.R. Owen that the millionaire's car was to be a raffle prize at the ball. Then there was the £171,000 of charity cash which Rosemary spent at the prestigious jewellers Boodle & Dunthorne, and the luxury new home in Kensington. She even sent her chauffeur to top people's store Harrods to buy fillet steak for her dog, Jeeves.

It was incredible that no one ever delved too deeply into Rosemary's spending. But, if they did ask questions, she had an answer for them. 'I'm an heiress,' she would reply coyly. 'I have an inheritance of £20 million.' No one disbelieved her. Hospital charity chairman John Young said Rosemary had a royal air about her and a 'great presence'. 'Lady Aberdour' would even cheekily arrive for work in her chauffeur-driven Bentley, regally waving at Mr Young.

There was no end to the fake lady's cheek. She wrote to Richard Stevens enclosing a cheque for £100,000 which, she said, was her gift towards a new hospital ward, adding that her trust fund had given her permission to make donations totalling £500,000 towards this worthy cause over five years. Rosemary asked that her donation be received 'anonymously'. This was hardly surprising when she had stolen the money from a charity headed by Mr Stevens himself.

Rosemary loved the high life. There was no limit to her spending. She would go on wild sprees with her credit cards and think nothing of disposing of £30,000 on a weekend shopping jaunt. She also acquired a new circle of friends, people she felt would not question her aristocratic status too closely.

Rosemary became renowned for her extravagant parties. As a supposed member of the aristocracy, a respected socialite and now a generous benefactor, she entertained lavishly. One party at her London home had a Caribbean theme. She employed professional party organisers to make sure every attention was paid to detail. Guests wearing grass skirts and Caribbean shirts arrived to find live lobsters in tanks of water, bars with Caribbean roofs made out of specially imported materials, two tons of sand, palm trees and champagne spouting from showers. It had taken seven days to build the setting for the party, at a cost of £40,000. As one partygoer said: 'It was Rosemary living a dream. It was her going to the Caribbean for the weekend.'

Rosemary was never to explain why she decided on 'Lady Aberdour' as her aristocratic pseudonym. But there was one particular family who felt she had a lot of explaining to do – the genuinely titled Aberdours. They only became aware of an impostor when a Sunday newspaper wrote about Rosemary. The writer thought it too audacious to question her face to face about her family roots, so he looked the family up in the aristocrats' directory, Debrett, found the

Aberdours and concluded that Rosemary was the twenty-first daughter of the Earl of Morton.

The Countess and Earl of Morton were concerned that their family name was being taken in vain and wrote to the *Sunday Times* to tell the paper so. They were no less anxious when they received a reply saying that there was obviously another branch of the family. 'We were slightly annoyed,' said the countess. 'It was a silly reply. There is no one in the family called Lady Rosemary Aberdour.'

The countess's son, Lord Aberdour, added: 'There is only one Lady Aberdour, and that's my wife Amanda. This woman is definitely a fraud.' Yet, even when the real Lord and Lady Aberdour found out that someone was living a lie and using their name, no one pursued investigations which would have revealed Rosemary's barefaced fraud.

It was now taking all Rosemary's nerve not only to maintain her fake existence but also to avoid discovery over rapidly dwindling charity funds at the National Hospital. A scheduled visit from auditors meant she had to put in overtime to balance the books. She had to adjust figures, produce forged documents and transfer cash. She even raised an overdraft on the Queen's Square Ball account. The auditors did not notice anything amiss.

'It was all done with stunning skill,' said John Young, who was again to fall victim to Rosemary's quick thinking. She forged his signature to get her hands on even more cash and, when a building society queried it, she told them that 'poor Mr Young' suffered from Parkinson's disease which made his hands shake.

By now Rosemary knew deep inside that all the money in the world could not buy love or friends. She had no real friends, just hangers-on, and even they were beginning to tire of the merry-go-round of parties. It was always the same crowd of people, the same old Rosemary determined to put on a bash more outrageous than the last and desperate to be the centre of attention. It was a sad fact that guests at her gatherings now comprised staff and the most casual of acquaintances. 'She left all her parties early,' said one partygoer, Hamish Mitchell. 'It was as if she wasn't having a good time.'

Ever blinkered to the harsher reality of life, poor little rich girl Rosemary decided to cheer herself up with the biggest party ever. In fact, it was a fortnight of parties. The venue for the two weeks of total self-indulgence was Thornton Watlass Hall, a magnificent country estate in Yorkshire. Every night the guests sat down to a gourmet dinner. There was live entertainment by top cabaret artists, firework displays, vintage car races and, as usual, the best champagne flowing non-stop.

Perhaps living such a complex lie began to take its toll on Rosemary or perhaps she realised at last that the good life would come to an end. Whatever her reasoning, she was determined to give up her 'career' with as much extravagance as she had pursued it. She rented a £123,000-a-year London penthouse with its own swimming pool, which was to be the venue for yet more of her flamboyant hospitality. Then she embarked on the spending spree of a lifetime. There were two £40,000 parties – first a Star Trek Voyage of Discovery party hosted by Rosemary, followed by a friend's birthday party which took the form of a medieval banquet at Conwy Castle in North Wales. Guests were flown in by helicopter. Then there was the Teddy Bears Picnic party, which cost £70,000 to stage at top London hotel Claridge's. Other personal indulgences included a £9,000 'RUA' personalised number plate for her Mercedes sports car, £78,000 to hire a yacht, £34,000 worth of vintage champagne and £54,000 on her favourite flowers, white lilies.

At the height of Rosemary's frenzied spending, in December 1990, she was getting through £15,000 every day. In just three months she spent £1,350,000. By April 1991 she had all but exhausted the charity donations. For the first time, she began to owe people money.

A few weeks later Rosemary knew it was all over. Charity director Richard Stevens found a letter in one of Rosemary's office drawers. It bore the forged signatures of both himself and the charity's chairman, John Young. The letter asked the Abbey National Building Society to transfer £250,000. 'It was a very good forgery,' admitted Mr Young. He confronted Rosemary, who, cool to the last, told him she had 'cash-flow' problems and that the matter would be sorted out that very afternoon. It never was. Rosemary boarded a plane for Brazil – and people started having serious doubts about their socialite friend and devoted charity worker. As Mr Young was to say later: 'The alarm bells rang.' Soon the swindling impostor, who had stolen almost £3 million of charity funds, was headline news.

After a week in Rio contemplating her fate, Rosemary was persuaded by her family and her boyfriend, Michael Cubbin, to return to face the music, and she flew back to London to give herself up to the police. After six months on remand – during which she had to get used to a new title 'Prisoner Aberdour, number TT184' – Rosemary appeared in court to plead guilty to 17 charges, including five of theft and 11 of obtaining property by deception. She had stolen and spent over £2,700,000.

Prosecuting barrister Brendan Finucane said Rosemary's spending had become an addiction. 'She spent all the money on such a grand scale,' he said. 'It was like the compulsion of a gambler. The money all went. She needed to fuel her fantasies and continued to do it until, by chance, she was stopped.'

Rosemary was sentenced to four years in prison. Newspaper reports labelled her 'Snooty Big Spender', 'The Girl Who Tried to Buy Love' and 'Phoney Aristocrat'. And the Essex girl returned to Essex to serve her time, at Bullwood Hall Prison.

Meanwhile, the National Hospital was left to sort out the monumental financial fraud she had perpetrated. Managers of the National Hospital Development Fund and the Queen's Square Ball fund refused to accept that the mess had been of their making. They blamed building societies and banks for failing to act the moment suspicions had been aroused. Under threat of legal action, the building societies involved paid back £1.5 million, the banks nearly £1 million. The charity was determined to recoup as much of its loss as was humanly possible, serving writs on those who had provided services or goods in return for their stolen money and fraudulent cheques. As one party organiser said: 'It all got pretty nasty.' Rosemary's furniture and paintings went back to the shops that had sold them and the money was refunded. Other possessions fetched around £100,000 at a sale organised by London auction house Christie's.

The Charity Commission was called in to investigate how it had all been allowed to happen. Its findings were simple: Rosemary had used charity donations for her own benefit, apparently answerable to no one. And her cunning accountancy meant auditors had failed to notice any discrepancies. National Hospital Development Fund director Richard Stevens left to become a fundraiser for Southampton University. Chairman John Young survived the scandal and became president of the fund. He later said: 'We shall never know how much Rosemary's fraud was planned. But she took people into her confidence and conned everyone, including her friends, family and fiancé. She was very cunning.' Rosemary's fraud was directly responsible for the passing of a new law concerning charity money; the 1992 Cheques Act meaning that such forgery is supposedly impossible.

Rosemary served two years of her sentence and was released in October 1993. The National Hospital's long-awaited new wing, with its eight wards, opened three months later. Fiancé Michael Cubbin, a helicopter pilot, stood by Rosemary. They made their home in a village in Oxfordshire. Rosemary was lucky to have a man like Michael. All her so-called friends had deserted her. Promises of million-pound book and film deals about her life had long vanished. The party really was over.

Michael and Rosemary married in November 1994. The wedding took place at Rosemary's local church, back home in Wickham Bishops. At 32 years of age, Rosemary had finally settled into a normal, honest life. The former 'Lady' may not have been able to buy love – but in her bizarre double life she had nevertheless found it.

JOHN BLUNT
SOUTH SEA BUBBLE

It takes a very special brand of confidence trickster to bring financial ruin on an entire country, and John Blunt was just such a man. The only ingredients he required to cause nationwide ruination were a staggering overconfidence in himself and a huge measure of greed and ignorance among his investors. It was a lethal combination which devastated a massive cross-section of British society, from lords to labourers, all taken in by the biggest financial scam in the nation's history, the so-called South Sea Bubble.

The South Sea Company was formed in 1711 with the then perfectly acceptable aim of shipping black slaves from Africa to South America. A concession to trade had been wheedled out of King Louis XIV of France, who had himself been given that right by the Spanish occupying parts of South America and the West Indies, to where the slaves were taken. The agreement was instantly hailed as a milestone in the improvement of Anglo-French relations. For the company, however, the first few years proved grim. The available concessions were restrictive and barely profitable, the slaves died by the hundred in appalling conditions during the voyage across the South Atlantic and pirates made matters worse by flooding the market with slaves at rock-bottom prices. Even the announcement that the British monarch, King George I, had become the company's governor failed to lift lacklustre balance sheets.

The turnaround came when John Blunt, a conniving director of the South Sea Company, seized on the idea of credit management, a system already being exploited well in France by the Scottish financier John Law. Law's theory was that governments should issue, through national banks, paper money instead of gold. The paper notes had to carry the pledge that they could be exchanged for gold at any time, otherwise the financial community would have no confidence in them, but once confidence was established a government could simply print more notes whenever it was short of cash. It seemed too good to be true – which, of course, it was. Today we know that such a policy is doomed to end in rampant inflation. But at the time, the likes of John Law, who almost single-handedly ruined the French economy, and his English counterpart John Blunt saw their schemes as economic miracles which could not fail.

Blunt persuaded his fellow directors at the South Sea Company to embark on a business plan in which they would take total responsibility for England's National Debt: the £50 million the government had borrowed from its own citizens. They would even pay £8 million for the privilege.

The plan went like this. Anyone with, say, £10,000 worth of government bonds could redeem them at the usual modest rate of interest or could instead choose to reinvest in South Sea stock with its promise of fabulous rewards. Each company share would be launched on the market for £100, and so the £10,000 investor would receive 100 new printed shares. But what if the publicity and excitement generated by this imaginative new venture was such that there was a huge demand? Shares would then naturally rise in price, perhaps even double to £200 apiece. The next £10,000 investor to come along would need only 50 shares from the company, leaving another 50 to sell to someone else. The instant profit for the company would amount to £10,000. The key was to keep the sale price of the shares rising so that there were always new investors ready to jump on board.

The idea went before Parliament on 22 January 1720 and, despite noisy objections from the Bank of England, which saw its own role being eroded, it was approved by a majority of four votes. Supporters believed the deal was good for the country because the government would pay the company only four per cent interest on loans rather than the then current five per cent. Within a quarter of a century, it was claimed, the National Debt would be wiped out and England would once again be able to trade with the world unfettered by the financial millstone around her neck.

Few of the investors in this new scheme really understood how credit worked. But at the time they didn't care. They didn't so much jump on to the bandwagon as fit it with a turbocharged engine. And at first it seemed they were right; the share price quickly rocketed to £400 before a few jubilant early profit takers damped it down to a steady £330.

Within a matter of weeks widows and pensioners were retrieving their meagre life savings from beneath mattresses to plough into the South Sea Company. Farm workers and fishermen rushed to buy their stake before the price spiralled again. And the landed gentry poured in every last penny they could find. Some even remortgaged their homes or borrowed from more circumspect friends to increase their exposure to this amazing new, no-risk wonder company.

The frenzy persisted even when three months after the

launch Blunt revealed another 20,000 shares were up for grabs. This was an illegal move as Parliament had decreed the only shares that could be sold were remainders left after government creditors and pensioners had received their full allocation. It didn't seem to matter. The new stock sold for £300 per share and a further 10,000 floated later in the month went for £400 each. Many people took their lead from the King, who let it be known that he had invested £20,000. George sold his stake for a handsome £86,000 profit early on and was so pleased with John Blunt's performance that he awarded him a knighthood.

Incredibly, none of the money that came in was reinvested by the South Sea Company. No one stopped to think that it should be put to work making things or providing services for consumers. The company's directors wallowed complacently in the belief that, if they needed more money, they could just print more shares.

Before 1720 was out, a host of other entrepreneurs were taking a slice of the action with their own hastily formed companies. Most of these were illegal because they were trading without a royal charter, but both the authorities and the general public were too busy getting rich quick to care. As a result anyone could buy shares in pirate-proof ships, cleaner lavatories, wheels which produced perpetual motion. Investors could get into the jackasses-from-Spain import business or silkworm production in Chelsea. One sincere-looking entrepreneur even sold shares in a company whose declared aim was 'carrying on an undertaking of great advantage but no one to know what it is'. He promised an annual return of £50 on every £1 invested and on his first day pocketed £2,000 from excited punters. The man vanished that evening, his undertaking of great advantage complete.

By August of that year the South Sea Company had taken more than £8 million from its shareholders. But, because many had bought under 'pay later' agreements, there was £60 million worth of payments still to come in. By now some of the new 'bubble' companies were starting to go bust, a factor that further slowed the flow of funds into Blunt's coffers. The mood was imperceptibly changing and Blunt failed to see it. He ordered the prosecution of four large rival companies which, he alleged, were trading without a royal charter. The courts backed Blunt and those companies' stocks became worthless.

Rarely in the field of great financial disasters has anyone misjudged the might of market forces so badly. Investors in the four bankrupt companies decided to solve their personal financial problems by selling their best assets – South Sea Company shares. Suddenly, instead of everyone wanting to buy, numerous big players wanted to sell. Word spread and smaller investors picked up the vibes. Confidence, the factor that drives any credit economy, was taking a massive nosedive.

Within days South Sea Company shares were in free-fall. Their value was reduced from £900 apiece to £190 and thousands of people stared ruin in the face. The Duke of Chandos saw £300,000 disappear almost overnight, while many famous figures, among them the poets Alexander Pope and Matthew Prior, also saw their life savings evaporate. Civil unrest loomed and at one point the King even considered bringing over his German troops from Hanover in case of riots. Outraged MPs and the public felt swindled and they demanded the perpetrators of this financial fiddle be brought to book. John Blunt was the obvious target and he was hauled before a parliamentary committee to be told his personal fortune of £185,000 would be reduced to £1,000. It was a mighty downfall – but matched pound for pound by the ruination of many of the great, the good and the gullible in the land.

VICTOR LUSTIG
THE BOUNCING CZECH

Millionaire André Poisson arrived at the fashionable Hôtel Crillon in the centre of Paris full of the joys of spring. He had every reason to feel especially good about himself because today was the day he was going to make history. Monsieur Poisson was due at the Crillon to buy the city's most famous landmark, the Eiffel Tower, and he was correct in the notion that he was about to make history, but not for the reason he expected. He was to go down in the annals of fraud as the victim of one of the most audacious hoaxes ever perpetrated.

The man Poisson was meeting that beautiful spring day in 1925 was Victor Lustig, or Count Lustig as he preferred to be called. A trickster of the highest order, Lustig had already been arrested 45 times and was now about to pull his most stunning stunt ever. He was born in Hestinne, Czechoslovakia, in 1890, and found himself in Paris after his father decided he should become a student at the Sorbonne. Lustig soon discovered that studying came a poor second to the Paris high life, financed by his skilful gambling.

His ability to speak several languages came in useful when he later joined transatlantic liners to fleece dollars from rich American card players. He was taken under the wing of Nicky Arnstein, an expert at 'working the boats', and soon learned how to spot an easy target. The pair remained partners throughout a series of frauds in America before Lustig returned to Paris and took a room at the Crillon. There he teamed up with a new partner, 'Dapper Dan' Collins. It was time for more money-making fun.

Their golden opportunity presented itself swiftly. Lustig was perusing his morning newspaper on 8 May 1925 when his eye alighted on a report that the Eiffel Tower was in need of repair. The cost would be so substantial that the French government was even considering it more economic to dismantle the famous Paris landmark. Lustig and Collins got into a heated debate. Collins thought the idea of tearing down the Eiffel Tower disgraceful. Lustig argued that, surprisingly, many French people thought the monument hideously ugly. His argument was supported by the fact that the newspaper report made no mention of public protest over the government's plans. What both men did agree on, however, was the potential for a splendid money-spinning adventure.

Lustig got to work quickly. He forged letterheads of the Ministère des Postes et Telegraphes, the authority responsible for the Eiffel Tower, and he found out who were the main iron and steel stockholders and scrap-metal dealers in and around Paris. He drew up a list of five suitably wealthy candidates for his confidence trick, although he already had one man marked down as the Eiffel Tower's perfect purchaser: Monsieur André Poisson. All five, however, received an official-looking invitation from the Ministère des Postes et Telegraphes to attend a meeting at the Hôtel Crillon. There they were warmly welcomed by the 'secretary to the deputy director', the dapperly attired Dan Collins. After a few minutes the 'deputy director' himself made his impressive appearance. It was, of course, Victor Lustig.

He started in fine style: 'I must emphasise, gentlemen, that what I am going to tell you must be treated in the greatest confidence. Indeed, I should point out that, before we sent you your invitations, each one of you was very thoroughly investigated. The nature of my news is so important, such a matter of national concern, that only the most trustworthy, the most serious, the most scrupulous businessmen in Paris are being let into my ministry's little secret.' There was a dramatic pause as Lustig waited to see what effect his words would have on the gathering. There was an expectant hush. Then he continued: 'No doubt you have read the newspaper reports. It is unnecessary for me to tell you that the Eiffel Tower, one of the more noble features of our noble city, has fallen into a serious state of disrepair. If all the work which is urgently needed is carried out, the bill will run into hundreds of thousands of francs. It is more than any of us sitting around this table could afford – and, dare I say it, more than France could afford.'

After giving the five businessmen an authoritative history lesson on the Eiffel Tower, Lustig came to the point of his meeting. Emphasising the crucial need for confidentiality to avoid 'political ramifications', he told his audience that the Eiffel Tower was being pulled down and that the resulting mountain of 7,000 tons of scrap iron was up for sale to the highest bidder. To give further credibility to his authority, he then proceeded to summarise the 'official' government specifications of the tower. It was 984 feet high, the base measured 142 yards in each direction and the interlaced girders were made of 12,000 sections joined together by over two and a half million rivets. The scrap-metal dealers were spellbound.

Lustig's introductory talk was followed by an invitation to the businessmen to avail themselves of one of the 'official cars' waiting outside the hotel and spend the afternoon viewing the Eiffel Tower. Lustig, the bogus man from the ministry, would then await the arrival of sealed bids at the Crillon. He told Poisson and the others that, because of the delicacy of the matter, the ministry could not be seen to be involved. The bids, therefore, should be addressed to 'Monsieur Dante'.

Lustig was right in targeting Poisson as the man most likely to buy the Eiffel Tower. Poisson was one of the provincial nouveaux riches anxious to make a name for himself in the Parisian business world. Back in his office, Poisson was already calculating how to raise the finance needed to make the Eiffel Tower his very own. He even considered remortgaging his home. In his imagination, he foresaw newspaper headlines such as 'André Poisson: the Man Who Bought the Eiffel Tower'. Even when Poisson's wife said she found it peculiar that such confidential meetings were held in a hotel room, Poisson remained unsuspicious. Lustig had had an answer for that too; he had emphasised the fact that the ministry must not be seen to have played any part in such controversial dealings.

Poisson was beside himself with joy when, a few days later, Lustig knocked on his door and told him his bid had been successful. He was now required to bring a certified cheque for a quarter of his bid price to the same suite of rooms at the Crillon. In return he would receive the necessary documents confirming his ownership of the Eiffel Tower and the terms on which he would be permitted to demolish it.

And so it was that Poisson found himself joyfully outside the Crillon on 20 May 1925. But, as he approached the room where he was to meet Lustig, doubts began to creep in. He remembered his wife's suspicions about the whole business. He fingered the cheque in his pocket. It represented nearly all his assets. Lustig sensed Poisson's apprehension and knew he had to act quickly. It was already after 2 p.m. and the banks in Paris closed at 2.30 p.m. That cheque had to be cashed today so that he and Collins could be on their way.

Lustig embarked on some clever play-acting. He adopted a nervous tone to explain that, although he was in an important and influential position, his salary was but a pittance. He had to rely on 'commissions' to earn a proper wage. Perhaps, he said hesitantly, Monsieur Poisson could see his way clear to offer a commission too.

'A bribe, you mean?' blurted out the astonished Poisson. Lustig merely smiled politely. Poisson relaxed. He knew all about bribes. They were a necessary evil he had come across in many a business transaction before. Now he knew the man from the ministry had to be genuine. Poisson reached inside his pocket, pulled out his wallet and removed the substantial wad of banknotes he always kept on him for such occasions. Lustig leaned over and, still smiling, helped himself to several thousand francs. Poisson returned his wallet to his pocket and then handed over his cheque to Lustig. They shook hands; it had been a very satisfactory meeting for both men.

That afternoon Lustig and Collins boarded a train to Vienna, where they lay low. Every day they avidly read the newspapers, waiting for the storm to break – but not a word about the hoax ever appeared. Poisson had obviously decided his pride was worth more than the bundle of money he had so readily handed over. The fraudsters waited patiently for two weeks for any repercussions. Then, safe in the knowledge that the police had not been informed of their con trick, they made new plans – to sell the Eiffel Tower all over again.

And so the dodgy duo headed once again for Paris. The same deception as before was put in motion. Only this time, the victim, realising he had been fooled, went straight to the police. Lustig and Collins fled the city, the two confidence tricksters at last parting company.

Lustig went to America and continued duping easy targets. These included wealthy but greedy Herman Loller, to whom he sold a 'money-making machine'. Lustig demonstrated how the machine could duplicate banknotes. A little careful preparation beforehand ensured the notes produced were genuine, so when Loller took them to a bank, their acceptance could not help but convince him the machine would make him even wealthier. Loller bought the machine from Lustig for $25,000. Amazingly, it was a year before he reported his worthless purchase to the police, having spent months believing that he had not properly mastered the machine. Lustig pulled the same stunt on a sheriff in Oklahoma. When the lawman tracked him down in Chicago to complain, Lustig 'made' some banknotes for him. Sadly for the sheriff, Lustig had used counterfeit money. The sheriff found himself on the wrong side of the law when he tried to use the cash, and was jailed.

Lustig's cheating career continued. He even bravely attempted to swindle Al Capone. He took $50,000 off the ruthless Mafia boss, telling him he could double it on Wall Street. In fact, Lustig could think of no scheme to double the money, so he boldly returned to Capone, handed the $50,000 back and admitted he had failed. Lustig's feigned humiliation at having let down such a great man impressed Capone. He peeled off a wad of notes and gave them to Lustig as compensation.

The arch conman went on to flood America with counterfeit money and was eventually arrested. He went on trial in December 1935 and was sentenced to 15 years plus another five years for an earlier escape from a federal institution. Even Lustig could not talk his way out of infamous Alcatraz, where he served 10 years before contracting pneumonia. Now an ailing man of 57, he was transferred to the Medical Center for Federal Prisoners in Springfield, Missouri, where he died on 9 March 1947. The death certificate did no justice to Lustig's colourful, cheating life. His occupation was recorded simply as 'Apprentice Salesman'.

COLLINS, LOWE AND FURGUSON
THREE KING CONS

The criminal career of Victor Lustig's artful associate, Dapper Dan Collins, continued long after his association with the master of fraud came to an end. Collins, born in 1885 as Robert Arthur Tourbillon, enjoyed an amazing career. His first job was as a lion tamer in a French circus. Known as 'The Circle of Death', his act involved riding a bicycle through a group of lions. Circus life was too tame for him, however, and he turned to crime while still in his teens. He gained the nickname 'The Rat', after his initials. At the age of 23 he emigrated to America and received his first prison sentence at 31 – convicted of 'white slavery', he proudly boasted later. Released from jail four years later, he was determined to specialise in one area of crime for which he seemed to have a natural talent: fraud. But first he needed a new image, so he kitted himself out with expensive clothes and set sail from New York for his native France. Dapper Dan Collins was born.

The fraudster's ready wit, good looks and charm meant there was no shortage of rich matrons on both sides of the Atlantic willing to finance his glamorous lifestyle. The infamous Eiffel Tower hoax in 1925, perpetrated with Victor Lustig, was but a brief break in his career as a

Casanova. It was bad luck that finally put Collins behind bars. Back in Paris after a string of money-making ventures in the USA, he had the misfortune to bump into two detectives. They were hunting an entirely different crook but could not ignore barroom talk about a man nicknamed Dapper Dan whose exploits sounded remarkably similar to those of 'The Rat'.

Collins was arrested and put on board the liner *France* bound for New York. During the journey he was treated as anything but a hardened villain. Instead, he hosted parties, gaily spending his money on the passengers, crew and his new detective friends. He believed that, since he was shortly going to be thrown into jail, he might as well spend the proceeds of crime while he was able. He might not have been so free with his money if he had known what would happen in America. For, incredibly, when Collins, under his real name of Tourbillon, appeared in court, he was acquitted of all robbery charges brought against him.

His good fortune was to run out, however. In 1929 one of his past misdemeanours caught up with him when he was charged with defrauding a New Jersey farmer out of $30,000 savings and was jailed for two years. He served 16 months and, when released, made clear his intention to return to France. No one knows if that is where Collins ended his days because, after walking through the prison gates to freedom, he was never heard of again – under any name.

One would think that, after Lustig and Collins's incredible Eiffel Tower hoax, no one would make the same mistake again. Yet, amazingly, there was one man, a wealthy Texan, who had not heard the story. Just after the Second World War, English conman Stanley Lowe managed to persuade him that the Eiffel Tower had been so badly damaged by the war that the city's officials had decided to sell it off, the historic monument's scrap value being a mere $40,000. The hapless Texan fell for the story. But, luckily for him, the attempted fraud was uncovered in time and Lowe was sentenced to nine months in jail.

Lowe's cheeky attempt to repeat a fellow confidence trickster's scam shows there is no limit to what a determined fraudster will attempt. The Eiffel Tower deception was just one in a series in Lowe's conning career. His speciality was disguise, and he regularly took on a persona selected from a variety of different characters.

Dressed as a cleric, Lowe once persuaded a Japanese tourist to contribute $100,000 to an 'appeal' to help restore London's historic St Paul's Cathedral. Another of Lowe's roles was as an Oscar-winning Hollywood producer called Mark Sheridan, seeking investors for a potential box-office success. On other occasions he would become Group Captain Rivers Bogle Bland, a former flyer working undercover for the British government on a top-secret mission. Despite the ludicrous name he had chosen for the fictitious war hero, he still managed to convince people to part with their money.

Lowe did not always want to prise cash from people, however; sometimes he just enjoyed inventing stories. It was a pastime he had perfected early in life, when his home was an orphanage in north London. He drifted into crime at an early age, quickly realising that you had to think on your feet to wriggle out of tricky situations. There was the time when the owner of a Mayfair flat caught him stealing. Calmly, he explained: 'Madam, this is an emergency. I was just passing when I saw a man attempting to hurl himself from the window.' Then he coolly walked off with his pockets full of the woman's jewellery.

It was Lowe's talent for escaping justice that enabled him

to lead a champagne lifestyle. He wore handmade shoes and shirts, stayed at the famous George V Hotel in Paris and went on exotic holidays. One of his plots was aimed at providing regular funding for this lifestyle. Lowe smooth-talked his way into a job as a footman at Marlborough House, home of Queen Mary, where he planned to lift as much as he could lay his hands on. But his taste for high living was his downfall. One day he arrived for his footman's job wearing an expensive suit and driving a brand-new Jaguar, which he had just stolen. Suspicions were naturally aroused, as Lowe's lifestyle seemed a little extravagant on a weekly wage of £6.

When questioned by officers of the law, the conman told them: 'The Queen is surrounded by priceless possessions and I had nothing. It's not that I'm disloyal to our beloved Royal Family. I just decided she should be punished for her greed.'

A prison sentence followed and, when he was released, Lowe seemed to have lost his confidence trickster's confidence. He was never the same villain again, eventually ending his days in a humble one-room flat. The glory days for the man who fancied himself as a modern Robin Hood – 'I want to rob the rich,' he once said – were finally over.

Stanley Lowe, Dapper Dan Collins and his mentor Victor Lustig are all strong candidates for the title 'King of Conmen', as is the modern-day trickster Peter Foster, but there is a fourth con artist whose barefaced cheek also makes him a candidate for the dubious award. Arthur Furguson was a canny Scotsman who found meagre fame and less fortune as an actor touring with repertory companies in his homeland and in the North of England. He deserved better, for, as an actor, he was extremely convincing.

Furguson had once played the role of an American duped by a conman, and this gave him the idea for what is perhaps the most brazen series of confidence tricks in history. Within just a few weeks in 1925 he conned three American tourists into 'buying' three of London's best-known landmarks: Big Ben, Nelson's Column and Buckingham Palace.

Nelson's Column was the first to go. Erected in honour of the great Admiral Horatio Nelson after his momentous naval victory over the French, the column stands in London's Trafalgar Square. Also standing in the square and gazing up at the column on this particular day was a tourist from Iowa. Furguson approached him. 'The statue atop that column is of England's greatest naval hero, victor of the Battle of Trafalgar in 1805,' announced Furguson. 'It's such a pity that it is having to be dismantled to help repay Britain's war loan from the United States.'

The American was horrified. In the conversation that ensued, Furguson established that the man was not only a 'lover of fine architecture' but also extremely rich. In that case, suggested the Scot, the visitor really ought to know that he, Arthur Furguson, was none other than the Ministry of Works official entrusted with the sad task of arranging the sale. There was already a long queue of potential buyers, warned the talkative trickster, but, if there was a chance of the monument going to such a fine new home as Iowa, then he guaranteed his best efforts to ensure that his new-found friend should acquire this great edifice to Britain's former glory.

The man from Iowa was hooked. He pleaded with Furguson to let him jump the queue for Nelson's Column. Eventually the Scot agreed to telephone his superiors there and then. Within minutes he was back with the good news that, for an immediate cheque in the sum of £6,000, the American could have the monument and dismantle it as soon as he liked. The cheque was written and a receipt exchanged for it, accompanied by the name and address of the 'authorised' demolition company. The afternoon was now drawing on and the company had closed for the day. But the next morning the American was on the phone to them — but all he heard from the other end were gales of laughter. Tourists are always told that, when in doubt, they should ask a London bobby. A bemused constable heard the American's story and led him to Scotland Yard nearby. There, at last, the penny dropped. But so did £6,000, for Furguson had already cashed the cheque and disappeared.

Furguson was now flushed with success, as well as whisky and grander plans. Within weeks Scotland Yard again heard of his amazing nerve when an American complained that he had bought Buckingham Palace for £2,000 yet the Royal Family would not allow him through the gates. Only days later a third transatlantic tourist told them he had paid good money for Big Ben, the clock tower alongside the Houses of Parliament. Furguson had accepted a knockdown price of £1,000 for it.

Police chiefs within the red-brick edifice of Scotland Yard were less than pleased that nearby historic buildings were being hawked on the streets of London. Might not they be next? However, attempts to trap the elusive Furguson came to naught. So impressed was the conman with the generosity of the American people that he had decided to emigrate there.

Once in the United States, the Scotsman's career of con artistry continued unchecked. 'Think big' was Furguson's motto, so he offered a Texan cattle rancher a 99-year lease on a large white building in Washington. The rent was

$100,000 a year, with the first year paid in advance. The Texan handed over the cash in exchange for a worthless lease on the White House.

Having attempted to dispossess the President of the United States, Furguson then attempted to do likewise to its most famous lady. In Manhattan he encountered a gullible Australian on a visit from Sydney, to whom he spun a yarn about New York harbour's waterways being widened. The unfortunate consequence of this modernisation programme, explained Furguson, was that the Statue of Liberty was to be dismantled and sold. If relocated to the southern hemisphere, would it not look just fine re-erected on Pinchgut Island in the middle of Sydney Harbour? The unsuspecting Australian was given a guided tour of the statue, a gift to New York from the people of France. He then asked a passer-by to take a photograph of himself with the famous torch-carrying lady in the background to show the folks back home. Unfortunately for Furguson, he too was in the picture.

The Australian's next call was to his New York bank, where he made an immediate application for a loan of $100,000, the price being asked by Furguson. The bank manager was more suspicious, however, and urged his client to check with the New York Police Department. After the Australian showed detectives the photograph of himself with the phoney 'city official', the police swooped on Furguson, who ended up with a five-year jail sentence.

On his release in 1930, Furguson removed himself to the gentler climes of Los Angeles, where he found the pickings modest but satisfactory. He perpetrated a further string of minor confidence tricks from his luxurious new home, avoiding the interest of the Californian police until his death in 1938.

Artful Fakers, Forgers, Charlatans and Cheats

ART FORGERS: PAST MASTERS

'You can sell anything to Americans and Englishmen,' said the grandson of French painter Jean-François Millet when convicted of art forgery in 1935. 'They know nothing about art. Even their experts know nothing. All you have to do is to ask a fabulous price.' Many forgers before and since would agree with Millet's verdict on the gullibility, ignorance and often greed of the luminaries of the art world. But the trade in fakes is not confined to duping 'Americans and Englishmen'. Nor, as we shall see, is it peculiar to the twentieth century.

There is nothing new about the forgery of works of art. Michelangelo not only created masterpieces such as the marble sculpture of *David* and the painting of the Sistine Chapel; he also dabbled in fakery. He first came to fame when he sold a marble *Cupid* to Cardinal San Giorgio, who then summoned him to Rome in 1496. What he never told the cardinal, however, was that he had first stained and buried the statue to age it for presentation as an antique. It produced much-needed funds for the struggling young artist.

One of the most prolific sculptors of all time was Giovanni Bastianini – and every one of his works was a fake. The nineteenth-century Florentine forger turned out terracotta busts by the dozen for a crooked art dealer. Before his death in 1868, Bastianini was heartened to see them displayed in museums and galleries around the globe. According to London's Victoria and Albert Museum, which took two of the forgeries, the faker's works were perfect examples of Renaissance sculpture.

A pair of forgers fell out over one particular work of art. The Tiara of Saitaphernes was an intricate golden headdress which reposed in the Louvre, Paris, admired by all and sundry as one of the minor wonders of the ancient world. In 1902, however, a Parisian painter claimed to have been the creator of this beautiful work of art. Administrators of the Louvre fiercely denied the claim, insisting that the artefact was genuine. The row created great publicity, reaching even Russia, where newspaper reports of the scandal were read by a goldsmith, Israel Rouchomowsky. He knew that the headdress was a fake — and was equally certain that it was not the work of the Parisian claimant. For the creator of the forgery was Rouchomowsky himself! The goldsmith travelled to Paris to lay claim to the dubious honour. When the Louvre officials adamantly refused to give him credit for his work, he produced his original designs for the tiara, which he had drawn up eight years earlier. Rouchomowsky finally proved the origins of the golden tiara beyond all doubt, by creating another one: a perfect match for the Louvre's most embarrassing fake.

Another artist who laid claim to his own work was an amateur sculptor who found his creation proudly displayed in Harrods, the top people's store in London's Knightsbridge. The store's antiques department is staffed by some of the leading experts in their various fields. But even they were bamboozled by the work of Frank Sedgwick, an ex-fitter whose hobby was woodwork and who had knocked up an 'antique' in less than a fortnight in his garden shed in Kent. The honest Mr Sedgwick had sold his wooden sculpture of a kneeling stag for £165 in 1972. It changed hands several times over the following five years until it turned up on display at Harrods with a price tag of £9,800. It was labelled as a 'carving from a French chateau, dated circa 1580'. In 1977 Sedgwick walked into the store and told the astonished assistant: 'That's all my own work.' Harrods removed it instantly.

Modern technology, rather than masterful knowledge, uncovered a fake that had been displayed as one of the most prized possessions of America's Cleveland Museum of Art. The museum believed that its wooden *Madonna and Child* had been carved in Italy in the thirteenth century. The work was indeed that of an Italian: it was carved by art restorer Alceo Dossena in 1920. In 1927 the *Madonna and Child* was X-rayed to discover whether such an ancient work was due for restoration. The discovery of modern nails embedded in the wood prompted the statue's sudden and embarrassed removal to the basement.

Within three weeks, however, the Cleveland Museum's authorities had found a suitable replacement for the fake. They purchased a marble statue of *Athena* for $120,000. Unfortunately this too was the work of Alceo Dossena. Sadly for the master forger, his expertise never made him a fortune. The Italian stonecutter turned sculptor produced a mass of sculptures during the early years of the twentieth century but sold them all through a pair of clever confidence tricksters. Jeweller Alberto Fasoliu and antique dealer Romano Palesi set up a studio in Rome for the young sculptor and paid him a small salary. There he spent 10 years slaving away at his forgeries for a pittance – while his crooked agents made themselves a small fortune.

Another gallery which paid handsomely for a string of fakes is New York's renowned Metropolitan Museum of Art. One particular statue, a two-metre-tall figure of an Etruscan warrior, held pride of place. One arm was missing, as was the thumb of his other hand. This was not surprising, as the statue had supposedly been buried since pre-Roman days. The museum had paid $40,000 for the Etruscan warrior in 1918. It was not until 1960 that Alfredo Fioravanti announced that he and five accomplices had created the statue half a century before. To prove that he was indeed the sculptor, Fioravanti produced the warrior's missing thumb – which fitted perfectly!

The Metropolitan Museum was again in trouble in 1975 when one of its most popular attractions, a beautiful bronze horse supposedly of the Greek period, was shown to be a fake and had to be withdrawn. In 1984 the museum was forced to re-examine many of its masterworks: elegant gold pieces embellished with jewels in the style of Benvenuto Cellini, the sixteenth-century Florentine goldsmith, sculptor and engraver. The alarm was raised when a museum curator came upon working sketches by a nineteenth-century German craftsman, Reinhold Vasters, for a gold cup depicting a jewel-studded dragon. This prompted the museum to make further examination of its own treasured gold cups, and it was realised that these had been soldered together in a rather too modern manner. Vasters, not Cellini, was the artist – and the embarrassed Met was forced to admit that no fewer than 45 of its golden treasures were fakes.

Perhaps the most astonishing scandal over art forgeries occurred in West Germany in the 1950s. It involved an art restorer turned forger named Dietrich Fey. Despite warnings that Fey was not to be trusted, he was nevertheless given the prestigious job of working on the frescoes of the Marienkirche in Lübeck. Scraps of the original thirteenth-century frescoes had come to light during the Second World War as bombs gutted the church. When his work was complete, Fey proudly declared that he had 'added nothing but merely preserved what had survived'. The work was unveiled before Chancellor Konrad Adenauer in September 1951. It was a momentous occasion, not only for art experts and historians but also for Christians, for the frescoes showed biblical scenes and saints as well as mythical beasts. A special five-pfennig stamp was even issued to commemorate the event.

Fey appeared to have done too good a job, however, and it was when he was awarded the nation's Cross of Merit for his work that a fellow art restorer on the project, Lothar Malskat, pulled his own masterstroke. Malskat was believed to have faked Chagalls and other modern masters before the war, and to have given them to Fey to sell. Now, embittered over lack of recognition for projects he had worked on, Malskat stepped forward in May 1952 to announce that the frescoes were all his own work. The claim threw the art world into turmoil but, after much debate, Malskat was simply dismissed as a troublemaker. Most critics agreed that neither Malskat nor Fey could possibly have created work of such beauty. Above all, the West German Association for the Preservation of Ancient Monuments did not want the embarrassment of knowing it had possibly spent £25,000 on dubious restoration work.

Even more frustrated that no one believed his confession, Malskat took drastic and incredible action. He instructed his lawyer to file charges against himself and Fey! At the court hearing, Malskat produced a film proving that the walls of the church had been almost entirely bare when he and Fey had begun work on them. He said the original paintings were so fragile they had crumbled to dust at the mere touch of a restoration brush. The only thing to do after that was to create the work of art from scratch.

Even now, there were those who refused to believe what they were hearing, but Malskat had one final trick up his sleeve to convince them. He led members of the court to the church walls and pointed out how the heavenly faces of a choir on the frescoes bore remarkable similarities to the not-so-saintly likes of Marlene Dietrich, Rasputin, Genghis Khan and even Malskat's own sister. If that wasn't enough proof, he told the astonished gathering, they could always visit Schleswig Cathedral and see his 'ancient' painting of a turkey – a bird unknown in Europe until after the discovery of America!

Dietrich Fey was sentenced to 20 months in jail and Lothar Malskat to 18 months. After his release, and satisfied with his revenge on Fey, Malskat returned to art restoration – but in an honest way.

Another quick-on-the draw artist was David Stein, who for a brief but mind-boggling four-year reign was undisputed king of the art forgers. Indeed his total income from his fakes was around £1 million. Stein, born near Paris in 1935, was a gifted artist, but he felt payments for his works simply were not enough – especially when he heard about the high prices other painters received. Forgery was too much of a temptation to resist. Working in watercolours or oils, he recreated the styles of some of the world's best-known artists, both living and dead.

The dead gave David Stein no trouble, but the living led to his downfall. On one occasion, while living in New

York, he rushed off three watercolours by Russian-born artist Marc Chagall, which he had promised to a dealer. Working furiously in his apartment, he took just seven hours to complete the whole fateful operation. During that time he treated the paper with cold tea to give it the impression of ageing, perfectly captured Chagall's style and put the finishing touch of the artist's signature to each painting. He finished at 6 a.m. and by lunchtime that same day he was handing his 'genuine' works of art, each with its own certificate of authentication, to a delighted art dealer. The dealer was so proud of his new acquisitions that he decided to show them to someone who had just arrived in New York – Chagall himself. Chagall's reaction was first bewilderment and then horror. 'They are not mine,' he said. 'And they are diabolical.'

Had Stein stuck to recreating Cézannes, Renoirs or Manets, he would have got away with it. Impersonating Chagall, who was alive and well and more than likely to come face to face with his faked work, was a bad decision. It also meant Stein had to abandon his New York gallery, financed, of course, by his ill-gotten gains. As the police arrived at his front door, he fled out the back, taking his wife Anne-Marie and their small child with him. They ended up in California. But there Stein's luck ran out. He was arrested and confessed to his handiwork. 'If only I had stuck to dead men,' he lamented as he was charged with 97 counts of grand larceny and counterfeiting. In January 1969 he was sentenced to three years in Sing Sing Prison.

While in jail, Stein shared his knowledge of forgery with the New York Police Department, helping them to create a special art forgery squad. With remission, he served just 16 months. His stay in prison had also given him time to think about a legitimate money-making venture. Stein had hit on the idea of painting famous people in the style of well-known artists. Only this time, he would declare his work as a genuine gimmick. For instance, a three-hour sitting with Brigitte Bardot allowed him to paint the actress in 25 different styles, ranging from Picasso to Van Gogh. Unfortunately for Stein, he then made the big mistake of setting up in business in France. The French police still wanted to interview him about his previous lifestyle. And, following their talk, Stein was back in jail – this time for two and a half years.

On his release, Stein concentrated only on paintings by Stein. But he was still bitter about what he considered the fickleness of so-called art experts. And he still reckoned he had had the last laugh. 'A lot of the art world is fake,' he said. 'And they may not know it, but there are about two or three hundred of my forgeries still on the market listed as originals.'

A touring exhibition of Expressionist works was one of the art world's most remarkable success stories of the early 1990s. American students flocked to see the 58 paintings, intrigued by the notion that these were works that Hitler had sought to burn as 'degenerate art' but which had miraculously escaped the Nazi torch. It was only when the paintings were on their twelfth stop, near Chicago, that a visiting art dealer called the police and alleged that all 58 were fakes. The tour was halted, the pictures impounded and one of the most astonishing art frauds of all time began to fall apart at the seams.

The tour of American colleges had been the brainwave of Bryn Lloyd Williams, a former art dealer from Chalfont St Giles, in Buckinghamshire, England. He had already induced 87 Irish art investors to put up £3.2 million to buy 'Old Masters' by the likes of Rubens, Rembrandt and Sir

Joshua Reynolds, which they were to sell on to guaranteed buyers for double the price. The pictures were modern fakes or nineteenth-century copies, yet enough money rolled in to enable Williams to acquire his next collection of worthless fakes: the supposed art treasures condemned by the Nazis but rescued by a Jewish nobleman who had fled Germany in 1938.

To boost the value of the 58 Expressionist works, Williams sent some on a tour of Germany, while the others went the rounds of American universities, where the cream of the nation's art academia lavished praise on them. When the works shown in America were finally exposed as fakes, the German police also impounded the European exhibition. The law finally caught up with Williams six years later when, in London's High Court in 1998, his long-suffering investors successfully sued the fraudster.

Most art fakers' talents are hidden, for obvious reasons. Eric Hebborn was different. The genial Englishman was among the most successful and prolific artists of his generation. His drawings can still be found in great private collections and in galleries and museums around the world. Yet Hebborn could never be honoured for his services to art. Instead, he was destined to become known as one of the greatest fakers of all time.

Hebborn copied almost every important European painter of the period from the fourteenth to the twentieth century and created more than 1,000 'Old Master' drawings which have been attributed to artists such as Van Dyck, Gainsborough, Poussin and Degas. In *The Art Forger's Handbook*, which he wrote a year before his death in Italy in 1996, he described his craft as 'a glorious game', a way of entertaining himself as well as of making money. Hebborn, an ex-Borstal boy who started his fakery as a penniless London art student, always insisted that he was no conman because none of his drawings was a copy; each was a fresh work that recreated the style of a great artist of the past. But he admitted his glee at deceiving the pundits. 'I have never tried to fool the man in the street,' he once said. 'Only the "experts" are worth fooling – and the greater the expert the greater the satisfaction.'

But it is art cheat Elmyr de Hory who is the recipient of the greatest accolade of anyone in his line of business. He was the subject of a book called *Fake!*, published in 1969. Not only that: it was written by fellow forger Clifford Irving (whom we report on elsewhere in this book as the creator of the 'Howard Hughes autobiography').

De Hory was a stateless Hungarian who was a fine artist in his own right. He was born in 1911, the only child of landowning parents who divorced when he was 16. De Hory first studied art in Budapest, then at the Akademie Heimann in Munich and finally at the Académie de la Grande Chaumière in Paris. He was a homosexual whose charm soon won him friends from the world of famous artists, including Matisse and Picasso – two twentieth-century masters whose work he would later have no qualms about imitating for financial gain.

Although he was making a good living and gaining in reputation as an artist, de Hory was to suffer a cruel fate. After returning to Budapest in 1938 after Hitler's annexation of Austria, he was arrested as a political undesirable. He was interned first in Transylvania and then moved to a concentration camp in Germany where he suffered badly at the hands of the Gestapo. The end of the war saw de Hory a broken and penniless refugee subsisting in Paris. However, a chance remark by a visitor to his studio was to set him on the road to profitable forgeries. Spotting a line drawing by de Hory of a young girl's head, the visitor asked: 'Is that a Picasso?' De Hory did not demur. Instead he accepted the equivalent of £50 for the picture – then went on to paint another half a dozen 'Picassos'.

In fact, de Hory became so adept at recreating Picasso's work that the great man himself was once fooled. De Hory had the cheek to ask Picasso to authenticate one of his fakes. Readily putting his name to the work, a nude, Picasso remarked: 'I remember painting her. It did take rather a long time to complete as I could not resist making love to her.'

After falling out with a partner in his crooked business, de Hory fled, first to Brazil, then New York and finally to Los Angeles. The same attributes that had won him friends in Paris soon earned him a place in Hollywood's smart set. He quickly realised that here was real money to be had. So he changed his name to Baron de Hory and turned out paintings purportedly by Matisse and Renoir, which were quickly snapped up by the rich residents of Hollywood.

In 1952, when a sharp-eyed dealer spotted a fake Modigliani, de Hory was forced to flee back to New York, where he sold three fake Matisse drawings for £500 each. Deciding to start a new life for himself, he went to Miami and attempted to exist only on his own work. But, when times got hard, he fell back on producing fake paintings of famous artists. He claimed he could paint a portrait in 45 minutes, draw a 'Modigliani' in 10 and then immediately knock off a 'Matisse'.

Over the next two years de Hory made nearly £200,000 from his fakes. And his colourful life continued. He was arrested and then freed after being suspected of a homosexual murder in Mexico City; he threw fabulous parties attended by glittering stars such as Marilyn

Monroe, and he attempted suicide after his criminal activities were exposed.

He said: 'The art dealers, the experts and the critics resent my talent because they don't want it shown how easily they can be fooled. I have tarnished the infallible image they rely upon for their fortunes.'

De Hory finally settled on the island of Ibiza. But he was not to find peace. He was in the clutches of a conman called Ferdinand Legros who controlled him and made a fortune out of his illicit work. The artist's tragic end came in December 1976 when all his misdeeds caught up with him. Everyone knew he was a crook, art dealers were demanding their money back and he had spent three months in jail on charges ranging from homosexuality to consorting with known criminals. All this painted a future too grim for Elmyr de Hory, the expert art faker, and in a fit of depression he killed himself.

THOMAS CHATTERTON
POETIC LICENCE

It is rare that the exploits of a fraudster or forger should have a tragic ending. The most their victims may suffer is financial loss and great embarrassment, while the tricksters themselves know the risks they run and in many cases even revel in the scandal that follows when they are exposed. This was not the case, however, for poor Thomas Chatterton, perhaps the saddest of history's forgers. He was just 17 when he died, driven to suicide by a series of events brought on by his deceptions and feelings of worthlessness.

Thomas Chatterton was born in Bristol on 20 November 1752, his father, a schoolmaster, having died three months earlier. Chatterton's mother was left in poverty with two children to support and so turned her hand to needlework to earn a living. From an early age Thomas was difficult, moody and a bit of a bully. He was also a bookworm, from the age of seven devouring works on such subjects as heraldry, music and astronomy. When he was eight he won a place a Colston's Hospital, a charity school for boys who were destined to become apprentices. This institution, housed in a former priory, first provided the young Chatterton with his curiosity about the Middle Ages, for the boys had to have their heads partly shaved and their uniform was a long coat and yellow stockings, styled very much on medieval fashions.

Chatterton was not happy at the school. He found it boring, became the school rebel and made it clear his mind needed more stimulation than his tutors could offer. He began to spend time alone and, at the age of 11, was writing serious poetry. There was only one teacher Chatterton had any time for: a young apprentice called Thomas Phillips, whom Chatterton was forever trying to impress. It was this desire which led to his first poetic forgery.

His free time was spent at the ancient church of St Mary Redcliffe, where his uncle was sexton. He could happily spend hours there, gazing at the medieval tombs and carvings, and running his fingers over their intricate forms. His fascination with the Middle Ages led Chatterton to believe he had been born into the wrong era. He felt more comfortable sitting in the quiet solitude of the church, casting his mind back to the fifteenth century and imagining what life was like then. And so, one morning as he sat pondering beside the tombs, Chatterton decided to reincarnate one Thomas Rowley, priest and poet of the 1400s, who had actually lived in Bristol around that time.

The man Chatterton so respected, Thomas Phillips, was the recipient of the first of many poems supposedly written by Thomas Rowley. Chatterton had, of course, penned it himself but claimed to have found it among other documents in a parish monument chest in the church he so frequently visited. In fact, such a chest did exist but its contents of manuscripts and parchments from the fifteenth century were used only as aids for Chatterton's clever forgery.

Chatterton called his first poem 'Elinoure and Juga'. His spidery lines written in brown ink purported to be a dialogue between two girls who lament the death of their lovers in the Wars of the Roses and end up drowning themselves. Deception aside, it was a remarkable piece of work from a boy of Chatterton's age. What was more, it earned him the attention he craved.

When he was 14, Chatterton met a local self-made man, a manufacturer of pewter called Henry Burgum, who was anxious to trace his family tree. Chatterton 'discovered' old parchments in St Mary Redcliffe which included the 'de Bergham' coat of arms and a family tree tracing the Burgums back to the Norman Conquest. He also 'found' a poem by his good friend Thomas Rowley which mentioned a knight named Johan de Berghamme. Adding a bit more colour to his discoveries, he included a branch of his own family that had intermarried with the de Berghams. It had all taken Chatterton time to create but he was well rewarded when a delighted Henry Burgum placed five shillings in his hand. And, after Chatterton was introduced to Burgum's partner, George Catcott, he too was the delighted recipient of some of Thomas Rowley's poems.

By now Chatterton had well and truly slipped into the art of skilful deception. And so, when he met a well-known surgeon called William Barrett who was compiling a work on the history of Bristol, he was more than happy to help. Thus various old parchments and plans of Bristol were 'discovered'. The young Chatterton found Barrett a stimulating conversationalist as he swapped historical information with the eminent surgeon old enough to be his father. Equally, Barrett made it obvious that he thought highly of the boy. So Chatterton gave him a special token of gratitude: more poems by the fifteenth-century priest Thomas Rowley.

After leaving school at 16, Chatterton was apprenticed to a local lawyer, John Lambert, whom he detested. The work was dull for someone with as sharp a mind and as strong an appetite for learning as the young lad. He spent his hours copying legal documents, wistfully yearning for a more challenging and rewarding way of life. The only respite from tedium he enjoyed was in the evenings. Then Chatterton came into his own. He had gathered a good coterie of friends around him and, already a promising poet, took great pleasure in writing verses to be presented to local girls of his acquaintance.

As a sideline, the bored clerk undertook an interesting escapade when a new footbridge was opened over a river. Chatterton arrived at the offices of the local newspaper with an account of a mayor first crossing the old bridge in 1248. Chatterton said he had copied it from a parchment removed by his father from St Mary Redcliffe. The newspaper willingly published the historical account.

Only two friends, John Rudhall and Edward Gardner, to whom Chatterton had shown the art of 'ageing' documents, knew the truth. They saw no reason to spoil the local newspaper's pleasure at such a historic discovery. Later, however, Gardner revealed: 'He would rub a parchment in several places in streaks with yellow ochre, then rub it several times on the ground, which was dirty, and afterwards crumple it in his hand saying that was how to antiquate it.'

The works by 'Thomas Rowley' that Chatterton produced were written in a pseudo-medieval style which seemed genuine enough to the local experts who examined them. The language of such poems was not authentic, however, and they were inspired not by medieval poets but by Tudor writers like William Shakespeare and Edmund

Spenser. Chatterton either invented medieval words or found them in dictionaries. Nevertheless, his work, such as these lines, convinced Bristol historians they were in possession of an important literary discovery:

> When Freedom dreste, yn blodde steyned veste
> To everie knyghte her warre songe sunge
> Uponne her hedde, wyld wedes were spredde,
> A gorie anlace bye her honge.

Chatterton was further endeared to the good people of his native city when some of the Rowley works he 'discovered' praised the city and criticised 'cowarde Londonne'.

In 1769 Chatterton had several of his own works accepted by magazines. This encouraged him to try to get the Rowley poems published, but without success. He then decided to approach Horace Walpole, author of the 1764 romantic novel *The Castle of Otranto*, his translation of a sixteenth-century Italian romance. Walpole was greatly interested in *A History of Painting in England* – or *The Ryse of Peyncteyne yn Englande* as it was called – by one T. Rowleie. Walpole agreed to publish the Rowley manuscripts but became suspicious at Chatterton's insistence on being paid. When Walpole discovered Chatterton's poor background and the fact he was dealing with such a youthful correspondent, he sought the advice of two acquaintances, who said they believed the manuscripts to be forgeries. One of these was the poet Thomas Gray.

Walpole wrote to Chatterton suggesting he continue working for John Lambert and to forget his aspirations to be a great writer. The rejection devastated Chatterton. He requested the return of his manuscripts in a bitter reply to

Walpole: 'Though I am but sixteen years of age, I have lived long enough to see that poverty attends literature. I am obliged to you, sir, for your advice and will go a little beyond it, by destroying all my useless lumber of literature and by never using my pen but in law.' Further enraged at neither receiving the courtesy of a reply nor the return of his manuscripts, Chatterton wrote to Walpole again: 'I cannot reconcile your behaviour to me with the notions I once entertained of you. I think myself injured, sir, and did not you know my circumstances, you would not dare to treat me thus. I have twice sent for a copy of the manuscript – no answer from you. An explanation or excuse for your silence would oblige.' But there was none forthcoming from Horace Walpole.

Reeling from what he saw as the ultimate blow to his ego, the highly sensitive youth sat behind his desk in Lambert's office on 17 April 1770 and wrote: 'The Last Will and Testament of me, Thomas Chatterton of Bristol.' The document was found by his employer and Chatterton was dismissed. He left clutching £5 and a bundle of unfinished poems.

Chatterton made his way to London in the hope of gaining some recognition either for work in his own right or for the discovery of that literary priest Thomas Rowley. At first he lodged with a cousin in Shoreditch. Life seemed happy enough as he mixed with writers and politicians, including the radical John Wilkes, and contributed to the Whig opposition party's journals and other publications. He even had a burlesque opera, *The Revenge*, successfully produced. He continued producing work from the literary priest Thomas Rowley. One poem of which the forger was particularly proud was 'An Excelente Balade of Charitie'.

Chatterton even won himself a female admirer, Esther

Saunders. The callow youth was intimidated by her advances and replied to her letters in an abrasive manner. This did not deter Miss Saunders and in April 1770 she wrote this letter to him: 'Sir, to a Blage you I wright a few lines to you but have not the weakness to Believe all you say of me for you may Say as much to other young Ladys for all I kno But I Cant go out of a Sunday with you for I ham afraid we Shall be seen to go Sir if it aggreable to you I had Take a walk with you in the morning for I be Belive we Shant be Seen about 6 a Clock But we must wait with patient for ther is a Time for all Things.' Determined to rid himself of Esther Saunders once and for all, Chatterton wrote back: 'There is a time for all things – except marriage my dear.'

Fortune was once more to turn against Chatterton. The Whig journals fell foul of the government and their proprietors were forced to choose between pursuing a more cautious line or suspending publication. The small payments Chatterton had been earning became few and far between. Further, having gained a new-found confidence from mixing with London's smart set, he unwisely turned on his home town in a satirical poem, 'The Exhibition', in which he pilloried most of his former acquaintances. His friends deserted him, including William Barrett, whom Chatterton had held dear.

Friendless and alienated, he rented an attic room in Brooke Street, Holborn. He hardly ate or slept for months as he desperately produced tales, scribblings, songs and poems from Thomas Rowley. He was always hungry and tired and his mental state was becoming troubled. In desperation, he turned to William Barrett for help, but his former friend refused him. In his letters home, the now virtually deranged Chatterton pretended all was well in his new, successful life. In one letter he wrote: 'I have an universal acquaintance; my company is courted everywhere ... the ladies are not out of my acquaintance. I have a deal of business now, and must therefore bid you adieu ...' But Chatterton's real feelings were expressed in his last poem, written two days before he died:

Farewell, my mother! – cease my mortal soul.
Nor let Distraction's billow's o'er me roll! –
Have mercy, Heaven! when here I cease to live.
And this last act of wretchedness forgive.

On 24 August 1770, Thomas Chatterton tore all his manuscripts to shreds and swallowed arsenic. He died in excruciating agony. In his will he wrote: 'I leave my mother and sister to the protection of my friends if I have any ...'

Following Chatterton's suicide, greater interest was shown in the work of Thomas Rowley. In Bristol the poems were passed around scholars of medieval works and their virtues discussed. Some were even included in Thomas Warton's *History of English Poetry*.

Horace Walpole learned of Chatterton's death when, at a banquet at London's Royal Academy, he heard Oliver Goldsmith praising some ancient poems that had been found in Bristol. He refused to feel any guilt over the boy – but he did not know then that he would be denounced as the heartless aristocrat who had driven Chatterton to suicide.

When the truth about Chatterton's fabrication of work by Thomas Rowley was revealed, he was reviled as a forger but praised as a poet on his own merits. Latter-day critics believe Chatterton would have been more accepted by the Establishment if it were not for his humble background. Edward Rushton, a contemporary of Chatterton, boldly

The face of the modern conman. (*Clockwise from bottom*) Peter Foster, the bane of the Blairs (and Samantha Fox); Major Ingram, almost walking away with a million pounds on ITV's *Who Wants to be a Millionaire* and Frank Abagnale, the master con artist who was played by Leonardo Di Caprio in the film *Catch Me If You Can.*

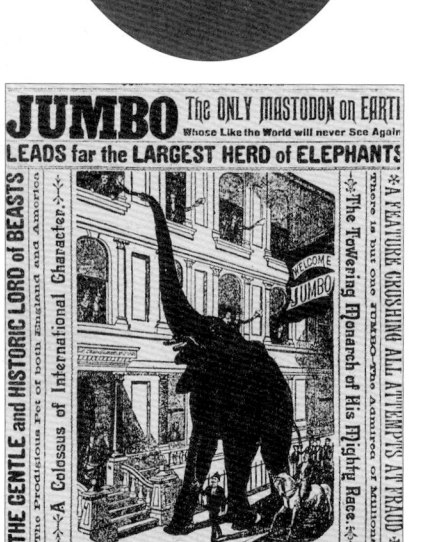

Above left: William Henry Ireland concocted bogus artefacts he claimed belonged to Shakespeare, including a 'lost play'.

Above right: A 'self portrait' of Shakespeare rendered by Ireland.

Below left: A poster advertising 'Jumbo', Barnum's famous elephant.

Below right: P. T. Barnum and Charles Sherwood ('Tom Thumb').

Above: Author Virginia Woolf and friends dressed as a delegation of Abyssinian royalty. Virginia Woolf is seated on the left of the picture.

Left: Horatio Bottomley, a dazzling orator, but out and out crook, who was so convincing he led one judge to suggest that he might join the legal profession.

The 'Cardiff Giant', created by George Hull, but believed, for many years by locals and visitors to the small town of Cardiff in New York State, to be one of a lost tribe of giants mentioned in *The Book of Genesis*.

Above: Arthur Orton, a semi-literate butcher, who nearly landed himself a baronetcy and a noble family's fortune by pretending to be the lost son of Henriette Tichborne.

Left: Princess Anastasia, only surviving child of Czar Nicholas II, or Franziska Schanzkowski, the poor Polish orphan?

Above: John Stonehouse, the man many tipped for the national leadership before he faked his own death in 1974.

Below: The Boing 727 hi-jacked by D. B. Cooper on Thanksgiving Day 1971.

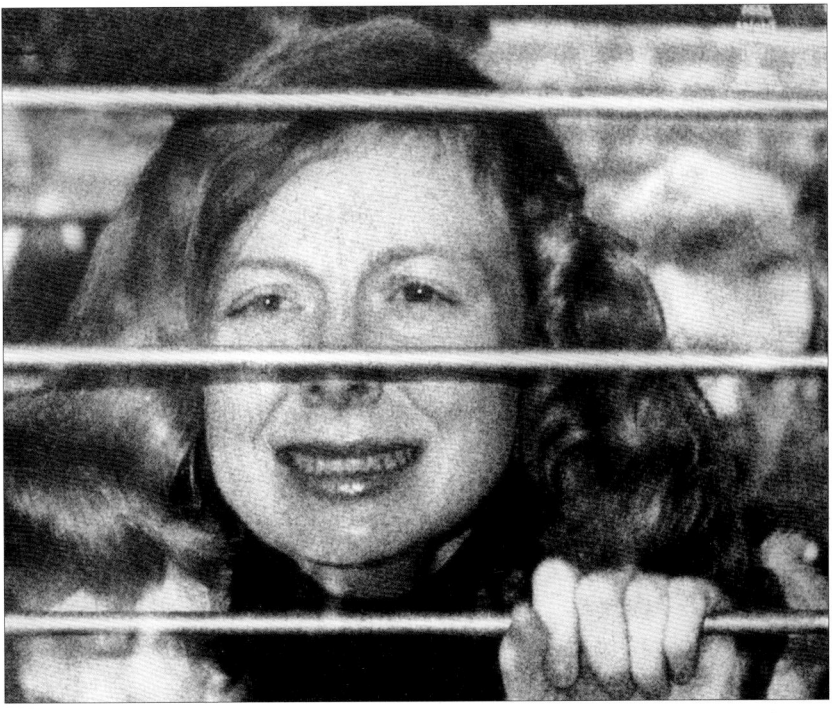

Above: 'Sex makes people happy.' – Cynthia Payne aka 'Madam Cyn'.

Below: Joyce McKinney, the kinky kidnapper of a Mormon minister.

Above: Bernie Cornfield the former American school teacher whose company controlled a fund of more than £1 billion of stocks and shares … before it went bust and he landed in jail.

Below: Tom Keating – the affectionately remembered forger – in front of one of his 'masterpieces'.

defended him. He compared the treatment he received with that of humble poet Thomas Percy and wrote: 'A Common Observer would imagine that both writers were in the same Predicament, but mark the Influence of Wealth and Situation; whilse the One is nothing more than the Innocent Artifice of an Honourable Author, the Other is loudly reprobated as the vile Forger of obscure Charity Boy.'

Others, too, found fine words with which to describe the tragic, talented writer. Dr Samuel Johnson called Chatterton 'the most extraordinary young man'. George Catcott, Chatterton's friend from Bristol, spoke of Chatterton's 'hawk's eye' through which 'one could see his soul'. Even William Barrett found it in his heart to forgive Chatterton and wrote colourfully: 'I had never seen such eyes, fire rolling at the bottom of them ... I sometimes crossed him just to see how wonderfully his eye would strike fire, kindle and blaze up.'

In 1777 the Rowley poems were published by Thomas Tyrwhitt, who left the question of their authorship open. The literary world divided into those who believed they were forgeries and those who believed they were genuine. Two years later Horace Walpole published an angry reply to accusations that he had been responsible for Chatterton's suicide. His fiercest accuser was George Catcott. In 1780 Herbert Croft's novel *Love and Madness* caused a sensation. It was based on the murder of Martha Ray, the mistress of the Earl of Sandwich, by a lovesick clergyman called Hackman. It contained a long account of the life of Chatterton and made him a household name.

Arguments over Chatterton's talent and the authenticity of Thomas Rowley's work raged on among the literary élite. Thorough examination of the poetry finally revealed it was not written by a fifteenth-century priest but by a misguided, disillusioned but gifted Bristol boy. Chatterton's work became recognised in its own right. And his life was captured by painters and fellow poets, not least by the words of William Wordsworth:

> ... *Chatterton, the marvellous Boy,*
> *The sleepless soul that perished in his pride.*

YVES CHAUDRON
THE MISSING MONA LISA

The enigmatic smile on the face of the *Mona Lisa* holds a million secrets which have intrigued art experts all over the world for hundreds of years. But the Van Gogh masterpiece once put a smile on other faces too – of the three conmen who not only sold forged copies of it but also stole the original. Those men were art forger and former picture restorer Yves Chaudron, trickster and self-styled marquis Eduardo de Valfierno and Italian burglar Vincenzo Perrugia. Chaudron and Valfierno had been partners in crime for many years. Their nefarious careers began at the turn of the nineteenth century in South America where they would offer to steal a painting for a crooked dealer, who would sell it on to a client without too many questions being asked.

This is how their amazing scam worked. Chaudron and Valfierno would visit an art gallery in the guise of supposed art experts (which, in a way, they were). They would target a particular painting and chat with the gallery owner about its merits. On a second visit they would arrive armed with a forgery of the 'target' painting, brilliantly executed by Chaudron. Again he and Valfierno would engage the gallery owner in conversation and eventually ask the unsuspecting official if they could examine the work more closely. When it was taken down from the wall, the deceitful duo would cunningly line the back of the canvas with the forgery.

On their third visit to the gallery they would have the crooked dealer in tow. He would be invited to make a surreptitious mark on the back of the painting that was to be stolen. He would, of course, be marking the back of the fake. On their fourth and final visit to the gallery, Chaudron and Valfierno would craftily remove the marked forgery. The gallery officials were never aware of their part in the confidence trick, since the genuine article remained in place. The crooked dealer, however, always greedily handed over the promised sum for the 'stolen' work of art.

If the dealer or the eventual purchaser of the forgery ever wondered why the original painting still hung on the gallery wall, Chaudron and Valfierno would let it be known that a copy of the original had taken its place while the theft was being investigated. In fact, as well as being great forgers, they were also great judges of human character. They knew that it was unlikely that the people they had tricked would ever realise their copies were fakes. Even if they suspected it, their pride and vanity would generally persuade them that they were too smart to be duped. And, after all, if it ever dawned on the dealers or the clients that they had been conned, they could hardly go to the police to admit being part of the shady deal. Their reputation as art connoisseurs and honest traders was at stake!

Since Chaudron specialised in faking the work of Spanish artist Bartolomé Estebán Murillo, it was not many months before Argentina, where he and Valfierno were then operating, became flooded with phoney Murillos. They moved on to Mexico City, where they perfected their techniques, even providing specially printed 'newspaper cuttings' reporting on the supposed thefts of the works they had replicated and sold. When Mexico City became too hot for the crooks they headed for Paris. There, naturally enough, they visited the world-renowned Louvre Museum, and saw its best-known work, the *Mona Lisa*.

The scam devised by Chaudron and Valfierno was of epic proportions. They realised they needed a third member for their gang, and recruited Vincenzo Perrugia, an Italian burglar and small-time crook who had once worked in the Louvre as a handyman. He knew his way around the gallery and had even put the glass in the screen that protected Leonardo da Vinci's masterpiece. Unbelievably, the gang of three then plotted to steal the *Mona Lisa*.

On 21 August 1911, dressed as workmen, Perrugia and two paid accomplices coolly wandered into the Louvre and secreted themselves in the basement. After dark they emerged from hiding and removed the *Mona Lisa* from the wall. Within minutes they had vanished into the Parisian night. And by morning Chaudron and Valfierno had been handed the art world's ultimate prize. The gang already had several prospective clients lined up. For, although it would have been a simple task to sell the genuine *Mona Lisa*, the thieves had a more ambitious plan. They would sell the masterpiece not once but over and over again – and not one of the paintings they unloaded would be the original article!

Before the year was out, no fewer than six American millionaires had each paid $300,000 for what each of them thought was da Vinci's masterpiece. It mattered little to them that the work had been stolen from the Louvre. Greed overcame any feelings of guilt when they could seize on such a priceless work at a knockdown price.

Chaudron and Valfierno made a little under $2 million selling their six expertly forged copies of the painting. But they never got the chance to dispose of the real thing. The newly hired member of the trio, Perrugia, grew greedy himself and ran off to Italy with the real *Mona Lisa*. On 13 November 1911 he tried to sell it to a Florence dealer who, for once, was honest enough to contact the police. The *Mona Lisa* was returned to the Louvre, where, behind thick glass panels, wired to several alarm systems and under armed guard, the masterpiece remains to this day. Chaudron, Valfierno and Perrugia found themselves equally protected from the general public – in their respective jail cells.

However, one lingering doubt remains about the world's most famous painting. No fewer than 60 other alleged '*Mona Lisas*' have been catalogued in various corners of the world. And they are not all forgeries. Most are believed to be genuine and are attributed, if not to Leonardo da Vinci himself, then to his school of painting. So is the masterpiece hanging in the Louvre today the original *Mona Lisa* after all?

FRANCES GRIFFITHS AND ELSIE WRIGHT
THE COTTINGLEY FAIRIES

Photographs taken by two young girls in the early 1900s were a fairy tale, if ever there was one. And they ensured that Frances Griffiths and her cousin Elsie Wright went down in the annals of great hoaxes. It helped, of course, that the great detective writer Sir Arthur Conan Doyle became involved with the photographs of fairies at the bottom of a garden. He, like everyone else, was taken in by the sweet little Yorkshire lasses and even went on lecture tours to proclaim that here, at last, was evidence fairies really did exist.

The story of the fairies began in 1917. Frances borrowed her father's camera to take pictures of Elsie with fairies dancing right under her nose in their garden in Cottingley. The veins in the wings were clearly visible. The photographs were developed by Elsie's father and Frances even cheekily sent one to a friend in South Africa. On the back she scribbled the message: 'Elsie and I are ever friendly with the beck stream fairies. It is funny, I never used to see them in Africa. It must be too hot for them there.'

Elsie's mother, Polly, took great interest in the occult and believed the photographs deserved to be shown to an expert. She took them to Arthur Gardner, president of the

London branch of the Theosophical Society. He accepted the pictures as genuine. So did Harold Snelling, a photographic expert, who commented: 'What gets me most is that all these figures have moved during exposure.'

It was the dark, grim days after the First World War, and the story of the Cottingley Fairies was just what a depressed Britain needed. Sir Arthur Conan Doyle, who had lost his son in the war and was eager to believe in the supernatural, heard about the fairy pictures while preparing an article on fairies for *Strand* magazine. Excitedly, he sent his agent to Yorkshire to meet Elsie, 16, and Frances, 10.

The girls were convincing about their 'friends' the fairies. They played with them often, they said. The tiny visitors were 'very shy but could be great fun'. They handed over the photographic plates and, although they refused to swear their story on the Bible, they did offer to take more photographs. Three more were produced, one showing a fairy offering Elsie flowers. The pictures, together with the girls' original ones, appeared alongside two articles by Sir Arthur in *Strand*, in November 1920 and March 1921. The headline on the first article was: 'An Epoch-making Event Described by A. Conan Doyle'. In the second, Sir Arthur wrote: 'It is at the lowest, an interesting speculation which gives an added charm to the silence of the woods and the wilderness of the moorland.'

Reaction was mixed. The tiny creatures were exactly what romantics imagined fairies to be and people wanted to believe there really were such gentle creatures. Others thought the detective writer should have known better. One photographic expert, Kenneth Styles, declared the pictures to be 'a most patent fraud'. Cynics said the fairies appeared to have been cut from a children's book and others pointed out the similarity between the Cottingley fairies and those that appeared in an advertisement for Price's Night Lights.

The *Manchester City News* reported: 'We must either believe in the almost incredible mystery of the fairies, or in the almost incredible wonder of faked photographs.' *Truth* magazine was more blunt. It said: 'For a true explanation of the fairy photographs, what is wanted is not a knowledge of the occult phenomena, but a knowledge of children.' None of this deterred Sir Arthur from pursuing his supernatural discovery, embarking on a round of lectures and even devoting an entire book to fairies.

Yet more fairy pictures were produced by Elsie and Frances. Their quality was poor but they helped convince a growing number of people who were becoming intrigued by the whole affair. Sir Arthur was delighted that he was at last being 'proved right'. In one of his lecture papers he wrote: 'If I am myself asked whether the case is to be absolutely and finally proved, I should answer that, in order to remove the last faint shred of doubt, I should wish to see the result repeated before a disinterested witness.'

It was not to be. Interest in the Cottingley fairies waned until, more than half a century later, modern technology and a belated confession by Elsie and Frances revealed the fairy story for what it really was – a great big hoax. Close examination of the photographs with computerised equipment showed that the fairies were 'dancing' at the end of a thread. They had, in fact, been copied by Elsie from *The Princess Mary Gift Book*, which was so popular at the time that it is incredible no one noticed. The girls had used hat pins to attach the fairy figures to leaves and twigs. They themselves found it hard to believe anyone could have been fooled.

Their admission finally came in a television programme in 1976. 'As for the photographs,' said Elsie, 'let's say they are figments of our imagination, mine and Frances's, and leave it at that.' She was even more forthcoming in later years. 'I felt that we couldn't tell Sir Arthur Conan Doyle they were fakes because it might have upset him dreadfully,' said Elsie. 'When we cut our fairies out, Frances had rather podgy hands and couldn't cut the fingers properly. So her fairies had thick-looking hands, and some of the experts got excited and said the fairies had fins. Fins, I ask you! I forgot to put wings on one fairy and that caused a great to-do as well.'

By the 1980s the two women were ready to write their autobiographies. They admitted neither had ever believed in fairies and never would. Apart from being given £20 each by a grateful Sir Arthur, Elsie and Frances received no great financial reward for their hoax. But they did find fame, for their story was told all over the world. Frances Wright once proudly remarked: 'It is perhaps every hoaxer's dream: the immortality that follows the perpetration of some well-staged and well-publicised piece of hocus-pocus.'

EDWARD SIMPSON
'FLINT JACK'S' FINDS

Victorian Britain's antique collectors were, typically, upper-crust men with servants, starched collars and waxed moustaches. Dabbling in ancient history was the height of fashion for the moneyed gentlefolk of high society. Yet rubbing shoulders with this élite was a man who looked and smelled no better than a tramp; he wore holed corduroy trousers, a cloth coat worn through at the elbows, a yellowing shirt and a scrappy neckerchief.

Despite his tatty appearance, this odd fellow was made welcome at the most noted archaeological events throughout the country. His currency was an apparently boundless supply of aged artefacts coupled with a specialist knowledge that set him head and shoulders above many. Only after the shabby itinerant melted away into the countryside did the well-heeled historians realise they had been duped. For their guest was none other than 'Flint Jack', one of the most successful forgers of all time.

Flint Jack had received a basic training in the identification and collection of fossils and had a genuine love of archaeology. However, the prospect of easy money to finance a costly drinking habit lured him into the shadowy world of fraud. By the end of the Victorian era, examples of his expert handiwork appeared in many of the country's leading collections. Even the British Museum was taken in and displayed some of Flint Jack's work.

He was born in 1815 at Sleights, a village in North Yorkshire. His real name was Edward Simpson, but he was also known as Cockney Bill, Bones, Shirtless, Snake Billy, Old Antiquarian or by the surnames of Jackson and Smith. As a teenager he found work with two eminent historians, acquiring skills that would serve him well in later life. When his second employer died, Flint Jack decided to make a living by scouring the country for fossils in which to trade. He soon discovered a new talent, however. He found he could make copies of old flint arrowheads using just a few basic tools. At the request of a local dealer, and with the use of a home-made kiln, he produced a range of sought-after items of 'ancient' pottery. For a while collectors did not suspect that the oddments they purchased were freshly sculpted. When their suspicions were aroused, Flint Jack left Yorkshire and embarked on a tour of Britain, taking his craftsmanship to new and different markets.

Encouraged by his success, he expanded his range. There was a Roman breastplate made from an old tin tray which he found on a roadside. Milestones, urns, seals and stones were all turned out with his magic touch. By 1846 he was moving from town to city selling sufficient amounts to finance the next leg of his tour. He visited Peterborough, Birmingham, Liverpool, Sheffield, Colchester, Hadrian's Wall, the Lake District, the West Country and Ireland. Word of his antics spread slowly. During the 1860s more and more collectors realised they had been fooled and warnings about him were published in specialist journals.

Yet Flint Jack was far more than just a scallywag. He would join archaeological digs and happily impart his voluminous knowledge to the experts. In 1862 he demonstrated his skills before a meeting of the Geologists' Association in Cavendish Square, London. His ragged appearance caused ripples of mirth and some consternation in the eminent audience. The *People's Magazine* gave a graphic account of what this roving fraudster looked like: 'He was a weather-beaten man of about 45 years of age and he came in dirty, tattered clothes and heavy navvy's boots, to take precedence of the whole assemblage. He wore a dark cloth coat, hanging in not unpicturesque rags about the elbows. It was unbuttoned over a cotton shirt which might once have been white but which had degenerated to a yellow brown. About his neck was a fragment of a blue cotton handkerchief. His skin was of a gypsy brown, his hair hung in lank black locks about a forehead and face that was not altogether unprepossessing, except for the furtive and cunning glances which he occasionally cast around him from eyes that did not correspond with each other in size and expression. His corduroys, which were in a very sorry condition, had been turned up, and their owner had evidently travelled through heavy clay, the dry remains of which bedaubed his boots.'

The quizzical glances of the eminent audience turned to looks of awe, however, when Flint Jack was introduced by the vice-president of the Geologists' Association. He explained that their guest, with only a bent iron rod, could produce the most amazingly realistic artefacts. The assembly then watched in total silence as Flint Jack went to work, casually turning out replicas of arrowheads one after the other.

By now he was notorious among serious collectors, many of whom could not forgive him for making fools of them. But the public loved him, particularly as he was disarmingly honest. If confronted, he always admitted he was a forger. In 1866 the story of Flint Jack's life appeared in the *Malton Messenger* and was so popular that it was published as a pamphlet and distributed nationwide. That's how Charles Dickens seized on the character for his story 'All the Year Round'.

By 1867 Flint Jack's notoriety eventually forced him out of the forgery business. In January of that year the destitute itinerant paid a visit to an old acquaintance, James Wyatt, a journalist and archaeologist. The details are recorded in Wyatt's diary. Flint Jack explained to him: 'When some species are scarce and people don't know them well, you must do your best.' He borrowed sixpence from Wyatt to tide him over until his next 'commission'.

However, as the diary recalls: 'It appears that he proceeded to the last house on the London Road but unfortunately that is a public house and he could not resist the temptation of entering. The consequence was that he got drunk and as the craving increased after his money was gone he came back to the town, opened the front door of a house near mine and took a barometer, but having been seen by a man outside, he bolted and threw the barometer away. Later in the evening, finding a light in the schoolroom attached to the Methodist Chapel he entered and stole a clock, which he tried to sell to the keeper of a public house, and finally left him with it as a deposit. The police got on the scent and ran him down to a low lodging house, and then removed him to the lock-up.'

For the crime, Flint Jack was tried on 12 March 1867 and sentenced to a year's imprisonment in Bedford Jail. Such was his standing in society that an archaeological magazine, *The Reliquary*, organised an appeal on his behalf. The journal's plea ended: 'The man possesses more real practical antiquarian knowledge than many of the leading antiquarian writers of the day, and he is a good geologist and palaeontologist. Is it meet, then, that he should be allowed to starve when a few mites from those that he may have duped but whom, at all events, he has ultimately benefited by his open disclosure and by his indomitable skill, would materially assist him, and perhaps turn his talents into a better and more honourable channel?'

The appeal fell on deaf ears. On his release from prison, Flint Jack continued his wandering lifestyle and faded from public gaze. It is thought he died in a workhouse in his native Yorkshire.

THOMAS GOUDIE
GAMBLING CLERK

One can imagine the pressure that the lowly paid clerk was under. His passion for gambling had left him in debt. And here, in his position of trust at the Bank of Liverpool, was his way out. So, in an era long before the advent of computers, a stroke of the pen on a ledger turned Thomas Peterson Goudie into a master forger.

Born in the Shetland Islands to a fine upstanding family, and with a good education behind him, Goudie had not found it difficult to secure a position at the bank, where he worked for six uneventful years. To his family, friends and employers, he was just a rather introverted young man with little interest in anything apart from his job. Every morning he would set off for work from a cheap lodging house near the docks. His adherence to routine and attention to detail made him more than acceptable at the bank. But what they did not realise was that Thomas Goudie was a compulsive gambler.

It was in 1898 that Goudie first turned to crime. No one could have any idea of his mounting debts. Indeed few had reason to suspect he was free with his money at all. He earned just £3 a week, £1 of which was needed to pay his keep at the lodging house. In fact, Goudie had enjoyed a very successful secret life as a gambler. He had even opened up an account at a London branch of Lloyd's Bank in the name of John Style. Around £10,000 had passed through it. Now, however, 27-year-old Goudie had nothing left. And he owed the bookmakers £100. He was being threatened that, if he didn't pay up, his shame would be exposed and he would lose his job.

The only way Goudie could have access to the money he needed was to take it from the very bank he worked for. He had charge of the ledger entries from 'H' to 'K'. Among the accounts in his care was one in the name of a Mr Hudson, who was connected with a large soap firm. Large sums of money regularly passed through Mr Hudson's account, it was from here that Goudie was to filter off an amazing £170,000.

The routine of the bank in those days was for cheques, after they had been passed by the clearing department, to be brought to the clerk, together with the journal in which they had to be entered. The ledger clerk then had to record the accounts in his ledger, indicate by a tick in the journal that he had done so, and then file the cheque. It was essential to Goudie's scheme that he should get hold of Bank of Liverpool cheques. So he simply opened an account in the name of 'G.P. Scott' and made out cheques to that fictitious person, forging Hudson's signature on them. The cheques went off to Goudie's bookmaker friends. When they came into the bank to be cleared, a clerk would debit the sum against Mr Hudson's account. When journal and cheque arrived with Goudie, he would tick off the amount in the journal but not enter it in his ledger. Instead of filing the cheque, he would destroy it.

Incredibly, Goudie got away with his cheating for three years. No one seemed to pick up on the continued discrepancies between the journal and the clearing book entries and those in the ledger. And, at audit time, Goudie would make an entry of a false debit. After the audit had taken place, he would then make an entry of a false credit. He was getting away with his forgeries, and his gambling spree continued. Goudie's downfall, when it came, was not the result of the bank's diligence or of clever detective work; it was caused by his unscrupulous acquaintances taking advantage of him.

The first were a couple of bookmaker's runners. They had encountered Goudie on a train journey and invited him to play cards. Noting how unworldly the bank clerk was, they decided to have some sport at his expense. Having learned that he was a regular gambler on horse racing, they would tell him that they had used their inside knowledge to place bets on his behalf, but sadly these had not been successful. Bizarre though it seems, Goudie was prepared to accept these stories. He paid the cheats a fortune – as much as £70,000 between them.

Word soon got round the gambling world that a G.P. Scott was placing big bets on the horses. Investigations by a bookmaker called George Mances revealed that, far from being a millionaire, Mr Scott was, in fact, a £3-a-week ledger clerk called Thomas Goudie. Mances quickly realised from where and how the betting funds were becoming available. It was, he decided, time to visit Mr Goudie. Mances dropped strong hints that he knew what the clerk was up to. And, although the word 'blackmail' was never mentioned, Goudie was soon placing futile bets with the bent bookie.

For one so smitten with horse racing, Goudie was remarkably naive. He believed Mances to be generous in allowing him to place £5,000 bets within an hour of a race. What this massive bet did, of course, was to make the horse in question favourite. At one time, his betting habits becoming addictive, Goudie wagered £25,000 in three days. What he was now doing was not gambling at all. He was simply giving away stolen money to crooks. And all he had to keep him going was the misguided belief that one day he would enjoy a substantial win.

On the morning of 21 November 1901 Goudie's falsified records were eventually discovered. An accountant at the Bank of Liverpool noticed that a cheque listed in the clearing book was not recorded as having passed through Mr Hudson's account. Neither was the cheque filed anywhere. Goudie was summoned to explain the discrepancy. He took the only action available to him. Saying he was 'going to look' for the missing cheque, Goudie walked calmly out of the Bank of Liverpool, never to return. The timid clerk managed to flee only as far as neighbouring Bootle before being apprehended. Soon everyone else involved in the sorry tale of betting, blackmail and theft was being hunted. Unhappily for Goudie, they had all disappeared.

Goudie's trial opened at the Old Bailey in London on 18 February 1902 when he pleaded guilty to fraud. The court heard that his misdeeds had all been deliberate and long-continued. The judge was told: 'But for the others, he would have been a criminal of a very ordinary type. It was as a tool in their hands and for their benefit he committed the series of crimes that made the total loss so great.' Defending Goudie, his counsel Lord Birkenhead said: 'In the whole history of crime there is not a case in which a man has enjoyed himself so little as the result of his misdeeds as is the case with Goudie.'

Goudie was sentenced to 10 years in prison. He died before finishing his term. It was a sad and sorry end to a man who betrayed the position of trust in which he was placed – and who in turn placed his trust in those who would only betray him and steal from him.

KONRAD KUJAU
THE HITLER DIARIES

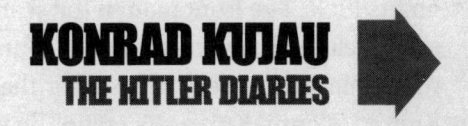

It was an explosive find. Details contained therein would provide an insight into the mind of the most evil dictator in history, the man who wanted to change the world, the man responsible for millions of deaths and whose name today still echoes with the fear he spread far and wide in the 1930s and 1940s. That man was Adolf Hitler. The earth-shattering discovery was a collection of his private diaries. They had never been seen before. And, written between 1932 and 1945, they spanned a watershed in history.

First to reap the benefit of these intimate revelations was the German news magazine *Stern*. Already envisaging its circulation rising to record figures, it was fully prepared to pay the equivalent of £2.5 million for the exclusive rights to the documents. Other prestigious publications were to follow: *Paris-Match*, *Newsweek* and even Britain's august newspaper the *Sunday Times*. But, in handing over small fortunes for the Führer's diaries, they were paying the price of being too hungry and too hasty for a scoop. The diaries were fakes and, as was later revealed, not even clever fakes. They were the work of a conman who succeeded in fooling hard-bitten newspaper executives and historical experts.

It was in 1983 that *Stern* and the *Sunday Times* announced the existence of volumes of Hitler's wartime jottings. No one had any reason to suspect they had been penned by a devious trickster who had teamed up with a chancer who was down on his luck. The front man in the scam was Gerd Heidemann, a 53-year-old award-winning journalist employed by a reputable magazine – none other than *Stern*. The forger was Konrad 'Konni' Kujau, 46, erstwhile waiter and talented artist with a fertile imagination.

Kujau was born in 1938 in the Saxon town of Loebau, which at that time was enjoying the prosperity of Hitler's Third Reich. From 1946 to 1991, however, it was part of East Germany. Kujau fled to West Germany in 1957 to avoid arrest after committing petty theft while employed as a waiter. He settled in Stuttgart and changed his name to Peter Fischer. But this didn't stop him getting into more trouble. Other minor misdemeanours led to two prison sentences. He then opened the Pelican Dance Bar in 1962, going into business with Edith Lieblang, a waitress and fellow refugee. When this failed, Kujau returned to being a waiter. But he was already set in his criminal ways and before long he was in prison once more, this time for forging luncheon vouchers. Edith stuck by him and, after his release, Kujau persuaded her to put up the money for the Lieblang Cleaning Company. The business prospered and only yet another spell in jail – after the authorities discovered 'Peter Fischer' was not who he said he was – marred their happiness.

A visit back home to Loebau gave Kujau a money-making idea. It was now 25 years since Hitler's death but there was a growing market for Nazi memorabilia. Kujau got his family to place adverts in East German newspapers. They read: 'Wanted for research: old toys, helmets, jugs, pipes, dolls etc.' The response was great and, although the East

German government had banned the export of objects made before 1945, Kujau managed to smuggle many into West Germany. He now supplemented his living by selling these relics from a shop in Stuttgart's Aspergstrasse.

Kujau never missed a chance to pull a fast one on eager collectors, cashing in on their cravings for historical material, and was not above manufacturing his own certificates of authenticity. A note authenticating a helmet as being worn by Hitler in 1917 was signed by Rudolf Hess. Kujau aged the documents by soaking them in tea – a technique that would prove of great value when the great Hitler Diaries Hoax was perpetrated.

Then Kujau moved on to paintings, specialising in the supposedly original works of Hitler himself. This business venture was to lead to his relationship with another keen collector of Nazi memorabilia, Fritz Stiefel. A wealthy owner of a local engineering works, Stiefel was an avid collector of militaria. He spent large sums of money at Kujau's store over a period of six years, for the shopkeeper seemed to have a never-ending supply of Nazi items any collector would love to own. There were 160 drawings, oil paintings and watercolours all by Hitler himself. Then there were the poems, notes of speeches and letters. Their manufacture kept Kujau very busy indeed. Poor Stiefel never suspected a thing.

Kujau decided that Stiefel deserved a real gem as a reward for his faithful custom. He would be offered a diary written in the Führer's own hand. It was now 1980 and news of the startling find soon reached the ears of Gerd Heidemann, who was also obsessed with the Third Reich. (His wife had left him when their apartment was taken over by Heidemann's collection of war games and toy soldiers.) It was more than just his obsession with the Nazis that attracted Heidemann to the idea of Hitler's private diaries being discovered. The purchase of Luftwaffe chief Hermann Goering's old motor yacht and a string of love affairs had left him heavily in debt. Heidemann was already realising the financial potential of Hitler's diaries.

Heidemann was put in touch with Fritz Stiefel, who told him there could be as many as 26 volumes of the diaries. Stiefel refused to name Kujau but acted as intermediary. Thus a deal was struck. Thomas Walde, editor of the historical department at *Stern*, became involved in the negotiations. Heidemann never doubted the authenticity of the new discovery. As any experienced reporter would do, he had embarked on background research and learned, to his great excitement, that on 20 April 1945, near the end of the Second World War, a courier aircraft had crashed near the Czechoslovakian border. The plane had been carrying Hitler's personal papers to his mountain retreat near Berchtesgaden. Heidemann concluded the diaries must have been among them.

He and Walde decided not to approach *Stern*'s editor, Peter Koch, with their incredible news, because Koch had repeatedly told Heidemann to drop his Nazi obsession. The two men instead took the first of Hitler's diaries and their background information to senior executives of Gruner and Jahr, the owners of *Stern*. A total payment was agreed. It was to be made in instalments as and when the diaries were received.

Kujau began his work in earnest. He compiled the diaries by drawing on his huge reference library. They bore a red wax seal of a German eagle. Heidemann was the go-between, but no one at Gruner and Jahr knew that, from every instalment of cash they gave him to pay to Kujau, he creamed off a cut for himself. The collation of the Hitler diaries took two years. Crafty Kujau – still using the alias 'Herr Fischer' – insisted he could only pass on the books when they arrived in his hands from his contacts in East Germany. Kujau, of course, needed a fair amount of time between 'consignments' to write the diaries.

Each time Herr Fischer insisted it was getting increasingly difficult to obtain the diaries, he was offered more and more money. It was no wonder that by 1983, the year of publication, *Stern* had paid £2.5 million. It seems incredible now that *Stern* and a host of eminent academics could have been taken in by the often childlike tone of the entries. Here are two of them:

'Ten thousand Communists meet in Berlin Sports Palace, pledge will fight fascism to last breath. Demonstration, many arrests. By Jove, we must stamp out the reds.'

'Meet all the leaders of the stormtroopers in Bavaria, give them medals. They pledge lifelong loyalty to the Führer, with tears in their eyes. What a splendid body of men!'

Of the famous bomb plot against Hitler by a group of German generals in 1944, Kujau recorded gleefully: 'Ha! Ha! Isn't it laughable? These people were bunglers. This scum, these loafers and good-for-nothings!'

Three experts who examined the handwriting before publication of the diaries agreed it was indeed Hitler's. The verdict from a police expert that some of the paper in the diaries was not in use until after the war was somehow lost in the excitement as *Stern*'s momentous publication day drew near. Meanwhile the *Sunday Times* offered $3.25 million for the English-language rights. *Newsweek* offered $3 million for American rights. As its big day, 3 May 1993, came closer, *Stern* demanded $4.25 million from both publications. But it had overplayed its hand. The asking price was too much. And, sadly for *Stern*, *Newsweek* had already secured enough of the diaries to go ahead and publish anyway. So *Stern* changed its publication date to 25 April. It wooed the *Sunday Times* back into a deal by accepting $1.2 million for the diaries. The British newspaper would announce its scoop on 24 April.

Stern, *Newsweek*, *Paris-Match* and the *Sunday Times* had now all bought the rights in good faith and started to publish extracts. *Stern*, when it published the astonishing scoop, explained that Heidemann had managed to obtain the historic material from East German contacts. The papers had been discovered in a hayloft, where supposedly they had been hidden after the plane crash. One correspondent was certainly fooled by what he read in the *Sunday Times*. In its fellow newspaper *The Times*, Frank Johnson wrote: 'At least when the *Sunday Times* published its first extract, your present correspondent, a lifelong amateur student of mid-twentieth-century European politics, had no doubt that the diaries were genuine; they were so boring. Hitler exerts his fascination with his deeds rather than his prose. On that Sunday, those of us familiar with *Mein Kampf*, the *Collected Speeches* and *Table Talk* knew that this was the authentic voice.'

However, new forensic evidence proved the diaries were fake. Experts at the Federal Archives in Koblenz were finally allowed to examine some of the writings. They declared them obvious fakes on post-war paper. Kujau had apparently got overconfident. Although he had checked facts and dates about Hitler before creating the diaries, he ended up making a ludicrous blunder. When he bought the Gothic letters in Hong Kong to stick on the diary covers, he mixed up the letters 'A' and 'F'. Adorning the volumes were the imitation metal initials 'FH' instead of 'AH'!

Kujau and Heidemann were arrested in May 1983.

Heidemann, his record as a star writer ruined for ever, was charged with defrauding the magazine of £2.5 million, paid in instalments between January 1981 and April 1983. He maintained throughout the 11-month trial in Hamburg that he had believed the diaries to be genuine. He told the court that Kujau had also offered him an unpublished volume of Hitler's autobiography *Mein Kampf*. He said: 'When I heard the diaries were fakes, I wondered whether to shoot myself then or later.'

The extent of Heidemann's obsession with Hitler was revealed after German police raided his home. They took photographs of objects which had once adorned Hitler's desk, including a swastika on a red background which Heidemann said was Hitler's 'martyr's flag'. Heidemann also had in his bizarre collection a pair of underpants that had once belonged to Idi Amin.

Kujau was charged with forgery. It had earned him £415,000. He pleaded guilty. Indeed he basked in the attention he attracted during the court proceedings. In his defence, he said that at first he had intended to write only three diaries in return for a uniform worn by Goering which Heidemann had shown him. 'I had to have it,' he told the court. He said he had forged one Hitler diary in 1978 because it annoyed him that the Führer had apparently left no records of his life. Kujau said he was sure Heidemann had rumbled his trickery after he had practised writing the word 'helmet' in Hitler's script on a piece of paper which Heidemann had spotted.

Kujau claimed Heidemann had first told him he wanted to discuss the diaries so that they could be sent to Martin Bormann, Hitler's former deputy in South America. He told the court: 'Heidemann said the diaries would help to rehabilitate Bormann but I began to doubt the story. Then in January 1982, Heidemann told me Bormann was seriously ill and I should hurry my work.' The court couldn't help but snigger when it heard that Kujau had once provided Heidemann with fake ashes of Hitler, supplied by a friend who worked in a crematorium.

The prosecution's case against the forgers filled 4,000 pages and involved 62 witnesses and eight experts. Eminent British historian Lord Dacre of Glanton (otherwise known as Hugh Trevor-Roper, author of *The Last Days of Hitler*), who had at first declared the diaries to be genuine, had the courage to admit his mistake. He expressed this doubt at a conference in Hamburg in April 1983, called by increasingly concerned executives of *Stern*. He also said he had tried to warn the *Sunday Times*.

As the trial dragged on, fascinating evidence was heard, producing copy as riveting as the fake diaries themselves. Professor Eberhard Jaeckel had published some of Kujau's earlier work before the big scandal broke. Experts had seen through them straight away, he said. *Sunday Times* writer Gitta Sereny said she had been dispatched to Germany after a tip-off about the diaries but had not been allowed to consult Jaeckel because of the extra cost it would have involved. The court also heard that *Stern* executives had given a page of the diaries to experts to study, without explaining why. The experts they had engaged did not know what they were looking for and passed the copies as authentic. This meant the ink and tea-soaked paper used for the diaries had not been tested until it was too late.

Heidemann and Kujau were both found guilty on 8 July 1985. Heidemann was jailed for four years and eight months. His friends said he had been used as a scapegoat by *Stern*, whose weekly circulation dropped by 100,000 when the deception was announced. Kujau was sent to jail for four and a half years. His faithful girlfriend, Edith Lieblang, had also been involved. She was accused of spending part of the proceeds and was given an eight-month suspended sentence. No one found out where all the money went.

Everyone else involved in the great Hitler Diary Hoax suffered some sorry fate. Poor Thomas Walde was humiliated in court for being so gullible. *Stern* editors Peter Koch and Felix Schmidt were fired, even though they had been kept in the dark about the diary dealings. Gerd Schulte-Hillen, managing director of Gruner and Jahr, had inherited the diaries from his predecessor Henri Nannen but had backed Heidemann, refusing to believe that he was involved in a major fraud. He did not escape a severe dressing-down but was allowed to stay on at *Stern*. Frank Giles, editor of the *Sunday Times*, retired to become 'editor emeritus'.

In *Selling Hitler, the Story of the Hitler Diaries*, author Richard Harris tells how Rupert Murdoch, owner of the *Sunday Times*, justified Giles's new title: 'It's Latin. The "e" means you're out and "meritus" means you deserve it …' But perhaps Harris best sums up the whole scam with the following anecdote. Murdoch, who ordered the *Sunday Times* to continue printing even when told Lord Dacre was sounding the alarm, did so with the words: 'After all, we're in the entertainment business!'

GEORGE HULL
GIANT FAKER

When it comes to really big hoaxes in history, no one deserves the title 'Giant Faker' more than George Hull. He thought big and he pulled off a literally gigantic fraud. What was to be known as the Cardiff Giant was discovered on a farm in Cardiff, New York State, in 1869. Weighing 3,000 pounds, the stone figure was indeed larger than life, and its discovery had epic significance to historians and archaeologists.

With his massive limbs and rugged features, the man mountain gave credence to tales of an ancient race of giants. The 'fossilised' find, as George Hull was keen to describe it, was hailed by some experts as a petrified man from the prehistoric period. Indeed four local doctors declared it to be a petrified body. Other experts believed it to be an ancient Phoenician idol (supporting their theory that Phoenicians had reached America). Yet another came to the conclusion that the giant was only 300 years old.

But the interest shown by archaeologists was nothing compared with the excitement of the people of Cardiff and visitors who arrived at the sleepy town in their hundreds. Even when scientists at Yale University raised doubts over the giant's authenticity, sightseers kept on coming. It meant boom time for Cardiff, with its population of 200 now boosted by tourists who came by rail and wagon to stay in the town, patronise its two hotels and, most importantly of all, spend money. As the people flooded in, new restaurants were opened and stalls selling cider were set up by Cardiff folk in front of their homes. It seemed the influx of curious visitors would never end. Week after week they crowded in, more than happy to pay their 50 cents to peer into the pit and take a peek at the Cardiff Giant. On one Sunday alone, 2,500 people came to stare.

Some time passed before the true origin of this amazing archaeological discovery was revealed. It was all George Hull's own creation. The cigar maker and conman, who came from Binghamton, New York, had hit on the idea of creating a giant three years earlier. He had visited Iowa in 1866 and fallen into conversation with a travelling preacher. From him he learned about the giants mentioned in the Book of Genesis. Hull went away and read up on the giants. It did not take him long to realise that if anyone unearthed an example of this ancient breed, he would surely make a fortune.

So Hull decided to make his own giant. On a return trip to Iowa, he visited the gypsum quarries near Fort Dodge, taking with him his partner, a Mr H.B. Martin. The two bought a block of stone 12 feet high by four feet wide and had it shipped to Chicago, where it took two sculptors three months to shape it into a man standing 10 feet tall. Then, after a clever bit of ageing using wet sand, ink and sulphuric acid, the Cardiff Giant was ready. He looked to all the world like a giant who had been buried for millions of years.

Hull shipped the figure to his cousin, Stub Newell, who, with great difficulty, managed to bury it five feet deep on his farm. The conspirators decided to bide their time before 'discovering' the giant. Then the main thrust of the huge forgery began to take shape. Newell would pretend to drill for water on his farm, sinking wells all over his land. It would be during this drilling that the Cardiff Giant would become their 'surprise' find.

No one suspected a thing when the discovery was eventually made. Newell erected a tent over the pit where the giant was found and soon began charging members of the public to take a look. Hull kept well away from the farm, fearing awkward questions, but he made sure Newell regularly paid him his cut of the admission fees.

So successful was the venture that Hull got Newell to raise the admission price to $1. People still crowded to the farm to see the Cardiff Giant with their very own eyes. Hull then sat down and wrote pages of 'scientific' notes on the discovery. He somehow managed to persuade the reluctant and far from eloquent farmer Newell to give a worthy lecture on the ancient figure, using Hull's 'authoritative' notes. Hull had no qualms about hailing the Cardiff Giant as the Eighth Wonder of the World. Indeed the giant was a fine figure of a man. His incredible proportions included feet that were nearly two feet long, thighs 13 feet in diameter and shoulders measuring more than three feet across.

Stories vary on just how Hull was finally exposed as a fraudster. One version has it that, when an archaeological expert, Oliver Wendell Holmes, bored a hole in the skull, he found it to be solid. Another report says a private investigator traced the connection between Hull and Newell and found out about a giant block of gypsum being shipped from Iowa to Chicago. Yet another declares that the end for Hull came when the giant was moved to Syracuse, New York. Experts there said that gypsum was neither an ancient stone nor local to where the figure was found. Therefore the Cardiff Giant was one big fake.

None of this mattered to Hull, for he had already extricated himself from the scam. Sensing he was soon to be exposed, he had sold his interest in the figure to a local businessman for $30,000. He had, of course, also made a great deal of money from the gullible folk who had paid to see the ancient figure.

Incredibly, even when the truth came out about the Cardiff Giant, people still flocked to see it, despite its now being nicknamed 'Old Hoaxey'. And another great fraudster, Phineas T. Barnum, made a replica of it for an exhibition. Hull had refused to sell him the original but that didn't stop Barnum saying his giant was the 'real' fake when he put it on show. The original giant ended up in the Farmers' Museum at Cooperstown, New York. It is still there today and enjoys the patronage of thousands of curious visitors every year.

WILLIAM IRELAND
FROM BARD TO VERSE

Such a thing was unimaginable. A work by Shakespeare booed and greeted by cries of derision. Words from the quill of the Bard drowned out by raucous laughter. And finally the curtain brought savagely down on the utterance of the line: 'And when this mockery is o'er.'

It was indeed 'o'er' for eighteenth-century forger William Henry Ireland – creator of the 'lost' Shakespeare masterpiece *Vortigern and Rowena*. All he could do now was confess to his stunning literary fraud. At first, like many other of history's tricksters, Ireland thought he had got away with it. For writing a play in the style of Shakespeare and pretending it was a lost manuscript seemed easy. It would also prove Ireland's own literary abilities.

The seed for Ireland's fraud was planted at a very early age. He was born in 1777, the third child sired by his father Samuel, who never married the woman he called his wife. She was Samuel's housekeeper and a former mistress of the Earl of Sandwich. William's father never had much time for his son. A prosperous architect, painter, author of travel guides and bookshop owner, he was also a devotee of Shakespeare, avidly collecting anything he could lay his hands on relating to the Bard.

William was dismissed as a dullard with no head for learning. So he was surprised but delighted when his father asked him to accompany him from their home in London to Shakespeare's birthplace of Stratford-upon-Avon. There his father bought a chair that once belonged to Shakespeare, a goblet carved from a mulberry tree planted by the Bard and a purse presented to him by his wife, Anne Hathaway. The Stratford dealers were more than happy to oblige Samuel Ireland with his request for such treasures but William, then aged 18, was doubtful that the relics he saw his father being sold were genuine. He did note, however, the joy Samuel Ireland showed over his purchases. And an idea began to germinate.

Now William began to take even less interest in his job as a solicitor's clerk in London's New Inn. Instead his thoughts turned to Thomas Chatterton, the astonishing young faker who had pulled off a literary fraud some 30 years before. William researched all he could about Chatterton. Then he decided to have similar fun with Shakespeare.

William bought some books which had been printed during the reign of Queen Elizabeth I, the text sandwiched between several sheets of blank paper. He carefully cut out these blank sheets, which were important to his scheme, having been around in Shakespeare's time. Taking a bookseller into his confidence, he asked what kind of ink Shakespeare would have used and what it contained. When he discovered the correct ingredients, he bought them from a pharmacist's shop and set about the first stages of his literary fraud, mixing the ingredients of this 'ancient' ink.

But this was just a practice run, and William knew he should tread cautiously. Forgetting Shakespeare for a while, he took one of the Elizabethan volumes and carefully wrote a 'dedication' from its author to the good queen. He presented the book to his father, who was overjoyed with the gift. Basking in that first-ever show of affection, William decided to find another suitable gift for his father. This turned out to be a terracotta relief head of Oliver Cromwell accompanied by an old parchment letter saying it had been presented by Cromwell to John Bradshaw, president of the court that condemned Charles I to death. Again William's father was deeply moved by the present, while at the same time proving that he was not as learned as he made out to be – for, according to historians, there was great animosity between Cromwell and Bradshaw.

It was time for William to move on to greater things. He had often heard his father quote a scholar named J.A. Boaden who had written a book about Shakespeare, in which he described the nation's passion for the Bard and expressed disappointment that so little was known about him and that so few documents or writings relating to him seemed to exist. Boaden included a list of documents which he felt must be hidden away somewhere. This was the key to William's scheme. He could react to Boaden's longing for Shakespearian relics by finding some. And in doing so he would find a place in his father's heart for ever.

Dipping his quill into his home-made 'ancient' ink, William practised Shakespeare's signature and handwriting until he achieved near-perfect results. His confidence growing, he wrote what purported to be a love letter from Shakespeare to Anne Hathaway. Then he wrote a business letter about a property deal between Shakespeare and an actor called John Heminge and provided a receipt for some money Shakespeare might have received. William realised he could not produce these historically significant items without providing a story to go with them, so he told his father he had met up with an elderly aristocratic gentleman in a coffee house. He and his new friend had got into conversation and their talk had turned to Shakespeare. Hearing of the Irelands' interest in the Bard, the gentleman had then invited William to his chambers to look through a chest of documents. 'I have one or two things I think might interest you,' he had supposedly told the young man.

Then, William related excitedly to his father, came the biggest surprise of his life. For there, stored away in one of the rooms, was a mass of documents written by Shakespeare – the literary 'treasure trove' Boaden believed must exist somewhere. And incredibly, added William, this generous, wealthy man said he would allow him to take away one of the documents to show his father if Samuel expressed sufficient interest.

Naturally this news enthused Samuel Ireland no end. He begged to be given the name of the remarkable gentleman with the incredible literary hoard but William explained that the old man wished to be known only as 'Mr W.H.'. Samuel Ireland did not question this, accepting that his son's new friend had good reason to wish to remain anonymous or was perhaps an aristocratic eccentric. All he was really concerned about was seeing one of the Shakespearian documents for himself. Two weeks later William brought home the property document: a deed of mortgage made between Michael Fraser and his wife, John Heminge and William Shakespeare. So overcome was Samuel at what he held in his hands that he could barely find words to thank his son. Instead he grabbed the bunch of his library keys, thrust them into William's hand and begged him to take whatever books he wished. It was a double triumph for William. He had created a fine forgery and he had won over his father at last.

Word of the precious document now in Samuel Ireland's possession soon spread. All his literary and artistic friends suddenly found reasons to call on him and they were all duly impressed. The forgery was convincing. It was written on parchment of the right period, Shakespeare's signature was unmistakable and the seal was authentic enough. The document was declared genuine and an extraordinary, exciting discovery. This spurred William on to produce the receipt for five guineas he had said was among the mystery gentleman's Shakespearian collection. To keep his story convincing, the receipt was from John Heminge and related to other business involving him and Shakespeare.

Samuel Ireland could barely contain himself. But now he was becoming greedy and curious. He implored William to tell him the full contents of this man's 'treasure chest'. William held back. Instead, he produced a letter from Shakespeare to his patron, the Earl of Southampton, and a reply from Southampton. Southampton's letter was written by William with his left hand in case the two sets of handwriting bore too much similarity. When Samuel Ireland's friends examined the Shakespeare letter and made loud exclamations about his genius, William was tempted to shout out: 'It's me. It is I who am the genius!' But he bit his lip and carried on writing fake texts on Shakespeare's behalf.

His next historical document was a letter from the Bard professing his devotion to the Church of England. This was particularly significant and guaranteed to send his father reeling. For William had often heard Samuel pondering over whether Shakespeare had been a Roman Catholic. Indeed, it had been the cause of great debate among scholars. Now here was the proof to demolish that theory. In Shakespeare's hand, William wrote what he considered to be just the right degree of piety: 'O Manne whatte arte though whye considereste thou thyselfe thus greatlye where are thye great thye boasted attrybutes loste forr everre inne colde Deathe …'

Even eminent Shakespeare scholars Joseph Warton and Samuel Parr failed to pick up on William's amateur attempts at the Bard's 300-word religious statement. Elizabethans did not put 'e' at the end of every word. And they paid more care to their punctuation!

With all these incredible manuscripts in his collection, Samuel Ireland became famous. The bookshop he ran near London's Strand became a mecca for Shakespearian enthusiasts. Even the Prince of Wales (later George IV) paid a visit. From time to time William added to the growing collection of relics. One of these additions was a lock of hair, said to have come from the head of the Bard. Then he told his father he had seen a full-length portrait of Shakespeare and that his friend 'Mr W.H.' had generously said he could have that for his collection too at some later date. William also acquired a collection of Elizabethan books and presented them to his father, saying they were from Shakespeare's library. Among them was a three-volume history of England, Scotland and Ireland entitled *Holinshed's Chronicles*, a work which was later to prove very useful to the forger as well as to his father.

William was now an expert not only at forging Shakespeare's writing but also at producing the kind of documents he might have received. One of these was to Shakespeare from Queen Elizabeth, thanking him for some of his 'prettye Verses'. It nearly proved William's downfall, for 'the Queen' referred to the Earl of Leicester and his presence at the Globe Theatre – yet the earl had died six years before the Globe was opened.

Incredibly, none of the so-called experts who regularly called at Samuel Ireland's bookshop to gaze in awe at his collection spotted these discrepancies. Only one man voiced his suspicions. Author and critic Edmond Malone, who was preparing a work entitled *Inquiry into the Validity of the Papers Attributed to Shakespeare*, was critical of William's Shakespearian spelling. Referring to the alleged deed between Shakespeare and Heminge, Malone also said: 'It is to be observed that we are not told where the deed was first discovered. It is said in a mansion house, but where situated is not stated.'

None of this stopped the flow of 'Shakespearian gifts' from William to his father. They included a drawing of Shakespeare's head from the hand of the Bard himself, a watercolour of Shakespeare in the role of Bassanio and a couple more love letters to Anne Hathaway. There was also a love poem that began:

Is there inne heavenne aught more rare
Thanne thou sweete nymphe of Avon Fayre
Is there onne arthe a Manne more trewe
Thanne Willy Shakespeare is to you.

One wonders how anyone could believe those words came from England's most celebrated playwright. Yet Samuel Ireland's appetite was insatiable and therefore William's output unstoppable – even when he was caught at work by a fellow clerk, Montague Talbot. Talbot had always believed William was up to no good. But, instead of exposing him, he found the world his colleague had created such fun that he became a willing supporter.

It is hard to comprehend how Samuel Ireland was so happy to accept such a succession of Shakespearian mementoes without fully investigating their source or authenticity. Why should a complete stranger hand over such treasures? Why wasn't the whole splendid hoard delivered in one go? And why, at a time when England was consumed with a 'Shakespeare revival', was this mystery man not demanding exorbitant prices for the Bard's bounty? None of this seemed to matter to Samuel Ireland. And when one day he mused out loud about the possibility of there being an actual, hitherto undiscovered Shakespeare play in existence, his son was more than happy to oblige.

First, however, William teased his father with fragments of genuine Shakespeare plays: first drafts written in the Bard's hand, complete with 'alterations' and 'deletions'. Thus Samuel Ireland found himself reading 'original' drafts of *King Lear* and *Hamlet*, all free of any bawdy language which his son feared might offend him. Some critics who saw the manuscripts scoffed at them. Derisory reports were written about them in newspapers, together with parodies of this early Shakespearian style. Nevertheless, the works convinced many. Diarist and biographer James Boswell saw them and fell on his knees and kissed them. He declared: 'I now kiss the invaluable relics of our Bard to thank God that I have lived to see them.' Boswell was particularly taken with Shakespeare's *Profession of Faith*.

One element of public speculation alarmed William somewhat: should these papers not belong to Shakespeare's own descendants? The problem was quickly solved. William supplied a Deed of Gift from Shakespeare to a contemporary who had once saved him from drowning. Amazingly, it did the trick.

It was now time to fulfil his father's greatest desire: the

discovery of an original, 'hidden' Shakespeare play. William's inspiration was found by way of a painting in his father's study. It depicted the Anglo-Saxon king Vortigern being offered a goblet of wine by his mistress, Rowena. William read up on the story of Vortigern in *Holinshed's Chronicles*. It seemed only reasonable, he reckoned, to use such a source of reference, for Shakespeare had found inspiration for the plots of some of his historical plays in the very same pages. And, of course, the *Chronicles* had been so helpful at the start of William's master plan.

William soon had his play mapped out in his mind. It was called *Vortigern and Rowena*. And he was confident enough of his giant hoax to cut corners. Not willing to spend the time writing the play in Shakespeare's forged writing, he wrote it in his own. William told his father that he was copying it piecemeal from the original. 'Mr W.H.' did not want to relinquish this piece of Shakespearian history but was prepared to let William copy it. William, for his part, was enthused by his work. He was later to say of his play: 'I became fired with the idea of possessing genius to which I had never aspired.'

Great interest was shown in *Vortigern and Rowena*. Drama experts said it was definitely penned by Shakespeare, but perhaps in his earliest period before he had developed his style. Theatrical managers clamoured to produce the play. The 'lucky' man who scored this coup was Richard Brinsley Sheridan, manager of the Drury Lane Theatre. After reading the manuscript, Sheridan admitted that although the work contained 'some bold ideas' it probably wasn't the Bard's best piece of writing. He said: 'It is very odd. One would be led to think that Shakespeare must have been very, very young when he wrote the play. As to the doubting whether it be really his or not, who can possibly look at the papers and not believe them to be ancient?'

Brinsley decreed that, for a successful public performance, the play would have to be shortened. The task was given to William, and so for the first time he actually got paid for his efforts, and his father acted on his behalf in drawing up the contract. Sheridan agreed to pay the Irelands £300 plus 50 per cent of the net profits. Highlighting Samuel Ireland's greed, William was actually to receive only £60 out of the £300 payment. Nevertheless, William was so overwhelmed at his literary success that he dashed off another Shakespeare play, *Henry II*.

Richard Brinsley Sheridan originally agreed to present *Vortigern and Rowena* at Drury Lane on 15 December 1795 but, having spent some time reading the play closely, he began to feel uneasy and kept postponing the date of the production. This discomfort was not helped by Samuel Ireland's publication *Miscellaneous Papers of William Shakespeare*, including the new version of *King Lear*. The publication was ridiculed.

A further drawback threatened the prospect of William Ireland's Shakespeare play reaching the stage. An historian unearthed an authentic deed signed by John Heminge the actor. Comparing the signature with that on the deed in Samuel Ireland's possession, he immediately saw they were vastly different. William had to think quickly. He said he would go away and get an explanation from 'Mr W.H.'. William was all smiles when he returned. He had solved the mystery, he said. There were *two* John Heminges, one of whom had been attached to the Globe Theatre and the other to the Curtain Theatre. Both, by an amazing coincidence, had had dealings with Shakespeare.

Preparations for the staging of *Vortigern and Rowena*

continued, although actor-manager John Kemble did not have his heart in the project. Having grave doubts about the work's authenticity, he wanted opening night to be 1 April 1796 so that everyone would see the joke! However, *Vortigern and Rowena* finally made it to the stage on 2 April 1796. The first act passed off reasonably well. Audiences were used to actors such as David Garrick rewriting Shakespeare and the often ridiculous result. And, as William had used *Macbeth* as his model for *Vortigern and Rowena*, some of the scenes had a comfortable feel about them. So the play passed happily into Act Two, the audience a little bemused but prepared to give it a chance.

It was in Act Three that things began to go disastrously wrong. An actor with a high tenor voice had to declaim: 'Nay, stop not there, but let them bellow on til with their clamourous noise they sham the thunder.' It brought the house down. Not with wild applause but with hoots of laughter. And, once the audience had discovered the play's unintentional comedy, they seemed to find everything about it amusing – especially when a comedian with an enormous nose who had been chosen to play a death scene flapped around the stage when the curtain accidentally fell on his neck. As far as the audience was concerned, the finale came with the next few lines:

O! then doest ope wide thy boney jaws
And with rude laughter and fantastic tricks
Thou clapp'st thy rattling fingers to thy sides
And when this solemn mockery is o'er.

Somehow the actors managed to make it to the end. The audience was having a wonderful time – until the announcement came that the play would be repeated the next night. Then there was uproar and people starting fighting with one another. *Vortigern and Rowena* would never be staged again. But the evening did reap some financial reward. Sheridan and Samuel each made £103 from it. William again fared worst with his £30 share.

The demise of *Vortigern and Rowena* also halted William's intention to complete a series of Shakespeare histories, covering all those periods the Bard had missed. Recalling this idea much later, he said: 'Had the play *Vortigern* succeeded with the public, and the manuscripts been acknowledged as genuine, it was my intention to have completed a series of plays from the reign of William the Conqueror to that of Queen Elizabeth; that is to say I should have planned a drama on every reign the subject of which had not been treated by Shakespeare.'

Following the spectacular failure of *Vortigern and Rowena*, the critics revelled in their caustic reviews. There was a strong suggestion that the play was a joke, the work of a prankster who had fooled everyone. What hurt Samuel Ireland most was speculation that he was the one behind this dramatic fraud.

The moment William had long dreaded finally came. He was confronted by his father and forced to confess to his catalogue of forgeries. His father stood there, transfixed as the whole story came tumbling out. But, to William's amazement, his father did not threaten to cut him out of his life for good. Instead, he simply accused William of 'arrogance and vanity' and of trying to be the centre of attention. Taken aback by his father's reaction, William decided to escape from the whole embarrassing affair. He told him that a rich, beautiful girl had fallen desperately in love with him and they were going to get married. For good measure, he added that, despite what the critics said, his good friend 'Mr W.H.' had sent all the actors in *Vortigern and Rowena* splendid presents and had decided to give William £300-a-year allowance. In these circumstances, William told his father, he would be off to make a life on his own. It was just a pity, he said, that he would not be around to see *Henry II* performed at Covent Garden. Even Samuel Ireland began to realise his son was probably entering the realms of fantasy. When he paid a visit to Covent Garden, he was told no one knew anything about the staging of *Henry II*.

Finally incurring his father's full wrath, William placed advertisements in newspapers stating that the terrible Shakespeare fraud that had been perpetrated was all his own responsibility and that his father was completely blameless in all respects. Despite this, his trusting parent still refused completely to believe that his son was capable of such a monumental confidence trick. William left the family house in Norfolk Street, London, never to return. In a letter to his father he made one final effort to convince him that it really was he who had created the bogus Shakespeare documents. It did no good. Samuel Ireland wrote back accusing his son of 'gross and deliberate impositions'. Father and son were never to communicate again.

As William was still only 20, his achievements as a forger must be considered quite remarkable. They had, however, earned him very little money. He lived off loans from family friends, secretly made without his father's knowledge. And, far from the beautiful female he had claimed was his true love, he married a short, ugly girl called Alice Crudge.

In a bid to earn some money with which to keep himself and his wife, William wrote a pamphlet called *Authentic Account of the Shakespearian Manuscripts*. But it was so badly written that it only seemed to confirm Samuel Ireland's belief that his son was an arrogant liar living in a world of his own. Even worse, the inferior pamphlet convinced the public and many historians that William could have had nothing to do with the forgeries – and therefore it must have been Samuel Ireland's work. Samuel hit back by publishing a pamphlet defending himself. One would have thought he had had enough of the whole sorry saga but, for reasons known only to himself, he actually published the finished *Henry II*. Just like *Vortigern and Rowena* before, it was greeted with derision. Samuel Ireland died in 1800, a bitter and frustrated man.

Meanwhile, William had made his home in France, where he embarked on a string of legitimate literary efforts. The year before his father's death he published a three-volume novel, *The Abbess*, which heralded a successful writing career for him at last, and 60 other books followed, including a three-volume book on the life of Napoleon. There was also a long poem, *The Neglected Genius*, containing an account of his hero, Thomas Chatterton. However, a book detailing William's Shakespeare forgeries caused only a ripple of interest. Everyone seemed to have forgotten the episode.

William died in 1835. His life had been a strange one, most of it 'lived' through a brilliant playwright from a previous century. Indeed, such a plot of scheming, misunderstandings and trickery would have been worthy of Shakespeare himself.

CLIFFORD IRVING
HOWARD HUGHES CON

Incredibly, Howard Hughes was the billionaire who found fame more for his hermit existence than for being the world's richest man. He became a mystery man, never being seen in public, never speaking to anyone outside his household and always the focus for bizarre speculation about his private life. So one can understand the excitement of a publishing house when it was offered the biography of this legendary character – indeed, an authorised biography, written with the co-operation of Hughes himself. Such a literary coup warranted spectacular reward for the author. And so it was that Clifford Irving earned for himself a record advance from giant publishing company McGraw-Hill. He also earned himself the title 'Howard Hughes Hoaxer'.

It was 1970. The last time Hughes had been interviewed was in 1958. Irving, an American expatriate living on the Mediterranean island of Ibiza, had just read an article about Hughes in *Newsweek* magazine. Entitled 'The Case of the Invisible Billionaire', it talked about problems in one of the tycoon's many companies, suggesting that Hughes was now in such ill health that he no longer had proper control of his empire. It also reported that he had shut himself away from the outside world. The article gave Irving a brilliant money-spinning idea. If no one could get to speak to Hughes, then how could they discover a proposed biography on him was fake? Irving put the idea to his friend Dick Suskind. They agreed to work as a team fabricating interviews with Hughes, offering the book to a publisher and even forging Hughes's signature on papers 'agreeing' to the project.

Irving was already an expert on faking and forgery. He had won some acclaim for his book *Fake!*, exposing the work of art forger Elmyr de Hory. His initial approach to New York-based McGraw-Hill was to say that he had sent a copy of *Fake!* to Hughes and had received a letter of thanks. He asked the publishers if they knew of any forthcoming books about the billionaire recluse. Knowing something more was needed to whet McGraw-Hill's appetite, he included letters addressed to him 'in Hughes's handwriting' suggesting interest in a book about his life. Irving had practised forging the tycoon's handwriting for many hours, having seen a photograph of it accompanying the article in *Newsweek*. One letter was nine pages long. Another said: 'It would not suit me to die without having certain misconceptions about my life cleared up and without having stated the truth about my life. I would be grateful if you would let me know when and how you would wish to undertake the writing of my biography you proposed ...'

An amazing coincidence then occurred which could have ended Irving's hoax there and then. On a visit to McGraw-Hill's offices, he was told that a letter from Hughes had appeared in another magazine, *Life*. The publishers had taken a quick glance at it and immediately become reassured that the letters sent to Irving were indeed genuine. Irving rushed away to buy a copy of the magazine and was astonished to see that Howard Hughes's handwriting in the reproduced letter was nothing like that which he had forged in his letters. It was incredible that McGraw-Hill had not made a direct comparison.

Happily for Irving, he now had an even better sample of Hughes's handwriting to copy. This he did with another two letters supposedly addressed to him from his billionaire friend. They too were sent to McGraw-Hill. Again no one thought to compare the second batch of Hughes' letters with the first. If they had, they could not have failed to spot the differences in handwriting.

Irving added one extra enticement to McGraw-Hill, giving them details of phone calls he said he had received from Hughes. They were hooked. The company's vice-president, Albert Leventhal, offered Irving $100,000 on signature, $100,000 on delivery of the transcript of interviews and $300,000 for the biography manuscript. It was 7 December 1971 and McGraw-Hill announced its intention to publish the exclusive Howard Hughes biography on 27 March 1972.

Such a deal seemed to demonstrate extreme naivety on the part of such an established company. No one questioned how Irving had managed to bypass Rosemont Enterprise Inc., the company the Hughes organisation had set up to make illegal the use or reproduction by anyone but Rosemont of the name Howard Hughes. And no one queried how Irving had suddenly become a close confidant of the billionaire when he had never even mentioned his name before.

McGraw-Hill, however, saw no reason to doubt Irving's sincerity. They had been the publishers of *Fake!* and now their loyal author was offering them what could possibly be the final account of Hughes's life from the mouth of the man himself. McGraw-Hill began capitalising on its investment. The company sold serial rights of the forthcoming biography to *Life* for $250,000. The contract stated that, if Hughes withdrew his authorisation of the biography at any date, that money would have to be repaid.

Irving's book deal included several provisos. Only top executives of the company should know about the project and there must be no attempt to contact Hughes; only Irving had his trust. And so sensitive was the book that it should be given the code name 'Señor Octavio'. Further, not a single soul outside of the select few should be told about the book. This restriction even excluded Frank McCulloch, the journalist to whom Hughes had given his last interview all those years before. McCulloch was still a working journalist. Indeed, he was employed by *Time* magazine – which shared a New York office with *Life*.

Hughes's public relations firm, those involved in his empire and a vast number of journalists were thrown into confusion about the proposed book. It was the first they had heard of it. All attempts to contact Hughes himself were blocked, as ever. Approaches made to his PR company about an impending biography were met with a firm denial. But this just made journalists more convinced the book existed. The Hughes organisation always denied anything about its master.

Meanwhile, Clifford Irving and Dick Suskind started researching Hughes in earnest. They acquired every single scrap of information they could about the man but soon realised that writing a book purporting to have had the full co-operation of their subject was a monumental task. Here fate dealt Irving a staggering piece of luck. An old acquaintance, Stanley Meyer, contacted him with news of an existing, half-finished book about Howard Hughes. It had been written by a journalist, James Phelan, in conjunction with a former employee and true confidant of Hughes, Noah Dietrich. The agent for the book had been none other than Irving's old friend Meyer. Author Phelan and agent Meyer had parted company after the manuscript had been blocked by Hughes's mighty legal team. But that did not stop Meyer passing a copy of the uncompleted manuscript to Irving, who photocopied every page before handing it back.

Irving was now able to inform McGraw-Hill that so successful were his interviews with Hughes that the book was developing into an autobiography, written almost firsthand by the recluse himself. And, contrary to rumours that Hughes was no longer mentally alert, he was, in fact, so wily that he was demanding an even bigger fee for his time and trouble. He wanted $850,000. The money, as originally agreed, was to be paid into the Zurich bank account of one H.R. Hughes. McGraw-Hill was on the point of refusing a bigger payment – until it heard a rival biography on Hughes was being prepared by another publishing house.

It was only a matter of time before Hughes himself decided to take a stand over the growing number of books all claiming to have been written with his authorisation. He gave his first press conference for more than 15 years. The telephone link-up organised between Hughes in Palm Beach, Florida, and journalists in a Los Angeles studio was hot with denial. Hughes did not know anyone called Clifford Irving. He had not met anyone called Clifford Irving.

Irving tried one last desperate attempt to save himself. He said the voice talking to the reporters was not that of Hughes at all. It was an impostor! But nothing could stop investigations taking place. James Phelan discovered that Irving's authorised biography was stolen from his own work and produced his manuscript to prove it. McGraw-Hill officially filed a complaint with the Swiss authorities to sort out the matter of the bogus bank account.

Hughes's own detective agency was called in and tracked down the Swiss bank which held the account of H.R. Hughes. It was amazed to discover H.R. Hughes was, in fact, a woman. She was called Helga and she made frequent visits to the bank to withdraw large amounts of money. That woman was Irving's wife, Edith. Edith Irving suffered more than the shock of being exposed. The exhaustive investigations into her husband's exploits revealed that, on the occasions when he had told her he was travelling the world to set up the hoax, he was actually in the arms of other women.

Clifford and Edith Irving and Dick Suskind appeared before two Grand Jury hearings on 7 February and 3 March 1972. They all confessed to their elaborate fraud. Between them, they owed more than $1.5 million to McGraw-Hill, the taxman and their lawyers. Irving received a 30-month jail sentence and Suskind six months. Edith Irving had 22 months of her two-year sentence suspended only to receive another two-year sentence in Zurich for her fraudulent banking habits.

An autobiography on Howard Hughes never did hit the bookstands. The eccentric billionaire died on 5 April 1976. At least that was the date given. Such was the secrecy surrounding Hughes at the end of his days that no one can be sure of the circumstances of his death.

On release from jail, Irving teamed up once again with Suskind. Together they wrote *Project Octavio*, the story of how they schemed to pull off the biggest publishing coup of the century.

TOM KEATING
'SEXTON BLAKES'

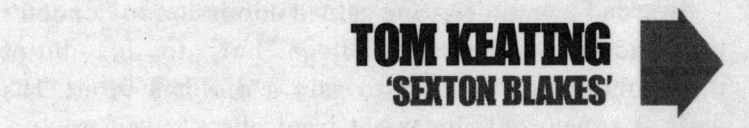

Cheeky Londoner Tom Keating literally had cheating down to a fine art. Between 1950 and 1971 he recreated on canvas the paintings of more than 100 famous artists. His output of about 2,500 fakes was an incredible feat which one may secretly admire. But what was even more amazing was the fact that no one in the art world recognised his blatant forgeries. And, unlike many other hoaxers, Keating did not wish to reap huge financial reward for his handiwork. He simply wanted to make a point to the self-styled elite who run galleries and art shops.

Born into poverty in Forest Hill, south London, in 1917, Keating left home when he was only 14 to pursue a painting career – although at this stage he confined his brush work to the outside of houses. He was following the trade of his father but later decided to better himself. Keating attended evening classes in signwriting and commercial art at two art schools, in Croydon and Camberwell. His artistic ambitions were halted, however, by the outbreak of the Second World War. The young art student now had to turn his hand to being a stoker in the Royal Navy. He served in the Far East, where he narrowly escaped capture by the Japanese after the fall of Singapore.

Keating was invalided out of the navy in 1944 because of nervous strain. And his wartime experiences were to blight him with poor health for the rest of his life.

Awarded a grant, Keating gained admission to London's prestigious Goldsmiths College but, to his bitter disappointment, he failed to gain a diploma in art. His work, he was told somewhat ironically, 'lacked original composition'. An acquaintance was later to state: 'Keating feels, like many art forgers before him, a resentment against the system and undoubtedly the extreme poverty of his childhood stimulated his sense of grievance. For a man with sufficient talent to "knock off" a Renoir in a couple of hours, the disappointment of being refused a final diploma from Goldsmiths College must have been the last straw.'

If it was this early setback that made Keating bitter and cynical about the art world, he was never to admit it. But his struggles as a young painter made him angry at the lack of respect he felt artists had to suffer. One particularly frustrating incident was when a gallery offered to exhibit his paintings but he was unable to afford frames for his work.

Keating also became enraged over the vast profits art dealers made from artists, selling paintings for as much as 100 per cent more than they had bought them for. He maintained he was a regular victim of dealers' greed, which was robbing him of the living he needed to support the wife and two children he now had. At one time he proclaimed: 'Those dealers are just East End blokes in West End suits. They don't give a damn about the paintings. All they're after is the profit.'

And so he set out to ridicule them all – and, in doing so, cracked the veneer of the art dealers' world. His limited success as an artist in his own right steered him towards a vocation which was to greatly aid his revenge. He became an art restorer and went to live in Scotland after his marriage ended. Here he diligently learned the finer points of art restoration and gleaned more knowledge through visits to Scottish castles and stately homes. Keating did not really approve of the need for art restorers, especially if several generations of them had had a go at a painting. He once declared: 'How authentic can you then say it is? If the old boys walked the earth again, they would not recognise their own work!'

By the early 1950s Keating was primed to produce his first fake work of art. He had already practised copying the work of famous painters and even sent the odd canvas to auction. Somewhat dramatically, Keating claimed his first fake was as much a shock to him as it was later to prove to the so-called experts. He said he awoke one morning to find what looked like a Degas self-portrait resting on his easel. Keating said he must have done it in his sleep. Nevertheless, he was wide awake when he commenced what was to be his 20-year 'fake period'. Indeed, he quite happily referred to his works of art as 'Sexton Blakes' – cockney rhyming slang for 'fakes'. He became a master at imitating the styles of Rembrandt, Goya, Constable, Turner, Gainsborough and Renoir.

Keating returned to London in 1960 for his most important commission – restoring the pictures in Marlborough House which had been empty since the death of Queen Mary in 1953. One day, as he was carrying out the restoration of a giant painting of the Duke of Marlborough by Laguerre, he was visited by the Queen. In his book *The Fake's Progress*, Keating recalls: 'The Queen came up the stairs and gazed in astonishment. She turned to me and mentioned that she had run up and down the stairs hundreds of times as a little girl but had not been aware these beautiful pictures were on the wall. "Well they are, madam," I said. "And there's a lot more under the black varnish on the other walls."' Then, according to Keating, the Queen watched him use a solvent to clean a section of the painting. Had anyone tried cleaning one of Keating's fakes in such a way, he would have immediately been exposed – the paint would have simply lifted off!

The restoration work at Marlborough House was just a necessary job for hard-up Keating. Most of the time he spent turning out his 'Sexton Blakes' by the score. What he didn't sell through auction rooms he gave away. He said one went to a tramp and another to a harassed mother of six he bumped into in a Woolworths store.

This cavalier attitude may explain why it took so long for Keating to be exposed. For the recipients of his gifts would probably have sold them to junk shops and it would often take years before the painting surfaced to more conventional art outlets. In any case, nobody took the trouble to check the paintings were real. With a constant need for new pictures by dead artists, the art world often believes it wisest not to delve too deeply into a painting's origin.

All it would have taken to discover Keating's fakes was closer inspection and an X-ray test. He would write in white lead paint the word 'fake', sign his own name or even write a rude word on the canvas before he painted over it. The words would clearly be visible under X-ray. In his fake Impressionist pictures, he often included tiny portraits of the artist whose work he was forging. His paintings were also coated with gelatine – hence the lifting of paint if cleaning was attempted.

In 1963 Keating met Jane Kelly, a pretty, convent-educated schoolgirl who was studying for her exams. In bohemian coffee bars, she and her friends would gather around the painter, treating him almost as a guru. After the death of her boyfriend in a road accident, Jane and Keating fell in love. She was 17 and he was 46. Jane became his mistress and the couple moved to historic Wattisfield Hall, in Suffolk, where Jane restored pictures and Keating carried on with his own creative brush work.

It was in 1963, too, that Keating read a book on the nineteenth-century artist Samuel Palmer and became captivated by him. He scoured the art galleries for examples of Palmer's work to copy. At the Tate Gallery, said Keating, he touched one 'and a strange sensation went through me like an electric shock'. He claimed the spirit of Palmer would guide his hand. 'I'd sit in my little sketching room waiting for it to happen,' he explained. 'I have never drawn a sheep from life but then Palmer's sheep would begin to appear on the paper. Then [came] *Valley of Vision Watched Over by the Good Shepherd in the Shadow of Shoreham Church*. With Sam's permission, I sometimes signed them with his own name, but they were his not mine. It was his hand that guided the pen.'

The fickle art world was so delighted that a market for Samuel Palmer had been created – thus allowing for inflation of the prices asked for his work – that, if it had any doubts about the authenticity of the paintings, it kept them to itself.

Keating had indeed become an art expert in his own way. He enjoyed his work with a passion. One reporter, Geraldine Norman, was later to write: 'I learned more in two weeks interviewing Tom than in seven years as *The Times*'s saleroom correspondent.' Supporting his claim of painting with a guiding hand, she added that 'the spirit of the artist whose style Tom was imitating at the time seemed to possess him as he worked'. In fact, it was Geraldine

Norman who pieced together the clues that led to Keating's exposure as a faker. She investigated the release of 13 previously unknown Palmers on to the market in 1976. Examination of the paper used revealed it was modern.

The game was up. But Keating just shrugged it off. He even happily co-operated with Geraldine Norman on *The Fake's Progress*, a tongue-in-cheek account of his career. And he willingly admitted: 'My aim was to get back at unscrupulous galleries and dealers. Five or six times, dealers approached me to do copies and I did them. I was conned. Once a gentleman offered £65 to do two pictures after the style of Krieghoff. He gave me £7.50 for them and hours later they were in a Bond Street gallery being offered at £1,500.'

Keating went on to claim that certain dealers had false signatures put on the paintings he had faked. Proving the ease with which a forged painting could be 'knocked out', he was later to appear in a television documentary producing a 'Samuel Palmer' in front of the camera.

In 1977 Keating appeared at London's Old Bailey, charged with criminal deception. The case was abandoned after five weeks because of his ill health. But there had been some entertaining moments when Keating, white-bearded and with a wicked sense of humour, took the witness box. At one point he was shown his most famous fake – a sepia ink wash of *Sepham Barn* sold as a genuine Samuel Palmer for £9,400. Keating turned to the jury and said: 'I am ashamed of this work.' He had no recollection of painting it, he said. Contrary to his usual attention to detail, the picture had been done using modern materials. And the main figure of a shepherd was 'un-Palmerish' and the flock of sheep 'unsheep like'. It was the sort of painting, he confessed, that he would normally have burned or thrown away.

In fact, *Sepham Barn* did have some significance for Keating. After its sale, he and Jane had gone to live in Tenerife. There Jane had met a Canadian whom she had married. Her appearance at the Old Bailey to give evidence was the first time Keating had seen her in seven years.

Presented in court with another work subsequently sold for £2,550, Keating appeared bemused and said: 'That must have taken me about half an hour. It's just a doodle. It has the ingredients of Palmer, but not his technical ability or aesthetic appeal.' The 'doodle' was of a barn at Shoreham which had been sold at a country auction for £35. It was later sold by a London gallery for £2,550 after restoration work by the National Gallery. As well as Keating's own revelations, the court heard colourful evidence exposing crooked dealers and ignorant experts. The discomfiture of the art establishment was immense.

Having escaped sentence, Keating became a celebrity. Those who wrote about him were careful not to call him a forger. An article in *The Times* described him as 'an artist and imitator of other painters'. And Keating continued turning out his paintings – for the right price. In fact, his notoriety had won him what he always craved as an artist: recognition. His works became highly prized. As one gallery owner said: 'Suddenly everyone wants to own a Keating. Prices have doubled in a month. His paintings are going around the world.'

Keating was offered a £250,000 contract by one London gallery and a £30,000 commission for a single portrait. He turned down both offers. 'I have enough work to make me rich beyond my wildest dreams,' he said. 'But I have met many millionaires and they have all been miserable. All I have ever wanted is to paint. I would give all the damn things away if I could afford to. Painting is God's gift, not mine, and it should be used to bring pleasure.'

Pleasure was the last thing felt by the art world. It had been ridiculed and acutely embarrassed. One gallery owner wrote to *The Times* stating that, far from being duped by Keating, it was the art cognoscenti who had exposed him. The writer suggested Keating had only escaped being sentenced because his mother had been a charwoman.

In December 1983 Keating had the satisfaction of seeing Christie's auction house sell 150 of his paintings for almost £100,000. Sadly, he died two months later, before he could see himself on television giving a colourful account of his life and times. TV director Rex Bloomstein, who got to know Keating well, said: 'He was a very emotional man. When painting, he would cry and shiver. He was the most fascinating, complex person I have ever met.'

In 1984 there was a major sale of Keating's work. It had been expected that many of the paintings would fetch between £100 and £200 but interest in Keating, described as 'staggering' by Christie's, made them revise their estimates and they finally sold 204 works for a total of over a quarter of a million pounds – four times the amount his paintings had fetched a year earlier. The highest prices were paid for a 'Monet' and a 'Van Gogh', which sold for £16,000 each. A self-portrait – the only 'genuine' painting in the sale – went for £7,500. Keating had made it as an artist in his own right at last.

In February 1992 a London pawnbroker bought what he believed to be a genuine 'fake' by Keating, only to find that it was a fake 'fake'. The artist who succeeded in exposing the art world sham could not have wished for a better accolade.

CHARLES DAWSON
PILTDOWN MAN

Nothing excites the archaeological world more than a real treasure of a 'find' – a revolutionary clue that can solve the mysteries of man's early days on earth. And it was with hysterical delight that one particular discovery was greeted in 1912. That discovery was Piltdown Man, so-called because his remains were found in a gravel pit near Piltdown Common, Sussex. Here it was claimed was crucial proof of Charles Darwin's controversial Theory of Evolution. When Darwin had published his *The Origin of Species* in 1859, he had been denounced as a crank and even a heretic. How dare he suggest that man originated from apes? What evidence did he have? But now, over 50 years later, here was that vital evidence. Piltdown Man was the famous 'Missing Link' between ape and man.

The world was alerted to the existence of Piltdown Man by a respected lawyer called Charles Dawson. He had been informed by workmen of bones in the gravel pit after a labourer had found an object there when digging in 1908. The workman had smashed it with his pick but kept a piece to give to Dawson, whom he knew to be a keen amateur geologist. Dawson identified the fragment as a piece of bone from a human skull and remarked that it looked very old indeed. The enthusiastic amateur then began a painstaking search for further pieces, but it was not until 1911 that he found four more fragments, which appeared to be from the same skull.

Dawson wrote to Dr Arthur Smith Woodward, keeper of the geology department at the British Museum in London: 'I have come across a very old Pleistocene bed overlying the Hastings beds between Uckfield and Crowborough which I think is going to be interesting.'

At Woodward's request, Dawson carefully parcelled the pieces up and took his finds to London. When he saw them, Woodward could not contain himself. Could this at last be the Missing Link? The two men returned to Piltdown to continue their dig. They found more fragments and called in other experts for advice. It was agreed that the pieces of bone made up a tiny brain area, an ape-like jaw and teeth, ground away just as human teeth would have been.

The geological group could come to only one conclusion. They had unearthed a creature that was half man, half ape and that had lived no less than 500,000 years ago. The discovery was reported at a meeting of the Geological Society in December 1912. And, although the skull was that of a woman, the find was officially named *Eoanthropus Dawsoni* – Dawson's Dawn Man.

The announcement threw archaeological experts into a frenzy. Piltdown was scheduled to be named a National Monument. Dawson was hailed a hero. Woodward wrote a book about the discovery of 'the earliest Englishman'. The British Museum displayed the skull to excited public horde. A pub in Piltdown changed its name from The Lamb Inn to The Piltdown Man. Visitors arrived by the coachload to view the site of the find.

Fired with great enthusiasm, Dawson continued his

excavation. Over the next few years he pieced together parts of a second skull. The finds ceased only when Dawson died in 1916, at the age of 52. After his death, and despite exhaustive digging, no other fossilised fragments were ever found again. This was hardly surprising, for Dawson had placed every one of them there himself.

The drying up of these revolutionary anthropological discoveries raised suspicion but it was not until 1948 that practical steps were taken to investigate further the mystery of Piltdown Man. Since Dawson's first discovery back in 1912, sophisticated scientific testing had been developed to decide the authenticity of such finds. Dr Kenneth Page Oakley, Woodward's successor at the British Museum, subjected the skull fragments to fluorine analysis, a form of test he had developed himself to determine the age of bones. He quickly realised the skull was only 50,000 years old, not 500,000. This news made scientists sit up and listen but did little to shake the faith of the general public; to them, the scientific debate seemed little more than nit-picking.

Eventually, in 1953, a further series of tests was carried out on the now infamous skull. It was these that finally proved Dawson had been the perpetrator of the greatest archaeological hoax ever. First, they revealed that even Oakley had been wrong. It was not just a question of the dubious age of Piltdown Man. The skull was quite simply a fake, a relatively 'new' skull that had been planted in the gravel in recent time. The jaw and teeth had come from a modern orang-utan and the teeth had been filed to make them look human. They had even been stained with oil paint to age them. There had also been a smell of burning when scientists drilled a hole in the jaw. This would not have happened with ancient bone. The same newspapers that had earlier reported on the discovery of the century now boasted other headlines, such as 'Great Missing Link Hoax Rocks Scientists', 'Experts Were Spoofed by Monkey's Jaw' and 'All the World Laughs at the Piltdown Man'.

Dawson, of course, was no longer around to answer any charges about his monumental hoax. But all the evidence pointed at him. Such an archaeological coup would have set him down in history for ever. The lure of such international and timeless kudos would have been enormous. However, there were other names put forward as potential hoaxers, including Sir Grafton Elliot Smith, one of the British Museum's leading experts, who had been called in to advise on the bones. This Australian-born scientist was known as a practical joker who had initiated a number of hoaxes, seemingly for no better reason than to enliven the museum's stuffy atmosphere. Another name put forward was that of William Johnson Sollas, professor of geology at Oxford University, who, it was suggested, might have wanted to have some fun at the expense of his old enemy Dr Arthur Smith Woodward. A further suspect was Sussex fossil collector Lewis Abbot, who thought pompous palaeontologists needed to be taken down a peg or two. Yet another name put forward as being behind the hoax was none other than Sir Arthur Conan Doyle, author of the Sherlock Holmes stories. He had been present when Dawson wrote that first excited letter to the British Museum.

One convincing clue to the true perpetrator of the Piltdown hoax, however, followed the bequest of Dawson's private collection of geological specimens to a museum in Hastings, Sussex. When tested in 1954, most of the life's work of the creator of Piltdown Man were also found to be painstakingly created forgeries.

BIDWELL GANG
ROBBING THE BANK

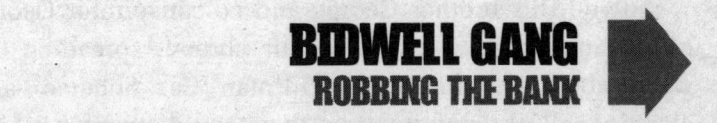

It was too incredible for the financial world to take in. That mighty monetary institution, the Bank of England, had been duped. It had fallen victim to a massive forgery and now, to the bank's great embarrassment, reports of the expertly executed crime were reaching out across the world. Behind it were four American financial wizards who in just six weeks had milked the 'Old Lady of Threadneedle Street', as the bank was affectionately known, out of £100,000, an incredible fortune at the time.

The scale of this carefully constructed plot was exposed when the four crooks, George Bidwell, Austin Bidwell, George Macdonnell and Edwin Noyes, went on trial at the Old Bailey on 18 August 1873. Prosecuting, Mr Hardinge Giffard began to outline exactly what the four conmen had done, even crediting them with 'consummate skill'. Their crooked scheme had been launched the previous November when Austin Bidwell, using the name of 'Warren Bidwell', had arrived at the bank's Western Branch, in the West End, posing as an American engineering contractor embarking on a project to construct Pullman railway carriages in Birmingham. Naturally the establishing of the necessary factory might require the granting of credit, he told the manager, Colonel Peregrine Francis. By way of cover, he opened an account, bought some genuine bonds and deposited them with the bank.

Bidwell, his brother George and co-conspirator George Macdonnell then went on a tour abroad, spreading the word about the fictitious 'Pullman Car Scheme' and gleaning all the information they could about banking practices. But they had already identified the chink in the armour of the Bank of England. This involved the issuing of bills by a finance house to raise capital. The purchaser of such a bill would be eventually paid with interest for his investment. But the owner of the bill could take it to a bank and exchange it for cash, at a discount on the cover value, before it was officially due to be bought back by the finance house. The bank would then keep the bill until the end of the financial quarter, when it was due to be repaid in full. However, the conspirators discovered that the Bank of England, unlike banks in their own country, did not check whether bills were genuine before buying. This was a very helpful practice if you were a forger, for it meant the conmen had plenty of time to get away before their crime came to light.

The gang acquired a number of genuine bills which were to be the 'models' for their future fakes and Austin Bidwell paid them into the Bank of England to establish his credit. He then got Colonel Francis to issue to him more genuine bills for larger and larger amounts. By New Year 1873 the conspirators were ready to move in for the kill. Bidwell informed Francis that his Birmingham factory had begun production and that he would be involved in some large financial transactions over the coming weeks. Bidwell himself would be tied up in Birmingham but his 'clerk' would present himself at the bank to make the transactions.

This involved the fourth member of the gang, Edwin Noyes, summoned from New York because his face was not known to anyone in the English banking world. He joined the crooked trio at their base, Grear's Hotel in St James's Place, where they faithfully copied their genuine bills of exchange.

From late January the fake bills made their appearance and were passed without suspicion. Gaining in confidence, Noyes changed cash into gold and Macdonnell exchanged gold for United States bonds. At the height of this activity, Austin Bidwell decided to get married. The newlyweds used their honeymoon to travel through France and Germany selling bonds and buying others. In a single week in January every bill sent to the Bank of England's Western Branch was a forgery. In all, the bank discounted forged bills to the sum of £102,217 – a staggering fortune at that period.

Time was now running out for the fraudsters. The first forged bill would become due on 25 March. It had been arranged that, during the time the forged bills were pouring into the bank, the genuine ones previously discounted were becoming due and were being paid. The gang had just three weeks left.

But, before the conmen could safely cover their tracks, chance intervened. Two bills purporting to be accepted by a Mr B.W. Blydenstein had been made payable at sight but the date had been accidentally omitted. The bank sent a clerk to Mr Blydenstein's office to sort out the problem – and there it was revealed that the bills were forgeries. Edwin Noyes was apprehended on his next visit to the Bank of England. It was soon discovered that Noyes had been operating under six different aliases, George Bidwell 16, Austin Bidwell six and Macdonnell 13.

The next day police notices appeared around London.

They offered £500 rewards 'for the apprehension in connection with forgeries of one Austin Bidwell (also known as Warren, Horton, Pierce, Albrecht, Walker or Nelson), his brother George Bidwell (also known as Burton) and George Macdonnell (also known as Swift or Sweet)'. All were wanted in connection with forgeries. Incredibly, without any of today's technological policing methods, all three men were soon apprehended. George Bidwell was arrested in Edinburgh, George Macdonnell in New York and Austin Bidwell in the Cuban capital, Havana. Swift extraditions followed.

At the Old Bailey, all four men denied fraud but prosecution witnesses included officials of banks and brokers from as far afield as Germany and the Netherlands, diamond merchants, Savile Row tailors and a selection of hotel waiters and cab drivers. Most damning was evidence from the hotel where the gang had committed most of their forgeries. They had tried to burn the evidence but, sadly for them, failed to destroy all trace of their illicit industry. Blotting paper impressions, lists of engravers who had made 'official' stamps and other incriminating papers were discovered by police.

Proceedings were disrupted when it was revealed that a third Bidwell brother, John, had tried to bribe warders at Newgate Prison, where the conmen were being held. Three warders were implicated and one admitted he had been paid enough gold to travel to Australia. Six armed policemen were recruited to keep a watchful eye on the prison.

Summing up the case, the prosecuting counsel said it was incredible that the forgers should have sought 'to taint the whole currency of commerce in Britain'. It took the jury just 15 minutes to return a 'guilty' verdict. The judge, Mr Justice Archibald, addressed each fraudster by name, stating that there were no possible mitigating circumstances and that they would all receive the maximum punishment of 'penal servitude' for life. Furthermore, the proceeds of their crime would go towards paying prosecution costs.

Edwin Noyes, Austin and George Bidwell and George Macdonnell now had plenty of time to contemplate their criminal folly in trying to cheat the Bank of England. In fact, Austin Bidwell was released after 17 years, Macdonnell and Noyes after 18 years, but George Bidwell, a conman to the last, convinced the prison doctor that he was near to death and was released on compassionate grounds after only six years in jail. As soon as he was freed, he made a remarkable recovery from his mystery illness. And who knows, perhaps he lived well off the Old Lady's money?

GEORGE PSALMANAZAR
'NATIVE OF FORMOSA'

George Psalmanazar arrived in London in 1701 claiming to be from Formosa, now Taiwan, a place about which little was known at the time. He actually labelled himself the 'Native of Formosa' and said he had been converted to Christianity by English missionaries to the island. Explaining his very Western looks, Psalmanazar said it was a simple fact that Formosans appeared more European than Oriental. No one questioned his story. It was a time of great exploration, and people were eager to meet those from far-off, exotic lands. Foreign travellers always had such fascinating tales to tell.

Psalmanazar was introduced to the Bishop of London, who was so impressed by the educated Formosan that he obtained a grant for him to study at Christ Church, one of the colleges of Oxford University. The idea was that Psalmanazar would train missionaries to be sent out to his heathen homeland. He also set himself a challenging task: the 'translation' of the Church of England Catechism into his native Formosan tongue. Being a complete and utter fraud, Psalmanazar could not actually do this, of course, but he burned candles in his window at night to convince people he was working on this important project.

It is not surprising that Psalmanazar declined an invitation to perform a similar translation of the Bible. However, he fooled everyone with his Catechism 'translation', for there was no reason for anyone to doubt his work. The language he produced was regular and grammatical. The alphabet he supplied looked suitably intricate and mysterious. Most of all, the language was so different from any heard in England before that no one was in a position to challenge it.

Creating a new language was not at all difficult for Psalmanazar. The one genuine talent he had was a fluency in languages and his knowledge of Latin. In fact, it was in Latin that Psalmanazar wrote *A Historical and Geographical Description of Formosa* in 1904. It was an immediate success, full of colourful tales about the Formosan way of life.

Most Formosans, he wrote, lived to be 100 years old because they ate raw meat and drank snake's blood. He said the religion in Formosa was more bloodthirsty than that of the Aztecs. Indeed, 18,000 boys, all under the age of nine, were offered as human sacrifices to the pagan gods every year. They were ritually slaughtered and their hearts burned out to appease the gods. This practice naturally led to a great shortage of males on the island and polygamy was rife. Drawing on his fantastic imagination, Psalmanazar wrote: 'The husband sends for one of his wives whom he has a mind to lie with that night. And in the daytime he sometimes visits one of them, sometimes another, according to his fancy. This kind of life is sweet and pleasant enough, as long as every one of them is of an agreeable humour. But if the husband begins to love one wife more than another, then arises envy and emulation.'

Laws were harsh, he wrote. Robbers and murderers were

hanged head down and then shot to death with arrows. Other offences were punished in ways which made medieval hanging, drawing and quartering mild by comparison. Describing the island itself, Psalmanazar said it was inhabited by elephants, giraffes and rhinoceroses. It was no wonder that such a work – a second edition of *A Historical and Geographical Description of Formosa* was published in 1705 – together with Psalmanazar's extraordinary background, helped make him a celebrity. He was lionised by London society, including Dr Samuel Johnson, who described him as 'a saved exotic'.

However, there was one man who was not taken in by Psalmanazar. A Dutch Jesuit, George Candidus, had actually been to Formosa and knew it well. So he was shocked when he sat down to read Psalmanazar's history of the island. Candidus did his best to explain what Formosa was really like. He wrote that, far from being a bloodthirsty society, the island had laws that were so lenient as to be almost non-existent. Robbery usually went unpunished. And, if adultery or murder was committed, the gift of a few hogs to the offended party was considered adequate compensation.

Incredibly, it was Psalmanazar's version that everyone chose to believe. There were two reasons for this. One was that Jesuits were hated in Protestant England at this time. The other was that, during these years of exploration, Psalmanazar's romantic account of bloodthirsty savages and untold riches was more appealing to an adventure-hungry public than poor old Candidus's true story. Even more incredible was the fact that belief in Psalmanazar's version of Formosa survived for 25 years. This was despite the fact that he had lost much of his credibility and was increasingly being treated as a figure of fun. Once handsomely supported and much sought after as an expert on the mysterious East, he was forced to take humble employment as a clerk to an army regiment.

In 1728, then in his fifties, Psalmanazar fell ill. Perhaps fearing punishment by a Christian God who would bar him from heaven, Psalmanazar decided to repent and confess his sins as an impostor. His confession, accompanied by much weeping, wailing and wringing of hands, begged for forgiveness for leading a life of 'shameless idleness, vanity and extravagance'. Such a soul-bearing act did not, however, prevent Psalmanazar from going on to commit another fraud. He contributed chapters on China and Japan to a book called *Complete System of Geography*. This contribution was almost entirely based on earlier writings of George Candidus.

Psalmanazar wrote his memoirs in 1752, but they were published only after his death in 1766. His last years were not unhappy ones. For once in his life, he undertook honest work, carrying out genuine research and submitting his own original articles to reference books. His only sin in his declining years was the drug opium, 'taken in a pint of punch' after long stints at his writing desk. Now greatly humbled, Psalmanazar refused to have his name ascribed to any of the books he wrote. And, when putting his affairs in order, he instructed that on his death his body should be buried in some obscure corner of a common graveyard, 'in a shell of the lowest value, without lid or other covering to hinder the natural earth from entirely surrounding it'.

Even after being revealed as a hoaxer, Psalmanazar kept his friends, who enjoyed his witty conversation and knowledge. He was also revered for his piety. Dr Johnson once even remarked: 'I would as soon have thought of contradicting a bishop.' But even Johnson, Psalmanazar's long-term drinking companion, never really learned the truth of his friend's origins. It was rumoured Psalmanazar was not his real name and that he had originally come from Avignon, France. Both these were secrets that the old fraud took to his grave when finally laid to rest, as requested, in a common burial ground.

HEINRICH SCHLIEMANN
GREEK MYTHOLOGY

Helen of Troy, Greek King Agamemnon, Ulysses – all are known to schoolboys who have swotted up on the ancient Trojan War. Yet no one knows for sure the full extent of the fact and fable that surround this classic piece of Greek history. Indeed, what poetic licence did Homer use in the *Iliad*? And who can say exactly where and how the Siege of Troy took place?

Normally one can rely on the discoveries of archaeologists to help unravel the mysteries of an age long gone. Sites have become hallowed historical havens as they yield artefacts which can tell us so much about those who lived before. And so it should have been in the case of the nineteenth-century German archaeologist Heinrich Schliemann. The excavations he carried out in that age of discovery looked set to put him on record for ever as the man who unearthed not only the city of Troy but also its wealth of lost riches, all of great historical significance.

For a while Schliemann did earn himself a formidable reputation as archaeologist extraordinaire. From the moment he set foot on the plain of Troy, in Turkish Asia Minor, his excavations went from strength to strength. He again disputed the beliefs of earlier scholars that Troy was sited three hours from the sea near a place called Bunarbashbi. Instead, he chose a huge mound near Hissarlik, an hour from the sea, for his excavations. The mound contained several cities and Schliemann decided Troy must be the lowest. Here a wealth of ancient, hidden artefacts seemed to have been awaiting discovery.

Furthermore, he was fortunate to fall upon the treasures of King Priam of Troy: a fabulous hoard of gold and silver cups, shields, vases, daggers, copper spears, gold diadems, earrings, ornaments. Completing his success as a world-renowned archaeologist, Schliemann was also able proudly to boast of the discovery of the grave of Greek King Agamemnon. But, while no one can deny that Schliemann uncovered city walls and the remains of an ancient Greek community, the authenticity of his other discoveries was to prove doubtful indeed. Every Greek legend became historical 'fact', borne out by Schliemann's amazing on-site finds.

Schliemann's own colourful past began with his birth in Neubukow, Germany, in 1822. He was one of seven sons of a minister. His mother died when he was very young. His father scandalised society by taking a maid as a mistress. Heinrich had a fiery relationship with his father but he soon became extremely ambitious. Although his first job was as a grocer's assistant, by the age of 20 he had progressed to the post of bookkeeper for a prestigious international trading company. He taught himself nine foreign languages and within two years he had so impressed his employers that he was sent as company agent to St Petersburg. Here Schliemann established his own business almost immediately. It became so successful so quickly that he was able to enjoy a more leisurely lifestyle. He found he had time on his hands to study Greek, and thus fulfil a boyhood desire.

Schliemann visited Greece for the first time when he was 37 and then travelled to Paris to take up his studies in archaeology. Later he returned to Greece and visited Mycenae. Schliemann's startling theory that the home of Agamemnon was to be found not outside the ruined walls of the citadel, as always believed, but inside earned him his doctorate from the university of Rostock. He claimed he wrote his thesis in classical Greek but this was later disproved.

But it was a fact that his curiosity about the Greek language, lifestyle and legend became an obsession. So ruled was he by all things Greek that, having divorced his first wife, a Russian, he was adamant that her replacement should be Greek. He enlisted the help of a Greek archbishop, who supplied him with photographs of suitable candidates. Out of these came wife Sophia Engastonmenos, chosen for her innocence and her knowledge of Homer. She was 16 and Schliemann was 47. The couple had two children, Andromache and Agamemnon.

The archaeologist made his home in a palace in Athens, and from this base launched expeditions throughout Greece and Turkey in search of ancient relics. In the 1870s he attained fame as the discoverer of Troy, that mystical place so magically described in Homer's epic poem. First at Troy and then at Mycenae, he unearthed some of the great icons of civilisation. He personally identified the Mask of Agamemnon, Priam's Treasure and Nestor's Cup.

Schliemann's seemingly single-handed discovery of every aspect of Greek life and legend meant he was lionised when he visited London in 1877. Victorian England revered him. Society gasped at photographs of his wife decked out in the gold jewellery he had so expertly unearthed. All agreed that she made a splendid 'Helen of

Troy' adorned in necklaces with 12,000 links of gold bearing 4,000 gold leaves. The treasures were part of what Schliemann claimed was the Priam hoard he had uncovered in 1873.

Sigmund Freud said Schliemann was the man whose life he most envied. Gladstone attended his lectures, spoke highly of him and wrote the introduction for one of Schliemann's archaeological books, although he did draw the line at agreeing to be Agamemnon's godfather.

However, others acquainted with Schliemann had differing opinions about his archaeological exploits. Some said his finds were authentic but that they had no connection with King Priam or indeed any other famous Greek. Others said Schliemann planted the artefacts at the Troy site, having 'imported' them from elsewhere. Yet others believed Schliemann was not even a proper archaeologist, but simply a spinner of stories to win enduring fame.

Schliemann would fly into a rage if anyone dared question his declarations. But slowly the truth about him began to filter through. There was doubt about whether the site he had been excavating was that of Troy at all. The palaces he claimed to have discovered were rumoured to have been pigsties. It also seemed remarkable that historically significant finds were only made by Schliemann. Worst of all, Schliemann may even have paid to have his legendary artefacts made to order.

Even this news did not entirely shake the faith of Schliemann's devout followers. Perhaps he was just overenthusiastic in his bid to piece history together, they said. But what cannot be denied is Schliemann's autobiography – a complete fantasy from start to finish. One touching extract relates how Schliemann dreamed of excavating Troy when he was just eight years old, yet no mention of this is made in the hundreds of letters and diaries he had painstakingly kept throughout his youth. His tales of meeting American presidents were proved false. Schliemann had worked hard to make his autobiography exciting. Even his description of seeing the great fire of San Francisco on 4 June 1851 was fabricated. The fire had taken place a month before he arrived.

Accounts of Schliemann's discoveries no longer rang true. People questioned why he had always seemed to be alone when making his major finds. For instance, he had claimed that his wife Sophia had been by his side when he made the significant Priam treasure discovery. Yet the truth was that she was nowhere near Troy at the time, having left the site weeks before. And it seemed odd that the most significant finds were always made at the end of a dig.

Entries in the diaries Schliemann kept on his archaeological work were less than reliable. After one discovery, the word 'Athens' was crossed out and 'Troy' was written in. It was also strange that Schliemann had written no description of any of the wonderful finds he claimed to have found. Moreover, he appeared to have been bribing local workers on his Turkish digs to keep quiet about any finds they made. He would promise them payment if the authorities were not told. It all helped him to build up a secret store of artefacts which he could later 'discover' *en masse* at the site of his choice – and link to whichever bit of Trojan history he liked!

Even more damning to Schliemann's credibility was one discovery he wished had never been made: that, before he took up archaeology, he had been sued for fraud while trading in St Petersburg. The dishonesty centred around his dealings in gold with miners. It was this particular line of business which had helped him amass his fortune.

What broke the hearts of genuine archaeologists long after Schliemann had finished at his Troy site was the discovery that one of the cities he and his motley band of diggers had destroyed in getting to the bottom of the great mound was almost certainly the Troy as described in the *Iliad*. Schliemann had apparently unwittingly found the lost city of his dreams – only to ruin it.

Schliemann's Trojan treasures were bequeathed to a Berlin museum. They disappeared in 1945 in the closing days of the Second World War and some ended up in the Pushkin Museum in Moscow. Schliemann died in 1890 and, of course, ended up just like the treasure he found – buried. He believed it only fitting that he should be laid to rest in a mausoleum built like a classical Greek temple. It was carved with scenes of the Trojan War.

HANS VAN MEEGEREN
WORKS OF IDLE HANS

Tongue-in-cheek fraudster Tom Keating went down in history as the man who rocked the art world in the 1970s and 1980s. But he was by no means the first to seek revenge for the arrogance exhibited in that elitist trade. Just like Keating, Hans van Meegeren despised art critics, dealers and so-called experts. And, just like Keating, the Dutchman was a master at faking paintings. It was only an amazing series of events after the fall of Nazi Germany in 1945 that exposed him. Until then, he really did believe he had got away with it.

Van Meegeren was born in Deventer, about 50 miles east of Amsterdam, in 1889, the second of five children. His mother was some 15 years younger than his strict schoolteacher father and it was from his mother that he inherited his artistic talents. But, while his delicate, sensitive mother praised his drawings and painting, his father would tear them up scornfully. This cruel behaviour did not deter the budding artist, however. Referring to those childhood days, van Meegeren once said: 'I invented a world where I was king and my subjects were lions.'

In his teens van Meegeren took up a place at the Institute of Technology in Delft, where he was a highly regarded student and gained the institute's gold medal for the best painting by a student. At the age of 23 he married Anna de Voogt, the Sumatran daughter of a Dutch government official serving in the East Indies, who soon became pregnant. Perhaps his sudden responsibilities affected his work because he was bitterly disappointed when he failed his final exams.

The couple moved to Scheveningen, then a little seaside town, where, during a lull in his painting, van Meegeren produced his first fake, a copy of the watercolour for which he had won the gold medal. (Later, during one of his lean periods, he sold the prize-winning painting for £100.) Anna refused to let him pass it off as the original and they argued fiercely. It was the first of their frequent rows, many brought on by van Meegeren's series of mistresses. The marriage fell apart and Anna returned to Rijswijk to live with her grandmother. So in 1917 the artist was alone again, struggling at his easel but not producing any acclaimed work. His paintings were described as being of high technical standard but lacking in richness and quality. One major exhibition in The Hague in 1922 received harsh reviews. The fiercest came from revered critic Dr Abraham Bredius – and van Meegeren was never to forget him, for one thing he could not stand was ridicule.

For many unrewarding years, the increasingly disillusioned painter was forced to design Christmas cards to make a living. He added to his income by doing some restoration work and selling portraits to tourists. Van Meegeren was now no longer an aspiring young genius but a broken, frustrated artist of 43. It was at this particularly low point in his life that he decided to become a professional forger. He chose the great Dutch master Johannes Vermeer as the artist to imitate in his great art-world scam. Van Meegeren could not help but smile as he realised the fun he could have at the expense of the critics and art experts he so despised. His choice of Vermeer had been deliberate: the seventeenth-century Dutch painter was the one most admired by Dr Bredius.

There was another reason. One of van Meegeren's close friends, Theo Wijngaarden, had been a victim of Dr Bredius's bullying. Wijngaarden had sincerely believed that he had discovered a Frans Hals painting and had even had it authenticated by art experts. However, Bredius dismissed the picture out of hand. But this was not the end of Wijngaarden's dealings with Bredius. Seeking revenge, Wijngaarden painted a 'Rembrandt' and four months later was again standing before the self-important art expert. Dr Bredius examined the pictured and pronounced it genuine. Wijngaarden then gleefully took hold of the painting and slashed it top to bottom with a palette knife just to witness the look of horror on his adversary's face.

After moving to a villa in the south of France, van Meegeren set about his secret work with great determination, application and patience. It was important that the materials he chose fooled everyone. And so anxious was he to make his master plan work that he spent four years hunting down the very same pigments that Vermeer himself would have used. This was by no means an easy task, for Vermeer obtained his characteristic blue colour from the semi-precious stone lapis lazuli which had been powdered. Van Meegeren did the same, paying extraordinary attention to detail, even grinding the pigments by hand so that the particles would look irregular when examined under a microscope. After great trial and error he found that mixing phenol resin and oil of lilac with the paints gave them the correct viscosity and fast-drying properties.

Providing the right canvas was also crucial. It had to look old. Van Meegeren simply bought old, genuine ones and either cleaned them or painted over the original pictures. And finally, not a detail overlooked, he even prepared special brushes which would reproduce the smooth texture of Vermeer's brush strokes. Even before he started on his first 'Vermeer', van Meegeren had the ageing of the work down to a fine art. The process was completed in a specially built oven with electric elements. Again much patience was needed to obtain the right temperature and time – 105 degrees centigrade for two hours – to bake the picture and harden the paint without causing any damage to the canvas. At last everything was perfect. Was it the lilac oil he could scent – or the sweet smell of revenge?

It took van Meegeren seven months to complete the great religious work *The Disciples at Emmaus*, his first and most brilliant forgery. In keeping with Vermeer's style, it was a strong, simple composition. Christ and his disciples were seated at a table near a window through which light poured in on the scene.

Van Meegeren had thought long and hard about the subject, for only one genuine 'religious' Vermeer existed for comparison. But the forger only considered this a greater challenge, and concentrated on every detail of the phoney work. He collected as many seventeenth-century items as he could, such as pots, plates and chairs, to ensure he was copying authentic articles for his picture. And, having spent so many years trying to recreate the great master's work, he had become not just obsessed with Vermeer but virtually possessed by him. 'It was the most thrilling, the most inspiring experience of my whole life,' he recalled later. 'I was positive that good old Vermeer would be satisfied with my job. He was keeping me company, you know. He was always with me during that whole period. I sensed his presence; he encouraged me. He liked what I was doing. Yes, he really did!' (What Vermeer would have thought of van Meegeren using a passing Italian tramp as a model for Jesus in his religious work, we shall never know.)

When *The Disciples at Emmaus* was finished, it underwent van Meegeren's intricate but perfected ageing process. After applying a coat of varnish, he had to set about 'cracking' it. As with all his other forgery techniques, van Meegeren had painstakingly practised this one over many weeks. Previous tests had proved that a genuine, worthless seventeenth-century oil painting could be stripped down to the last layer of paint. The last thin layer had the authentic cracks and van Meegeren had found that, as he painted the new picture over an old one, these original cracks came through. For good measure he used a cylinder around which he rolled the painting, and then he filled in all the cracks with black Indian ink to give the appearance of the accumulated dust of three centuries. The final touch was another coat of varnish, this time in a brownish colour. Only when he was certain the picture would stand up to detailed scientific examination was he ready to make the public aware of this great 'missing Vermeer'.

Van Meegeren first paid a visit to a member of the Dutch Parliament and explained how a Vermeer had come into his possession. It belonged to a Dutch family now living in Italy, he said. The owners wished to remain anonymous for personal reasons and had asked him to make the necessary approaches to determine the painting's authenticity. Naturally, van Meegeren continued, an expert would have to be called. Perhaps – and he could barely bring himself to say the name – that famous Dr Bredius might like to cast an eye over this mysterious work. The parliamentarian agreed to act as mediator and took the painting to Dr Bredius. The art expert made great play of first holding the painting at arm's length and then peering at it so closely his nose almost brushed the canvas. With a final examination of the signature, Bredius was happy to agree the painting was indeed a Vermeer and to issue a certificate of authenticity.

The discovery soon became big news in the art world and the prestigious Boymans Museum in Rotterdam bought the picture for £58,000. When the 'Vermeer' went on show in 1937 it caused further excitement in the newspapers, one hailing it as 'The Art Find of the Century'. Dr Bredius, naturally enough, took all the glory for discovering a Vermeer masterpiece. He went as far as to announce the discovery in the *Burlington Magazine* in 1937: 'It is a wonderful moment in the life of a lover of art when he finds himself suddenly confronted with a hitherto unknown painting by a great master, untouched on the original canvas and without any restoration, just as it left the painter's studio. We have here a – I am inclined to say, the – masterpiece of Johannes Vermeer of Delft.'

Van Meegeren, who had, quite wisely, not made his involvement in the matter too public, could nevertheless not help paying a visit to the museum on a day he knew Dr Bredius and fellow experts would be there. The master forger took one look at the 'Vermeer' and pronounced it a fake. He was ignored. This was the reaction van Meegeren wanted. He now knew the money he had received for the painting was quite safe. And any intention he originally may have had about admitting the forgery and returning the money had disappeared. He would instead have further fun at the expense of the pompous elite of the art world.

With the same precise attention to detail, van Meegeren painted two 'de Hooghs', which he sold for £46,000 each.

Returning to the artist whose work had helped him wreak such satisfying revenge, he then painted no fewer than five Vermeer forgeries. They sold for fantastic prices. Among the purchasers were the fabulously wealthy collectors D.G. van Beuningen and W. van der Vorm.

Van Meegeren received the equivalent of £20 million or more for his works at today's prices, which enabled him to lead a very fine life. He had artist's models more than willing to become artist's mistresses; he became a regular diner at nightclubs and, although again reports vary, he was the proud owner of up to 50 properties throughout the world. Rather ironically, he also owned many fine and original works of art.

It does seem incredible that his sudden, not inconsiderable wealth was not challenged. The manic artist told many tales about where the money had come from, including winning the state lottery three times! Sadly, however, van Meegeren was not enjoying life to the full. He was sliding into alcohol and drug addiction.

With the outbreak of the Second World War and the German invasion of the Netherlands, a more sinister explanation of van Meegeren's riches began to surface. Could he perhaps be involved with the Nazi regime? In fact, van Meegeren had already made a dangerous mistake in this direction. He had sold one of his Vermeer forgeries, *The Woman Taken in Adultery*, to Nazi leader Hermann Goering for almost £200,000.

After the collapse of the Third Reich in 1945, Goering's priceless art collection was uncovered at his Bavarian mansion. Most of it had been looted from churches, galleries and private collections as the Nazis swept through Europe. Among the collection was, of course, *The Woman Taken in Adultery*. Investigating agents soon discovered it had been purchased from a dealer in Amsterdam – van Meegeren. The artist was to be arrested, not for the crime of forgery, but for being a collaborator. He was accused of selling a national treasure to the enemy.

Van Meegeren was presented with a bitter dilemma. The idea of being thought a collaborator both offended and terrified him. If found guilty, he could face the death penalty. The alternative was to confess to his faked works of art and risk ruin. For several weeks van Meegeren maintained that he had bought the painting from a family and then sold it. He had had no idea it would end up in Nazi hands, he told his accusers.

Eventually, however, he admitted the painting in Goering's possession was not only a fake but a fake painted by him. At first his astonished interrogators refused to believe him. Then a novel test of his claim was devised. Van Meegeren was ordered to paint a copy of *The Woman Taken in Adultery*. He refused to do this, saying he didn't copy works; he created them. To prove his innocence as a collaborator but his guilt as a forger, van Meegeren would paint a new 'Vermeer' before the very eyes of witnesses.

Thus *Christ Teaching at the Temple* came to be. Undertaken in the somewhat stressful conditions of custody, it was not one of van Meegeren's better forgeries, but it was convincing enough. On its completion the faker declared to anyone who would listen: 'I had been so belittled by the critics that I could no longer exhibit my work. I was systematically and maliciously damaged by the critics, who don't know the first thing about painting.' The experts, he added, were 'arrogant scum'.

A commission was set up to evaluate other paintings van Meegeren said he had forged. Such a commission was sorely needed, for he claimed to have faked no fewer than

14 paintings which had all been declared genuine and sold at prices reflecting their 'authenticity'. Van Meegeren's work had been so skilful that even ultraviolet and infrared photography revealed no clues. The pictures also stood up well to chemical tests. And all the pigments, thanks to van Meegeren's fastidious care, were genuine. Well, all except one. When he painted *The Woman Taken in Adultery*, he used cobalt blue for Christ's robe. It was unbelievable that, after such methodical and painstaking research and experimentation, the counterfeiter could have made such a grave and basic error. For that particular pigment was not used until the nineteenth century.

This mistake cleared van Meegeren of treason – but exposed him as a master forger who had 'corrupted' the art world. The court hearing lasted just one day in 1947. Van Meegeren, although charged with deception and forging signatures, was determined to clear his name as a traitor. He shouted from the witness box: 'Fools! You're like the rest of them. I sold no Vermeer to the Germans – only a van Meegeren, painted to look like a Vermeer. I have not collaborated with the Germans. I have duped them.'

Van Meegeren was found guilty as charged. He was sentenced to a year in prison. But he never served his time. Neither did he ever paint again. For before starting his sentence he suffered a heart attack and died six weeks later.

Shortly before his death van Meegeren explained why he had devoted his latter years to reproducing the work of other artists in a bid to fool art experts and dealers. He said: 'I had to prove, once and for all, their utter incompetence, their shocking lack of knowledge and understanding.' Not long after his death, the true story of his dealings with Goering was revealed. Far from collaborating with the Nazi leader, van Meegeren had courageously forced him to strike a bargain. Goering was allowed to take possession of the fake Vermeer only if 200 works of art looted from the Netherlands by the Germans were returned. Incredibly, because he was so anxious to get his hands on the Vermeer, Goering agreed.

One description of van Meegeren's life and work was this: 'He epitomised that heroic figure, the victorious underdog; a little man, a forgotten failure and outcast who had accumulated by guile a vast fortune and fame at the precise expense of those who had refused him recognition.' His death had brought him recognition not only as an acclaimed artist but also as a national hero. And that was not a bad epitaph for a convicted forger.

Daring Rascals, Rogues, Interlopers and Impostors

FRANK ABAGNALE
THE HIGH-FLYING FAKE

Walter Mitty or arch confidence trickster? Or, indeed, a bit of both? In Frank Abagnale's case, no one is quite sure. His reported escapades are so amazing that a Hollywood movie was made about him, starring Leonardo DiCaprio as the resourceful trickster. But whether the storyline of the successful Spielberg movie *Catch Me If You Can* is all truth or partly fiction is still somewhat in doubt.

Certainly Abagnale's background is an unlikely one for a flawed genius. Born in 1950 and brought up in the New York suburb of Bronxville, where his family ran a stationery shop, he made his father his first victim when, at the age of 15, he used his gas-station credit card to buy tyres, batteries and anything else he could sell for a wad of dollars to impress girlfriends. The fraud was discovered only when the credit-card company asked Abagnale senior why he had bought 14 sets of tyres and 22 batteries in three months.

Frank was sent to a private reform school but it had little effect and within a year he had moved to New York City, where he learned the art of 'paperhanging': cashing cheques issued on empty bank accounts. The only problem was that bank tellers asked too many questions of a 16-year-old, so he set about creating a new identity for himself. An airline pilot, seen as a glamorous profession in the 1960s, was, he correctly judged, the perfect guise.

Not for Frank the normal years of study and training. The teenager 'aged' a few years by greying his hair, then simply rang Pan Am pretending to be a pilot whose uniform had been stolen and asked where to get a spare one at short notice. The airline directed him to the Well-Built uniform company, where he was fitted out in the blue suit of a first officer – all on Pan Am's account. Then, using logos taken from a model aeroplane kit, he forged a staff ID card. Abagnale was suddenly a Pan Am 'co-pilot'.

Abagnale got away with this double life for two years, jetting around the world, staying in luxury hotels and wining, dining and bedding hundreds of women along the way. He would sign into hotels used by aircrew, charging his room and all expenses to Pan Am and other airlines. He socialised with airline staff and dated attractive stewardesses. The hotels also cashed personal cheques for crew and Abagnale took full advantage of this.

Then the conman took to the skies. Airlines allowed each other's staff to travel free, a perk known as 'deadheading', and this often placed 'co-pilot' Abagnale in the jump seat at the back of the cockpit. On several occasions the real crew invited him to take over the controls, putting thousands of passengers briefly in his hands. The first time this happened was on a Pan Am flight between Paris and Rome when, with the aircraft cruising at 30,000 feet, the captain left the cockpit to mingle with passengers in the first-class compartment while Abagnale, the perfect image of the confident aviator, slid into his seat. Frank was just 17 and had never flown a plane before!

Almost as audacious was the stunt he pulled when he

conned Pan Am into putting him in touch with a group of school leavers who had applied to be stewardesses – and hired eight of them, all Arizona university students, to travel around Europe with him dressed as Pan Am crew. He told them it was part of a promotional tour but he was using them to boost his credibility, allowing him to cash ever-larger phoney cheques.

Abagnale's aerial career ended with a close call when he was quizzed by a suspicious FBI man at Miami Airport and, although the conman talked his way out of trouble, he decided it was time for a career change. By the time he was 21, he had worked as a doctor, a lawyer and a sociology professor, while conning banks, airlines and hotels out of $2.5 million, the equivalent of around $36 million (£23 million) today. As a 53-year-old ex-jailbird, the conman again hit the jackpot in 2003 with the release of a $40-million Steven Spielberg screen adaptation of his book *Catch Me If You Can*, starring DiCaprio as Abagnale and Tom Hanks as the FBI officer chasing him.

'The true story of a real fake,' was how the film was billed. 'Every scam he pulls in the movie is what he pulled in real life,' Spielberg stated at the launch. 'There's an awful lot of authenticity in it,' added Hanks. And DiCaprio described the film as 'more fantastic than anything Hollywood could make up'. Wherein hangs a mystery, because some critics alleged that a lot of Abagnale's life story had been made up – by the conman himself.

The film and the book that preceded it told how Abagnale used a forged medical certificate to convince a hospital in Georgia that he was a senior paediatrician. When asked for a diagnosis, he would always quiz a trainee doctor, then nod sagely and say: 'I concur.' Abagnale got away with this for nearly a year, only stopping when he was asked to give emergency treatment to a sick baby, finally realising he was out of his depth.

Again he moved on, working as an attorney in Atlanta before using forged papers to become a professor of sociology at a university in Utah. By reading one chapter ahead of his students, he was able to add his own wisdom to a subject and claimed that he was so convincing the university considered offering him a permanent post.

The FBI finally caught up with him after he had returned to his pilot's role. After an ex-girlfriend tipped off police, he was arrested in Paris and extradited to the USA. But, slippery to the last, he escaped from the aircraft at New York by removing the toilet and lowering himself through the hole on to the runway. He evaded capture yet again when two FBI agents confronted him on a street in Washington DC – by persuading them that he too was an undercover FBI man.

A month later the conman fell for the oldest trick in the police manual. When two detectives spotted him strolling down a New York street, they called out his name and he made the mistake of looking back. He was sentenced to 12 years for his crimes but was offered parole after only four on condition that he advise the FBI how to deal with the sort of crime he had committed himself. Shortly after his release he met his wife, Kelly, whom he described as his salvation and with whom he had three children.

But has Frank Abagnale been telling the truth, the whole truth and nothing but the truth ever since? After he appeared on Johnny Carson's *Tonight Show* in the 1970s and confessed to an extraordinary bank robbery that netted him thousands of dollars, journalists began investigating his claims. Abagnale told Carson that he had placed an 'Out of Order' sign on the First National City Bank of Boston's night deposit box at Logan International Airport while standing nearby in a guard's uniform with a portable box to collect the day's takings from airline and shop staff. But the bank doesn't exist and a spokesman for the similar-sounding First National Bank of Boston said: 'It never happened at our bank, never happened in Boston and never happened to the only bank that has a night deposit box out there.'

Another Abagnale boast was that he taught sociology students at Brigham Young University in Provo, Utah, after convincing his employers he was a professor. But sociology professor Barry Johnson, who has taught at the prestigious college since 1965, said: 'It's news to me. To even be considered for a position at the university you must have ecclesiastical references. Without them, you just aren't going to get in.'

Another of the major confidence tricks in Abagnale's life story has him spending a year as 'Dr Frank Williams' at Cobb County General Hospital, near Atlanta, Georgia, where he claimed to have headed a staff of seven interns and 40 nurses. However, administrators said they had no record of any Dr Frank Williams.

When Abagnale was questioned about his stories, he replied: 'I impersonated a doctor for a few days, I was a lawyer for a few days. People have asked me to prove it but, due to the embarrassment involved, I doubt if anyone would confirm the information.'

Whatever parts of Frank Abagnale's story are truth and whatever fiction, the arch confidence trickster has done well out of his criminal career. Although he received just £20,000 for the film rights to his book, the silver-haired smooth talker who was once America's most wanted conman ended his life of fraud as a millionaire businessman advising companies on white-collar crime.

JOYCE MCKINNEY
KINKY KIDNAPPER

Scotland Yard's statement was unsensational. A young Mormon missionary, said a Yard press spokesman, had vanished 'in most unusual circumstances'. He added: 'We cannot rule out the possibility that he has been abducted.' The statement, on 15 September 1977, was enough to arouse the curiosity of a few seasoned crime reporters. Investigating further, Fleet Street's finest discovered that the American missionary's name was Kirk Anderson, aged 21, from Salt Lake City. He had apparently received a call from a man who had expressed an interest in turning to Anderson's faith. The young priest had met the caller at the Mormon church in East Ewell, Surrey, and joined him and a friend to show them the mile-long route to the church offices. None of the three had been seen since.

So far the story was intriguing, though hardly front-page news. Within hours, however, new revelations had Fleet Street's editors champing at the bit. Salt Lake City police wired Scotland Yard to warn that before visiting Britain Anderson had suffered persistent harassment from a woman who seemed mentally unstable. Even more fascinating was the suggestion from Mormon Church officials that he had been kidnapped because he 'scorned a wealthy woman's love'. It appeared the woman concerned had hired a small army of private detectives to pursue him across America. The trip to Britain was his way of escaping her.

Within three days Kirk Anderson turned up and confirmed that the story was true. The woman and two accomplices had kept him handcuffed and manacled for 72 hours in a remote cottage. Detective Chief Superintendent Hucklesby, head of the CID's 'Z' Division, announced that police were searching for two Americans travelling as man and wife. One was Keith Joseph May, also known as Bob Bosler and Paul Van Deusen, aged 24. The other was Joyce McKinney, also known as Cathy Vaughn Bare and Heidi Krazler, aged 27. McKinney had long, blonde hair and a strong Southern accent. Hucklesby was asked by journalists if it would be right to describe her as attractive. 'Oh yes,' he replied, 'very.'

Later that same day the two suspects were picked up by police in the West Country driving along the A30. Officers had also discovered the secluded holiday cottage near Okehampton, Devon, where Anderson claimed he had been held in chains. There were already rumours coming out of Devon that 'unusual discoveries' at the cottage had left the local police in stitches. Understandably, Hucklesby found himself swamped with questions from the curious media pack. Off the record, he admitted that the Devon and Cornwall Constabulary had found 'certain equipment' at the cottage. 'I can't go into details,' he said, 'but I'll tell you what: I've never been lucky enough to have anything like that happen to me.'

On 22 September Joyce McKinney, described as a 'former beauty queen', and Keith May, a trainee architect, appeared in court accused of forcibly abducting and imprisoning Kirk Anderson and possessing an imitation .38 revolver with intent to commit an offence. The 'Sex in Chains' scandal was well under way.

At her next appearance the following week McKinney showed she could milk publicity with the best of them. As the prison van drew up outside Epsom Magistrates Court, she managed to fling four notes at the waiting pressmen. They read: 'Please tell the truth. My reputation is at stake!', 'He had sex with me for four days', 'Please get the truth to the public. He made it look like kidnapping' and 'Ask Christians to pray for me.' Fighting then broke out as McKinney, wearing a flimsy cheesecloth outfit with loose neckline, tried to make a dash towards the reporters. Police restrained her but in the mêlée she managed to reveal her ample breasts to photographers. Clearly she was in no mood to let British justice take its normal course.

Over the next few weeks the police became more and more baffled by the bizarre case. Not least of the puzzles was McKinney's claim that, far from locking the missionary up in a Devon love nest for four days, she, May and Anderson had twice been out shopping and dining together in London's West End.

The court committal hearing opened on 23 November with prosecutor Neil Dennison QC explaining how McKinney had developed a 'consuming desire' for Anderson when they first met in Provo, Utah. They had sex but, as this was contrary to Mormon beliefs, Anderson later told her the relationship was over. She refused to accept his decision, blaming the doctrine of his church. And so her epic attempt to pursue and seduce him began. When the trail led to England, McKinney and May, a man described as her friend and mentor, hatched a plot to kidnap the missionary at gunpoint and drive him to Devon.

In the witness box, Anderson took up the story. He told how he had been chained spreadeagled to the four corners of the bed, after which McKinney ripped off his pyjamas, performed oral sex on him to arouse him and then proceeded to full intercourse. Later they had two further sessions of love making. Anderson went on: 'She said she was going to get what she wanted, whether I wanted to or not. She said she might keep me there for another month or so until she missed her period.' McKinney's counsel, Stuart Elgrod, was unimpressed.

Elgrod: 'I am suggesting that at no stage were you ever tied up in that cottage except for the purpose of sex games.'

Anderson: 'No, no, that's wrong.'

Elgrod: 'The next day you were joking about it. It came off with a can opener. You were completely unfettered.'

Anderson: 'I was bolted in.'

Elgrod: 'You didn't even try to escape?'

Anderson: 'No, I knew I was going back soon anyway.'

The case was adjourned and lawyers from both sides decamped to consider strategy. It certainly didn't look good for the prosecution. Anderson had admitted asking McKinney to rub his back. He also agreed that he had thrown his so-called jailer across the bed in a fit of pique. Then there was the trip to London during his 'confinement' when he, McKinney and May had lunched at the Hard Rock Café. It did not sound like the experience of a man captured and held against his will.

McKinney was now spilling out her side of the story to police. She told how she and Anderson had enjoyed a three-year relationship in which he had made much of the running. How she had stocked up on his favourite food at the Devon cottage. How she bought his blue pyjamas, complete with name tag, and packed see-through nighties for herself. And how she even remembered to bring the quilt on which she and Kirk first had sex. She had invented the bondage game, she said, after studying the books of Dr Alex Comfort, author of *The Joy of Sex*, and talking to men with 'sexual hang-ups' in an attempt to understand why Anderson had spurned her.

McKinney said: 'They [the men] had said the sexual bondage game, where the woman was the aggressor, was the way to get over the guilt feelings of men who do not enjoy intercourse. When I came to England, I was looking for a real romantic cottage where we could have a honeymoon, and I decided to play some of those bondage games with him. We had such a fun time – just like old times.'

Despite her protestations of innocence, Epsom magistrates decided McKinney did have a case to answer. They committed her for a full Crown Court trial, but also granted her request to make a statement in court. She jumped at the chance and produced a 14-page document which covered her life story. In her strong Southern drawl she spoke of her conversion to Mormonism while studying at the Tennessee State University, her love affair with Anderson, her bizarre methods of satisfying his sexual guilt complex and, finally, how she became a Mormon outcast. Her statement ended: 'This man has imprisoned my heart with false promises of love and marriage and a family life. He has had me cast into prison for a kidnap he knows he set things up for. I don't want anything more to do with Kirk. He does not know what eternal love is. All I ask is that you do not allow him to imprison me any longer. Let me pick up the pieces of my life.'

The court agreed to bail after sureties were put up by McKinney's mother, and at last Joyce was free. She became an instant celebrity, being escorted to the finest restaurants by reporters and photographed wherever she went in London. Behind the scenes, a hectic auction was going on as the press clamoured for the rights to her life story. The bidding, she advised, ought to start at £50,000. Such was her love for Anderson, she told reporters in a memorable quote, that she 'would have skied down Everest backwards with a carnation up my nose for him'.

It was a heady lifestyle for the girl from Avery County, North Carolina, and it could not last. The media wanted to keep the story hot but the forthcoming trial meant they were heavily constrained as to what they could print. Inevitably they used the time to dig dirt, and it was in Los Angeles, where in 1975 McKinney had been chasing Anderson, that they found it.

McKinney had needed to pay the private detectives she had hired to follow Anderson's movements. She took to posing for bondage magazines and then graduated to providing sexual services for, as she put it, an 'upper income clientele'. One of her adverts in the *Los Angeles Free Press* read: 'Fantasy Room. Your fantasy is her speciality! – S&M (sadomasochism), B&D (bondage and dominance), escort service, PR work, acting jobs, nude wrestling/modelling, erotic phone calls, dirty panties or pictures, TV charm schools fantasies etc.' The ad closed with a P.S.: 'Joey says: Ah love shy boys, dirty ol' men and sugah daddies!' The enterprise earned her around $50,000 dollars a year.

While McKinney was awaiting trial, a file of photographs showing her performing perverted sexual acts was obtained by the London-based *Daily Mirror*. The paper sat on its exclusive – but, as it turned out, McKinney was to provide an even bigger story. On the eve of her trial she and Keith May packed their 14 suitcases, picked up their British passports (made out in false identities) and flew to Shannon, Ireland. From there, posing as deaf mutes, they flew to Canada and later slipped back across the US border. McKinney stayed on the run for 15 months before the FBI tracked her down in North Carolina. She was convicted of using false passports, given three years probation and fined. That, it seemed, was the end of her extraordinary story.

But there was an epilogue. In June 1984 McKinney was arrested in Salt Lake City and accused of disturbing the peace by 'shadowing' Anderson, who complained that she had been following and photographing him. McKinney retorted that she was simply writing a book and wanted to know what he was doing with his life. The case was thrown out of court after her lawyer entered a plea of 'extremely not guilty'.

COUNT SAINT-GERMAIN
AGELESS MYSTERY MAN

He breezed in from nowhere and captivated the courts of Europe. Graceful, charming, dressed like a dandy, his pockets full of glittering diamonds, he became one of history's most enigmatic men – not least because he claimed to be over 150 years old!

Count Saint-Germain first appeared on the European social scene in the mid-eighteenth century. He was guaranteed to make an impression with the flowing black and white silk clothes he habitually wore, an austere display for times when brightly coloured dress was the fashion. He set off his sombre clothes, however, with a magnificent array of diamonds which he wore on his shoe buckles and on his fingers and which decorated his snuff box. He boasted of always carrying them in his pockets in lieu of money. He was quick-witted and engaging, but it was his allusions to his own immortality that drew to him the attention of Europe's intellectual and social elite. To many he was a charlatan, a clever talker, an eccentric. To others, among them the great French writer Voltaire, he was 'a man who knows everything and never dies'.

Even now, the story of the man who called himself Count

Saint-Germain remains a mystery, perhaps because the stories he told of himself may have actually been true.

Where did the mysterious Count Saint-Germain come from? One report says that he was born in Italy in 1710, the son of a tax collector. Another has him born in Bohemia, the son of an occultist. Little is known of his early life, apart from his own reports of his travels and experiments in alchemy. Certainly he was master of more than six foreign languages and there is no reason to disbelieve his claim that he studied jewellery and art design at the court of the Shah of Persia.

If his younger years were indeed spent absorbing the mysteries of the occult in faraway places, it would explain why there is so little independent record of him before his rise to fame in Austria. In 1740, historical records describe him as a mature man, somewhere between 45 and 50 years old, whose charming manner won him recognition among the higher echelons of Austrian society. The first of many to fall under his spell were Count Zabor and Count Lobkowitz, two leading Viennese socialites and dictators of fashion, who took him under their wing. For whatever reason, they generously installed him in a stylish apartment.

By now well known for his astonishing claims to have powers over death, Saint-Germain was sought out by a sick general, the Maréchal de Belle-Isle. The nature of his ailment was not recorded, but it seem that after a visit from Saint-Germain he was completely cured. In gratitude, Belle-Isle funded Saint-Germain on a trip to Paris and set him up in a laboratory. There he embarked on his weird alchemy studies.

It was in Paris in the early 1740s that the legend of Count Saint-Germain really became celebrated. Parisian society was fascinated by him, although they knew little about his antecedents except that his age appeared to be about 50 – although he claimed to be over 100! We know this from the anecdote of an aged French countess who, on meeting the mysterious newcomer, recalled that as a young woman in 1670 she had heard the name Saint-Germain announced by a footman. 'Was that your father?' asked the countess. 'No, Madame, that was me,' he replied. Astonished, the countess told him that it was impossible. The Saint-Germain she had known was then about 50 and would now be over 120 years of age. Saint-Germain said that he well recalled her beauty from that ancient meeting and ended by saying: 'Madame, I am very old.'

The story helped Saint-Germain in one of the two goals he was pursuing in Paris – the search for the elixir of life, or 'the secrets of eternal wealth and eternal beauty', as he once described it. His other obsession was as far-fetched, if equally predictable: the pursuit, as old as time itself, of the secret of turning base metals into gold. Claims about these and many other astonishing subjects guaranteed that he became the talk of Paris, some in society pronouncing him a genius, others a devil.

It was inevitable that his renown should come to the attention of the omnipotent Louis XV. In 1743 the Bourbon king summoned Saint-Germain to his opulent Palace of Versailles, where the monarch and his mistress, Madame de Pompadour, questioned him at length about his outrageous claims. They both ended up totally entranced by the alchemist as he related to them his tales of mysterious meetings with Italian occultists and Indian mystics. He also related to them how he had unravelled the secrets of the Pyramids.

Perhaps Saint-Germain wished he had kept his boastful mouth shut. For Louis XV immediately employed this supposed globe-roving genius – as a spy! The count travelled to England at a time when revolution was being fomented to restore the Roman Catholic Stuart family to the throne. With help from Louis XV, Charles Stuart – 'Bonnie Prince Charlie' – had rallied an army in the Scottish Highlands and launched the Jacobite Rebellion, which was eventually savagely crushed at the Battle of Culloden in 1746.

Nevertheless, spy fever swept the nervous English aristocracy. Every French-speaking stranger was seen as a Jacobite sympathiser and many were arrested, including Saint-Germain. On him were found pro-Stuart letters. In the case of any normal man, retribution would have been swift and final. But, amazingly, Saint-Germain sweet-talked his prosecutors and convinced them that the letters had been planted on him. Not only did he escape with his head, but he also began to attract the curiosity of English society and politicians, one of whom, Horace Walpole, wrote of him: 'The other day they seized an odd man who goes by the name of Count Saint-Germain. He has been here these two years and will not tell who he is or whence, but professes that he does not go by his right name. He sings and plays on the violin wonderfully, is mad and not very sensible.'

The count could have been as big a star in England as he had been at the French court. But wanderlust overtook him and he moved back 'home' to Austria, where he made his base a new laboratory in Vienna, funded by wealthy patrons. From there he travelled twice to India, in 1747 and 1756, where he boasted about learning new arts from Indian mystics. In one letter to Louis XV, he claimed that he had perfected the arts of alchemy and could now 'melt jewels'. The hint that he was on the verge of a breakthrough in his attempt to turn base metals into gold was sufficient to bring a fresh summons from a rapt French court.

Saint-Germain again settled in Paris, where Louis funded a new laboratory for his experiments that never quite came to fruition. There was another commission for the count, however. Louis sent him on a mission to the Netherlands in 1760 to raise financial support for France's Seven Years War against Britain. Again the scheming count failed to realise when he was on to a good thing. Instead of helping his French patrons make war, he made secret representations to English diplomats, supposedly seeking peace between the two countries. His conspiracy was uncovered by the French foreign minister at the Hague, the Duc de Choiseul, who reported back to Louis. The king was furious and ordered Saint-Germain arrested and sent back to Paris. The count, as ever, was one step ahead of his foes. He took ship to England and stayed there until the fuss died down. In 1764 he felt safe enough to return to the Netherlands, where he remained for two years, opening laboratories which produced a myriad coloured paints and dyes but no gold. When again his patrons demanded some tangible results from their investments, he fled to Belgium under the name of 'the Marquis de Monferrat'. A year there and he was off again, on an amazing odyssey across Europe.

His first stop was the court of Catherine the Great. In 1768 the Russian Empress had declared war on Turkey, and the glib-tongued traveller soon found himself advising a spellbound Catherine on the conduct of the war. In recognition of his services, he was given a title, and the name he chose for himself was 'General Welldone'.

His tour of Europe continued from 1774. In Germany he raised fresh funds and established laboratories in Nuremberg, which became his base. From there he travelled to Berlin, Frankfurt and Dresden, dabbling widely in Freemasonry and the occult, as well as his alchemy. On one of these trips he encountered one of the few people to have dismissed Saint-Germain as a phoney. He went to Prince Frederick Augustus of Brunswick, claiming to be a Mason. The prince knew his claim was false, however – because he himself was Grand Master of the Prussian Masonic lodges.

The brazen count also tried to reintroduce himself to the French court, now under the old king's successor, Louis XVI. He sent a warning to the king and his wife, Marie Antoinette, of a 'gigantic conspiracy' which would overtake them and sweep away the old order of things. Saint-Germain was showing remarkable foresight, for in 1789 the French Revolution broke out and four years later dispatched them to the guillotine.

Saint-Germain's final port of call was Eckenförde, in Schleswig, Germany, the home of Prince Charles of Hesse-Cassel. The count, by now well into his sixties, is said to have died there in 1784. Certainly a tombstone in the local churchyard records: 'He who called himself the Comte de Saint-Germain and Welldone, of whom there is no other information, has been buried in this church.'

And that was the end of the story of Count Saint-Germain. Or was it? A year after his death a group of occultists holding a conference at Wilhemsbad reported that he had appeared before them. In 1788 he was supposedly warning the French nobility of the looming peasants' revolt. In 1789 he was said to be at the court of King Gustavus III of Sweden. And an old friend, Madame d'Adhémar, said she continued to be visited by the count, the last occasion being in 1820. That would have made him more than 100 years of age! French Emperor Louis

Napoleon III was so obsessed by the legend of Count Saint-Germain that he instituted a special commission to study his life and works. The findings of this inquiry were destroyed in a fire in 1871. The latter-day followers of the count believe that this was no accident but an act for which the count himself was responsible!

Adventurer, explorer, inventor, alchemist, mystic, healer, clairvoyant, diplomat and socialite – or spy, dandy, leech, fraud and confidence trickster? History has not provided us with the answer to the question of whether the charismatic Count Saint-Germain was a charlatan or a genius – or both.

ANNA ANDERSON
ROMANOV FORTUNE SEEKER

At midnight on 6 July 1918, Tsar Nicholas II and his family were awoken by their Bolshevik guards at the house in which they were being held at Ekaterinburg, east of the Ural Mountains. The Tsar was told that anti-revolutionary forces were approaching the town and that orders had come from Moscow that they were to be moved. The imperial royal family and their servants were taken to a cellar in the requisitioned merchant's house which served as their prison. There they were told to await transport to a more secure area.

The guards had until two days earlier been peasant soldiers and, while not overly familiar, neither had they been unfriendly. However, on 4 July they had been replaced by secret police under the command of fanatical revolutionary Yacov Yurovsky. And his men were not gaolers; they were executioners.

The Tsar and his household waited in that dingy cellar, with a heavy iron grille protecting its only window, for the transport that never came. Then Yurovsky and his men entered and informed them that they were to be shot. As the Tsar rose to protest, Yurovsky fired a bullet into his head. A fusillade cut down his young wife, the Tsarina Alexandra Feodorovna, and three of her daughters, along with two servants and the family doctor. The soldiers then turned their bayonets on any other adults still standing. The Tsar's son Alexis had been wounded and when he stirred was stamped to death by soldiers. Yurovsky administered the *coup de grâce*, placing his pistol to the boy's ear and firing two shots. Even the family's dog had its skull smashed in by a rifle butt.

The bodies were bundled into lorries and driven along the lonely route to a mineshaft, where they were mutilated and buried. They did not remain there long, however, because the anti-revolutionary White Army was counter-attacking in the area. So, a day or two later, the remains of the imperial Romanov dynasty were clumsily removed to a secret resting place deep in the neighbouring forest. And that is where the legend began of a single royal survivor from the massacre. According to the legend, one of the Tsar's daughters, 17-year-old Anastasia, escaped the carnage, and over the years several women have claimed to be the princess and hence the heir to the Romanov fortune.

Principal among these was an American, Anna Anderson, and the picture she painted of the horror that overwhelmed 'her family' was even more horrific than the historians' version of events. She said that every member of the group in the dungeon was violently raped before death, with the exception of Prince Alexis, who was saved by the Tsar himself volunteering to submit to the ordeal to protect his son. Anderson claimed that she awoke as she bumped along in the lorry carrying the bodies to the mineshaft. A conscripted peasant soldier heard her soft moans and spirited her away in the darkness. She subsequently bore him a son, later adopted.

Anna first came to public notice when the following brief bulletin was published by the Berlin police on 18

February 1920: 'Yesterday evening at 9 p.m. a girl of about 20 jumped off the Bendler Bridge into the Landwehr Canal with the intention of taking her own life. She was saved by a police sergeant and admitted to the Elisabeth Hospital in Lützowstrasse. No papers or valuables of any kind were found in her possession and she refused to make any statements about herself or her motives for attempting suicide.'

Although German-speaking, the poor girl refused to give her identity and, at her own request, was committed by police to a mental institution at Daldorf, where she remained for two years. It was not until 1922 that she eventually announced that she was the surviving Romanov, the Tsar's youngest daughter, the Grand Duchess Anastasia.

One or two sceptics suggested that Anna was really Franziska Schanzkowski, a Polish orphan who had disappeared from a Berlin boarding house at the time of the suicide attempt. However, relatives and servants of the Romanovs visited the mysterious claimant in the Daldorf institution and confirmed that she bore a strong resemblance to Anastasia. She certainly had detailed knowledge of the lifestyle of the Romanovs. She had scars that could have been the results of bullet and bayonet wounds. A handwriting expert averred that her writing and that of Anastasia were identical. And the two shared a physical peculiarity: Anastasia's middle finger was the same length as her index and ring fingers.

On leaving the institution, the claimant, by now something of a celebrity, travelled to the United States and adopted the name Anna Anderson. She was persuaded to return to Berlin to launch a legal claim on the title, and 30 years of litigation through the German courts followed. If she had been successful, she would have won prestige and riches. The Tsar was always rumoured to have salted away millions in foreign banks in readiness for an escape from the Bolsheviks.

In 1967, however, she sat despondently in a secluded retreat in Germany's Black Forest after her final court action had ended with a judgment that she had been 'unable to provide sufficient proof for recognition'. She said hopelessly: 'All I ever wanted was a name. It's the right of everyone in this world except for me. I suppose the only thing left to do is to die.' In fact, Anna Anderson did not die. She had married an American university professor, Dr John Manahan, and they settled down in Charlottesville, Virginia. She died in hospital there in 1984 and her body was cremated 24 hours later. Her husband survived her by six years.

Right up to her death, Anna was still believed by many to have been a survivor of the slaughter of Ekaterinburg. It is only since then that scientists have been able to determine if there was any truth in her claims. The reason is two discoveries: one was the introduction of DNA testing, or 'genetic fingerprinting', the other the discovery of a secret grave. Even those two breakthroughs could not have totally resolved the mystery without a third chance discovery: that, despite the obvious destruction of Anna's remains in the cremation, a tiny part of her body had been removed and preserved. Five years before her death she had had an emergency operation to remove an intestinal blockage. Microscopic slides of her diseased tissue had been kept in paraffin-wax blocks in the pathology department of Charlotte's Martha Jefferson Hospital.

In 1991 a collection of bones were unearthed by accident in a shallow burial pit in the forest 20 miles from Ekaterinburg. Proof that they were those of the Romanov family was achieved by DNA testing, assisted by the British Royal Family. In 1993 genetic scientists studied blood samples from Prince Philip, who is related to the Russian royal family, and were able to confirm the fate of the Tsar, the Tsarina and three of their five children. However, the DNA tests left a question mark over whether Anastasia and Tsarevich Alexei were among the remains. Tantalisingly, the tests could not at that time distinguish between the sisters.

That is when the lucky discovery in the pathology department of the Charlotte hospital finally allowed scientists to crack the DNA code. After legal obstructions in America, the slides of the tissue taken from Anna were eventually handed over to genetic investigators in London. At last they were able to match the tissue samples with the Russian bone samples – and match the claims of Anna Anderson against the truth. The 75-year-old mystery was about to be ended.

The jubilant British team passed their findings to their counterparts in Moscow and on 6 September 1994 Russia's Deputy Prime Minister, Yuri Yarov, revealed the final, foolproof report of the DNA scientists. He announced that the bones found in the burial pit were those of five skeletons. The Tsar, his wife and three of their children had been positively identified – including Anastasia.

So all the 'Anastasias' who had emerged over the decades had been impostors. Despite Anna Anderson's lifelong protestations, she died not a princess but a conwoman. As one mystery was solved, however, another one opened. If the remains of Anastasia's sister, Maria, and those of the Tsar's heir, Alexis, were not in the grave, where were they?

MAUNDY GREGORY
HONOURS FOR SALE

It was a system which appealed greatly to a snobbish, self-seeking and shallow stratum of British society – discreet payment for the peerage or knighthood which would elevate them to the top of the aristocratic classes. And there was just the man on hand to fulfil their dreams: Maundy Gregory, a rascally entrepreneur only too happy to cash in on the aspirations of the rich and famous. Born in 1877, the son of a clergyman, he had spent much of his early life in the theatre. While portraying fantasy characters for the audience, he also wove fantastic stories about himself. By his thirties he had climbed the social ladder by deceit and had established himself as a 'fixer' in the political world.

His get-rich-quick scheme was simple. It was just after the end of the First World War and Liberal Prime Minister Lloyd George was quite blatantly selling peerages and other honours to those who wanted them. This had two benefits: the money received was useful to boost party funds and, of course, recipients of the grand titles were only too happy to pledge their eternal political support in the House of Lords. Gregory realised that this was a 'no questions asked' arrangement and decided to sell titles too.

Oozing confidence and charm, Gregory inveigled his

way into the circles of the wealthy and ambitious. From these people he soon learned who was most likely to earn a mention in that all-important Honours List. Armed with this information, he would then approach those most likely to receive an honour – and offer to 'sell' them what they would have freely received anyway.

Gregory had a different story for each group of his new-found friends. To some, he was a high-ranking member of the Foreign Office; to others he was head of the Secret Service. Above all, they believed Gregory had great influence with people powerful enough to ensure certain names turned up on that all-important Honours List. Just in case anyone did express an interest in Gregory's family background, he had a ready-made answer: a 'family tree', four feet long and showing his ancestry right back to Edward III.

Completing his façade as a man of impressive social status, Gregory set himself up in luxurious offices not far from the Prime Minister's London residence in Downing Street. He even had his own commissionaire standing guard at his office front door. To impress visitors even more, Gregory organised phone calls to 'interrupt' meetings and visitors would sit enthralled as Gregory 'advised the Prime Minister' on matters of state. Gregory also used the premises to launch a fiercely patriotic and anti-communist magazine, *Whitehall Gazette*, to which many of his visitors, including judges, ambassadors, civil servants and barristers, willingly contributed articles. It all helped elevate his social standing even further.

Through flattery and bribery, Gregory soon drew up regular 'Honours Lists' of his own. These comprised not only those already in line for an honour but also those desperate enough to pay for one. Likely candidates were sent letters suggesting a meeting to discuss a matter of 'great confidentiality'. These meetings almost invariably ended with Gregory's guests parting with anything from £10,000 for a knighthood to £100,000 for a peerage. They were all too greedy to realise that they would have been quite likely to have received their honours in any case.

Gregory's reputation grew. Soon rich businessman, anxious to earn themselves an honour, approached him directly with their requests. In most cases, those hopeful of an honour were only too happy to part with their money straight away. On one occasion, however, a cautious businessman wrote Gregory a cheque for £50,000, but signed it with the title he wanted Gregory to put his way. This of, course, meant that Gregory could only cash the cheque if he fulfilled the deal.

As Gregory's promises of honours became more widespread, so did people's suspicions. His business took a knock, too, when Lloyd George ceded power to the Conservatives under Stanley Baldwin, whose government in 1925 passed legislation outlawing the trading of honours. But it was not enough to deter the arrogant Gregory, so in 1927 the Conservative Party called in Scotland Yard's Special Branch to launch an undercover operation against him. Police infiltrated Gregory's organisation and obtained a list of people who had paid for honours – and made sure they never got them.

In 1933 Maundy Gregory was prosecuted under the Honours (Prevention and Abuses) Act. One charge was that of attempting to obtain £10,000 from a Lieutenant Commander E.W.B. Leake DSO, a notable figure in sporting and social circles, who had reported Gregory's illicit offer of a title. Gregory at first denied all charges against him. He then changed his plea to guilty – a move that had much of

British society sighing with relief. For such a plea meant there would be no long drawn-out court case, no names and no scandal. Gregory was sentenced to two months in prison and fined £50. He served his time at London's Wormwood Scrubs Prison.

On his release he survived another scandal following the death of a woman friend, Mrs Edith Rosse, who had suspiciously changed her will in his favour. It was accepted as legal, even though it was written on the menu of a London restaurant, and her money enabled him to enjoy a very agreeable lifestyle 'in exile' in Paris. Mrs Rosse's bequest wasn't the only financial gift received by Gregory, however. He was also secretly paid a sum of money and a pension by the government – to keep his silence over exactly who had sought and received honours from the arch fixer.

MARY BAKER
PRINCESS CARABOO

The arrival of a such an exquisite, exotic stranger caused much excitement in the village. Local gentry could not wait to be introduced to the princess who had come to them from distant shores, telling tales in her foreign tongue of pirates and kidnap. The charitable-minded wanted to do all they could to make the enchanting visitor feel at home. In all, the presence of Princess Caraboo created quite a stir. But Princess Caraboo was a fake, the romantic invention of a wretched girl from Devon. She fooled everyone she met and, even though she was a fraud, one had to admire her play-acting – right down to the strange language she used and the bizarre behaviour she adopted.

The story of the make-believe princess began in April 1817 in the Gloucestershire village of Almondsbury. A clergyman answered a knock on the door and encountered on his doorstep a young woman who immediately started babbling away in a language he could not understand. Noting her plain black dress, ruffles around her neck and a black turban wrapped about her head, the clergyman did not know what to make of her.

She was obviously exhausted from her travels and the kindly man knew he could not turn her away. After letting her rest a while, he took her to the Overseer of the Poor, a Mr Hill. Even he was at a loss as to what to do when the stranger refused his offer of a shilling to find herself a bed for the night. So the two men put the girl into a carriage and took her to Knole Park, the grand home of Bristol town clerk Samuel Worrall and his wife, Elizabeth. The sight of the house seemed to frighten the girl, and it was only with Mrs Worrall's gentle persuasion that she went inside.

The learned couple were baffled when the girl failed to understand what they were saying. Instead, her black eyes would look at them in puzzlement; her full lips every so often breaking into a broad smile. After studying the girl for a while, Mrs Worrall announced that she must be a foreign gypsy. It was only after some effort that the good lady managed to extricate a name from her house guest. Mrs Worrall repeatedly pointed to herself, saying: 'Elizabeth, Elizabeth.' The girl finally responded, pointing at herself and saying gravely: 'Caraboo, Caraboo.'

Caraboo, accompanied by one of the Worralls' maids, was sent to a local inn to spend the night. There she refused to touch the supper laid out on a table for her. But she greedily grabbed a cup of tea, covered her eyes, gabbled some sort of prayer and noisily devoured the contents. The sight of a bed mystified her and she curled up on the floor instead. The landlord's daughter showed her what the bed was for. Only then did Caraboo lie down on it and drift off to sleep. When Mrs Worrall arrived at the inn the next morning, Caraboo ran to her, squealing and holding tightly on to her hand. Mrs Worrall felt obliged to take the girl back to Knole Park.

Word quickly spread about the enchanting visitor staying at the 'big house'. There were strange stories, too, such as how the girl had cut the cross from a hot cross bun and stuffed it inside her dress. And how she performed peculiar war dances, swam naked and darted up trees like a wild animal.

Still she showed bewilderment when anyone tried to talk to her and still she uttered odd-sounding words. Even when someone tried to catch her out, running into her bedroom and shouting 'Fire!', Caraboo stared blankly at them. The Worralls' family doctor voiced his suspicions, saying Caraboo's skin was too white for a foreigner. Her features, he said, were European. Mrs Worrall, however, refused to accept the doctor's claims, saying he was wrong to cast such doubts on the poor girl.

It was the arrival in the village of a Portuguese traveller that seemed to solve the mystery. Manuel Eynesso had spent some time in the Far East and supposedly knew the Malay language. He was invited to Knole Park, where he 'spoke' to Caraboo at length before declaring she was a princess from an island called Javasu. Her language, he said, was a mixture of dialects used on the coast of Sumatra. This surprised even Caraboo, since the language she was speaking was totally made up!

Eynesso described how Caraboo had been kidnapped by pirates and had escaped overboard in the Bristol Channel. The Worralls seemed satisfied with the explanation, not realising that Eynesso was almost as great a charlatan as Caraboo herself. In fact, it was later suggested that the two of them had been in cahoots all along, the Portuguese visitor hoping to cash in on a share of the phoney princess's fame and fortune.

Princess Caraboo was then introduced to a friend of the Worralls. A retired naval captain, he used sign language and a smattering of words she seemed to understand. An even more remarkable story emerged. Not only did she come from Javasu in the East Indies, but her father, Jessu Mandu, was a high-caste Chinese, so revered that people fell to their knees in his presence. Lowly men carried him around on their shoulders and he wore a headdress made of peacock feathers. One of his four wives was Caraboo's mother, a beautiful Malay who blackened her teeth and wore jewels in her nose.

The story continued of how Caraboo was in her garden when she was seized by pirates, bound hand and foot and carried off to sea. After more than a week the pirate chief sold her to the captain of a brig who, because of his huge whiskers and evil eyes, so terrified Princess Caraboo that she jumped overboard. It just so happened that the brig was off the coast of England at the time, so she could safely swim ashore. At the time of her escape Princess Caraboo had been wearing a fine silk dress, spun with gold. However, this was given to a peasant girl in exchange for more simple clothes, and she used a shawl as a turban to wrap around her head. The princess then roamed the countryside, lost and frightened in a strange land. She slept in barns and survived by begging until she eventually found herself in Almondsbury.

When the naval captain who was relaying this fantastic story showed Caraboo a book on Java, she reacted with delight, pointing animatedly at the pictures. It was obvious that this was her homeland.

Yet another visitor came to inspect Princess Caraboo. Dr Charles Wilkinson was considered an intellectual and an expert on foreign affairs. After meeting the princess he announced: 'Her manners are extremely graceful, her countenance surprisingly fascinating. If before suspected as an impostor, the sight of her removes all doubt.'

The Worralls and their friends could not help but be

impressed with their 'royal' guest and it was agreed that she should make Knole Park her home for as long as she wished. Having Princess Caraboo living with them, however, meant the Worralls had to get used to her strange habits. She would stalk around with a bow and arrow. She prepared her own food, showing a particular love of rice and hot vegetable curries. She ate little meat and drank only water and tea. Once, after stalking a pigeon, she caught it with one hand, cut its head off and buried it, together with the bird's entrails, in a strange ceremony. She then plucked the rest of the pigeon, curried it and ate it. The princess was also very religious. When shown the drawing of an idol from the South Seas, she threw it to the ground, declaring Allah-Tallah as the only god she would worship. She set up a temple in the shrubbery, saying her prayers there every morning and evening.

All was going well until Dr Wilkinson began writing about Princess Caraboo in journals and newspapers. Then the princess disappeared. Feeling he was responsible for scaring her away, Wilkinson tracked her down in Bath, where she had made new friends among the guests at the fashionable spa. The women wanted to touch her; the men gave her £10 and £20 notes to help towards her passage back home to Javasu. The princess did not take the money, however. She apparently did not know what to do with it. It was one of Dr Wilkinson's newspaper reports that revealed the princess for what she really was. A Mrs Neale recognised the girl's description and told friends that she was the same person who had stayed at her lodging house in Bristol. The girl had amused herself by wearing a turban and making up her own language.

Word got back to Mrs Worrall, who was shaken by the news. She confronted Princess Caraboo on her return to

Almondsbury. Then she made her come face to face with Mrs Neale, who shrieked: 'Yes, that's her. That's Mary Baker!' Instantly dropping her regal façade, Mary Baker burst into tears and, in a strong north Devon accent, begged Mrs Worrall to forgive her.

That same year, what was claimed at last to be the true story of Mary Baker was published in a pamphlet called *Caraboo: A Narrative Of A Singular Imposition Practised Upon the Benevolence Of A Lady*. The fact that Mary herself had provided the information to author John Matthew Gutch made it somewhat implausible but it was nevertheless colourful reading. The pamphlet told how she was born Mary Willcocks, one of many children born to a poor but respectable couple in the village of Witheridge, near Crediton, Devon. She received little education and ran wild until she was eight years old. Then she was taught to spin. When she was 16 her parents found her a job at a nearby farmhouse, looking after the farmer's children and doing manual work.

Rural life as a humble domestic servant was not good enough for Mary, who was already dreaming her wild dreams and making up fantastic stories about herself. Sometimes she pretended she was Spanish or French. On other occasions she was a gypsy. After two years at the farm, Mary asked for a pay rise. The farmer refused and she returned home. Furious that she had so readily left gainful employment, Mary's father thrashed her, so she ran away. Then, so Mary's story went, she really did live with a band of gypsies until becoming ill and being admitted to St Giles Hospital in London. Eventually she found a good position with a Mr and Mrs Matthews at their house in Clapham Place. Mr Matthews taught Mary to read and write, even allowing her to use his library. She spent her leisure time with her head buried in books about far-off lands, weird and wonderful customs and romantic tales.

After three years Mary was dismissed and took to the road again. Sometimes she dressed as a man to deter robbers. Then she became a servant to a fishmonger's wife in Dark House Lane, Billingsgate, in the City of London. It was a tedious job for Mary but the one thing she did enjoy was going out on errands. This gave her an hour or two of freedom and she could browse around the shops. In a book shop she met a stranger who introduced himself as Herr Bakerstendht, a well-travelled gentleman. Mary said she married him, shortening her surname to Baker. Others say the couple simply lived together and he deserted her when she had a child. The baby was apparently handed over to a foundling hospital.

It was around this time that Mary decided to become Princess Caraboo. She practised mannerisms, rehearsed strange behaviour and wove a fantastic story around herself. It was incredible that the Worralls and everyone else who came into contact with Mary could have been so easily taken in. But her charade was greatly enhanced by the 'language' she spoke. It comprised mainly Malay and Arabic words which she had picked up from Bakerstendht, together with a smattering of Romany from the gypsies. Her knowledge of foreign parts had come from the time spent reading books, courtesy of Mr Matthews.

It was even more remarkable that, when Princess Caraboo was revealed as a fraud, no one turned against her. Instead, the forgiving Mrs Worrall helped Mary fulfil her dreams of going to America. She gave her money and clothes and paid for her passage on board a ship from Bristol. In return, Mary was to be in charge of a group of missionaries. It is believed that Mary's dreams of an exciting new life in America were not fulfilled, however. She was disappointed when she failed to get the recognition she felt she deserved and she set off on her travels once again.

But that was not the last anyone heard of Mary Baker, the fake princess. A letter appeared in the *Bristol Journal* in September 1817 from Sir Hudson Lowe, governor of St Helena, the island where Napoleon was being held prisoner. Apparently, watching one day from shore during a fierce storm, Sir Hudson saw a ship in trouble just a short distance away. Moments later he noticed a small boat entering the harbour. Going down to the beach to investigate, he came across a young woman getting out of the boat. She told him her name was Princess Caraboo and that she desperately wanted to see Napoleon. Mary Baker was up to her old tricks again. And once more her self-spun fantasies seemed to have been believed. According to the letter from St Helena, Napoleon was so captivated by this pretty creature that he asked if she might be allowed an apartment in his house. No one knows how their relationship ended.

Princess Caraboo made two subsequent appearances. Mary Baker paid a return visit to London and assumed the character of the fake princess while attending a Bond Street art gallery. She then disappeared again, re-emerging in Bristol – a full seven years after she had left the city for America – where she tried to exhibit herself as Princess Caraboo for 'a shilling a peep'. Her fantasy life had now run its full course, however. She spent the next 20 years collecting and selling leeches to the local hospital. It was only when she died, aged 75, that Mary found fame again – with an obituary on her colourful life in the top people's newspaper, *The Times*.

ARTHUR ORTON
THE TICHBORNE CLAIMANT

Arthur Orton was a semi-literate butcher from Wagga Wagga in the Australian Outback. Also known as Thomas Castro, this fat, obnoxious ne'er-do-well had emigrated from the East End of London to escape his creditors. Now married with two young children, Orton was returning to Britain with £20,000 of borrowed money to lay claim to a noble family's fortune. The chances of his pulling off such a blatant confidence trick seemed non-existent – for he had to convince a wealthy woman he was her long-lost son. Yet, incredibly, by bravado and determination, the two sharpest tools of a conman's trade, Orton came within a hair's breadth of succeeding.

Orton chose well when he targeted the Tichborne family for his dastardly deception. For at stake was not only a fortune but a baronetcy too. James Tichborne and his wife Henriette had lived in Paris and had had four children, but only two boys survived. When James's brother, the tenth baronet, died, the eldest son, Roger, was in line to take the title. But James, irritated by his wife's obsessive love for her son and anxious that the young lad should be whipped into shape, had other plans. James invented a family funeral and insisted Roger accompany him.

Once safely on English soil, James sent his son to Stonyhurst, a famous Roman Catholic boarding school in Lancashire. Four years later he secured a commission for Roger in the Sixth Dragoon Guards. Roger was now in his early twenties and he turned to more romantic interests. He fell in love with his cousin, Katherine Doughty, but their romance was doomed. The Catholic Church did not allow first cousins to marry, and Katherine's family did not consider Roger a suitable match. Her father, Sir Edward Doughty, forbade the two to meet for three years. He told them that, if they obeyed his instructions and their feelings were still strong for each other when the three years had passed, he would reconsider. He would even try to obtain dispensation from the Church so that they could marry.

Katherine and Roger were distraught, but reluctantly agreed to comply with her father's wishes. They bade a tearful farewell, never realising it was the last time they would ever see each other. When Katherine had gone, Roger sat down and wrote a moving letter to her. It read: 'I make on this day a promise, if I marry my cousin Katherine Doughty this year, or before three years are over at the latest, to build a church or chapel at Tichborne to the Holy Virgin in thanksgiving for the protection which she has thrown over us, and praying God that our wishes may be fulfilled.'

We shall never know whether Roger believed fate might deal him a tragic blow, but for some reason he made a copy of his letter. He gave it to a trusted friend, Vincent Gosport, for safe keeping. Roger then resigned his commission and boarded a boat bound for South America. He spent 10 months trying to forget Katherine, scraping a living in Chile and Argentina. He then decided to head for America, and in 1852 he joined a small British trader, the *Bella*, leaving Rio de Janeiro for New York. But Roger was never to complete the journey. The *Bella* went down in fierce Atlantic storms. The only trace left of her was the logbook. There were no listed survivors.

Roger's mother was overcome with grief on hearing the news. She blamed her husband for sending their beloved son away. Never recovering from the loss, James Tichborne died soon afterwards. Three years later Roger Tichborne was officially declared dead. The family estate and title was passed to Roger's young brother, Alfred. He too died not long afterwards. His baby son Henry became the twelfth baronet.

Henriette felt the whole family was cursed. She had lost all four children and her husband. But in her tortured mind she started to believe that somehow her darling boy Roger would one day return to her. Despite strong dissuasion from friends, Henriette began the search for Roger Tichborne. Her tragic quest started with advertisements placed in newspapers everywhere between South America and Australia asking for information about her son. One of these adverts fell into the hands of Arthur Orton. His poor literacy prevented him fully understanding the meaning of the advert but with a little help from better-educated friends it eventually became clear.

Orton now embarked on his fortune-seeking plot. It was a deception that was to grow and grow. Clutching the advertisement, Orton made his way to Wagga Wagga's local lawyer, William Gibbes. He told Gibbes that, although he was living under the name of Thomas Castro, he was, in fact, the missing Roger Tichborne. As proof, he showed the lawyer a pipe carved with the initials R.C.T. Gibbes was taken in by his story, and Orton returned home to pass on his good news to a waiting wife and children.

In May 1865 Gibbes wrote to Henriette in Paris, telling

her that her son might indeed still be alive and living in Australia. Henriette was overjoyed, replying immediately. She begged to learn more, asking that 'Roger' write to her himself. With some difficulty, Orton penned a letter addressed to 'My dear Mother' and a regular correspondence between mother and 'son' began. Henriette, in her desperation to believe her son was still alive, apparently did not question the nature of Orton's letters. She ignored friends' intervention when they pointed out that the degree of literacy in the letters conflicted with the education Roger had received at Stonyhurst.

Eventually Henriette wrote to Orton to tell him to hasten to Sydney, where he would meet an old family servant by the name of Bogle. The Negro servant was so excited at being reunited with young Roger Tichborne – or had been promised some reward in maintaining the pretence – that he confirmed that Henriette's son was indeed alive and well. Henriette sent money to Orton. He had also raised £20,000 himself on the strength of his inheritance. Orton, accompanied by his family and the faithful Bogle, set sail for England.

Trying to avoid an early meeting with Henriette, Orton first headed for Hampshire, where the Tichborne family home was situated, and attempted to stake a claim to the title of baronet and the Tichborne fortune. He failed dismally. Even the village blacksmith saw through Orton, saying: 'If you are Sir Roger, you've changed from a racehorse to a carthorse!' For the blacksmith last remembered Roger Tichborne as a slim man with a long pointed face, sallow complexion and straight, black hair. Yet here before him was an obvious impostor, with a florid face, greasy, waved hair and weighing at least 24 stone. Roger's old tutor, Henri Chatillon, also saw through Orton straight away. He could not accept that the skinny little runt called Roger Charles Tichborne whom he had taught could ever have become such an obese, uncouth and common person. Not only that: this man was much older than Roger would have been. He bore no tattoo on his arm as Roger had. And he did not understand French, the language Roger had been so expertly tutored in.

Orton was not to be put off. He had come this far and he was determined to receive recognition and reward for his pains. If he could not persuade these stupid people in England that he was the missing heir, then he would have to face the one person who really mattered: Mrs Henriette Tichborne herself.

He made arrangements to travel to Paris. The reunion between mother and 'son' took place in the hotel where the lonely Henriette now lived. Aged, frail and confused, she did not question Orton's plea that the room be darkened because he was ill. Henriette accepted Orton as her son without question. For, in failing health, she was desperate to be reunited with the child she had loved above all others.

Orton had also done his homework. He had used his time in England well, gleaning every piece of information he could about Roger and the Tichborne family. He could not physically become Roger Tichborne but he could put up a damn convincing charade. Even when he made the odd mistake – such as forgetting the names of schoolteachers and school friends – Henriette chose to ignore it, saying: 'He confuses everything as in a dream.' Henriette immediately made Orton an annual allowance of £1,000. Her unquestioning acceptance of him made the fraudster even bolder. Now was the time, he decided, to go after the inheritance with a vengeance.

Orton returned to England to set about claiming the

family estates. He was still reading as much as he could about the finer details of the Tichborne history and family life. He even cheekily bounced the two-year-old twelfth baronet on his knee, in a convincingly avuncular manner. And, once established in Hampshire, he invited two old troopers of the Dragoon Guards to join the household as servants. From them, he learned all about Roger Tichborne's life in the regiment. Finally he agreed to sign a sworn affidavit that he was indeed Roger Charles Tichborne, who had had the good fortune to be rescued from the stricken *Bella* by the Australia-bound *Osprey*, which had transported him to his new life. Orton even managed to convince the Tichborne family solicitor, Robert Hopkin, of the justice of his cause.

One person Orton did not convince, however, was Roger's loyal friend Vincent Gosport. Gosport asked Orton about the contents of the letter he had been given. Of course, Orton knew nothing of such a letter – and Gosport knew straight away that the man in front of him was an impostor.

Despite this drawback, Orton was ready to go before a court and swear that he was the true Sir Roger Tichborne, heir to the Tichborne estates, and the real twelfth baronet. Progress was by no means as swift as he would have liked, however, and it took four years for his claim to be heard in the Chancery Division of London's High Court. During this time two crucial witnesses on the Tichborne side had died: Henriette and family solicitor Robert Hopkin.

Orton went to great trouble and expense to assemble his evidence, one extravagant example of which was to lead to his downfall. He took a lawyer all the way to Chile to prove that he, Roger Tichborne, had stayed at certain villages during his time in South America. This visit could have paid off because Orton had indeed been to South America.

But he was recognised as being plain Arthur Orton – and those who remembered him also recalled that he had been around three years before Roger Tichborne's arrival there. This was enough to arouse the lawyer's suspicions. Further digging revealed the story behind Orton, including how, as a seaman, he had jumped ship in Chile and eventually turned up in Australia, where he had adopted the name Thomas Castro.

The hearing began on 11 May 1871. There were several witnesses who swore Orton was the man they had known either as a child or in the Dragoons. Even Roger's former governess said Orton was definitely the child she had cared for. In all, Orton called 100 witness to support his claim. The Tichborne family could produce only 17.

However, two pieces of evidence proved once and for all that Orton was not Roger Tichborne. The first came from Roger's beloved Katherine Doughty. The court was hushed as she read out the letter she had kept all those years. The second was the absence of the tattoo on Orton's arm. There was also the question of Orton's speech. It was certainly not that of a gentleman. And as Orton himself declared afterwards: 'I would have won if only I could have kept my mouth shut.'

After a hearing which lasted 103 days, Orton was declared an impostor and was arrested and charged with perjury. With cheers ringing in his ears from those who still firmly believed he was genuine, he was released on bail. He spent the year before his trial travelling around Britain giving talks at music halls, public meetings and church fêtes. A subscription fund was set up to pay for his defence.

Orton eventually appeared in court to answer 23 charges of perjury. The trial lasted 188 days – the longest criminal hearing in British legal history. This time a desperate but

290 ◀ THE STING

fiercely determined Orton called 300 witnesses, some from South America and Australia. The Crown called 210. As part of its case, the prosecution submitted a notebook which contained Orton's handwriting. He had written a strange motto: 'Some men has plenty money and no brains, and some men has plenty brains and no money. Surely men with plenty money and no brains were made for men with plenty brains and no money.'

The jury eventually decided that, whatever brains Orton thought he had, he deserved no more money or sympathy. They found him guilty and he was sentenced to 14 years' imprisonment. He was released in 1884 after serving 10 years. He sold his story to a newspaper for £3,000. But, despite attempts to resurrect his career in public speaking, Orton discovered that people were no longer interested. He died in a humble boarding house, a broken man, on 1 April 1898. He was 64. To the end, the rough and grasping butcher from London insisted on being addressed as Sir Roger Tichborne. Indeed, that was the name on his pauper's coffin.

PHINEAS T. BARNUM
ONE BORN EVERY MINUTE

P.T. Barnum was born on 5 July 1810 to a grim Puritan family in Bethel, Connecticut. For some reason they named the child Phineas, a biblical name that means 'Brazen Mouth'. Little did they realise how apt that title was to become. For Barnum's boasts were to make him the most famous showman in the world. He is also considered the father of modern advertising because of his remarkable talent for grabbing the attention of the public. What Phineas Taylor Barnum is also famed for is his expertise as a garrulous trickster. For big-mouthed Barnum would tell the most outrageous lies to lure his audiences. He is credited with coining the phrases 'Never give a sucker an even break' and 'There's a sucker born every minute'. By following these two adages, Barnum made two fortunes on the backs of his gullible customers.

The role of showbusiness swindler did not immediately apply to Barnum, however. A discontented Jack-of-all-trades, he was a store clerk, ran lotteries, sold men's hats, edited a newspaper and was joint owner of a grocery store. Despite this modest success, he saw himself as a failure. In the first real surge of his adventurous spirit, he sold his interest in the grocery shore and embarked on a bizarre adventure into showmanship. Barnum had learned the most elementary lessons while working in a barter store in Bethel. Here goods were paid for not in cash but in kind. Because so much suspect merchandise was being offered, the store's policy was always to offer faulty goods in return. As Barnum recalled: 'Everything in that store was different from what was represented.' Burned peas, for instance, were offered as coffee beans and cotton in place of wool.

With this insight into fair trading, 33-year-old Barnum, now married to Charity Hallett and the father of two children, took his family to New York and opened a sideshow on Broadway. His first exhibit was an ugly and withered black lady named Joice Heth whom he had come across in a similar sideshow in Philadelphia. Joice, blind and partly paralysed, assured him that she was 160 years old and had once been George Washington's nursemaid. Barnum bought her on the spot for a pittance.

Then he plastered Manhattan with posters announcing: 'The greatest curiosity in the world and the most interesting, particularly to Americans, is now exhibiting at the saloon fronting on Broadway; Joice Heth, nurse to General George Washington, the father of our country, who has arrived at the astonishing age of 161 years, as authentic documents will prove, and in full possession of her mental faculties. She is cheerful and healthy though she weighs but 49 pounds. She relates many anecdotes of her younger master.'

Displaying his great flare for publicity, Barnum dreamed up incredible tales for the press and learned the lesson that free editorial space is much more cost-effective than expensive advertising. So astute was he that he even wrote anonymous letters to the newspapers calling into question the claims about Joice. He reasoned that it was better to have people talking about you than not and, as many confidence tricksters have reaffirmed since, bad publicity is better than no publicity. Crowds queued along the sidewalks of Broadway to see the 'female Methuselah'. And they certainly got their money's worth with her phoney memories of Washington, the many errors in her narrative being excused because of her extreme antiquity.

When initial interest in his 'Methuselah' died down, Barnum took an advertisement in a newspaper to announce that Joice Heth was not a real person at all – but a robot. The crowds flocked back when he proclaimed: 'What purports to be a remarkable old woman is simply a curiously constructed automaton, made up of whalebone, india-rubber and numberless springs ingeniously put together and made to move at the slightest touch.'

Long after she retired through ill health, Barnum took great care of her. On her death in 1836, however, he found a new way of making money out of the old hag. He hired a surgeon to perform an autopsy on Joice in front of an invited audience. Barnum had long known that Joice was nothing like her advertised age, but he roared with laughter when it was revealed that the old lady had fooled even him. The surgeon pronounced Joice to be no more than 80 years of age. 'I, like you, have been duped,' said the irrepressible Barnum, and his name remained in the news for another few weeks.

Joice Heth had not been Barnum's only exhibit. There was his 'Feejee Mermaid' – fished out of the Pacific in 1817, he claimed. In fact, it was, in his own words, 'an ugly, dried-up, black-looking and diminutive specimen' which he had bought from a Boston showman in 1842. He kept his acquisition secret at first while he distributed 10,000 leaflets arguing that mermaids existed and displaying engravings of beautiful specimens disporting themselves on rocks. No mention was made of Barnum's own ugly specimen until, public interest having been awakened, he announced its arrival at the museum. Thousands of people handed over their 10 cents to see what was nothing more than a monkey's torso attached by amateurish taxidermy to the tail of a large fish.

There were even more blatant frauds. Barnum persuaded spectators to pay to view 'the horse with its tail where its head should be' – only to encounter an ordinary horse tethered in its stall back to front, with its tail in the feeding trough. Barnum even exhibited an ordinary black alley cat, advertising it as 'the world's only cherry coloured cat'. When his customers complained, they were told that the animal was the colour of black cherries!

Richer from displaying Joice Heth and his other fraudulent acts, Barnum took to the road in the late 1830s with America's first canvas-top circus.

When love of his family drew him back to New York, he found the show-business game tougher than ever. A string of short theatrical ventures led him finally to a go-for-broke gamble that would have frightened other men.

Scudder's American Museum was up for sale, a five-storey shell of a building that had been a money loser for years. With nothing for collateral but his dreams, Barnum convinced the owners that he could ride their white elephant into fields of glory. And he did. From the date of its opening, Barnum's American Museum was destined to become the new wonder of the Western World. He displayed educated dogs and jumping fleas, fat boys and giants, dwarfs and rope dancers, performing Indians and the first Punch and Judy Show ever seen in New York.

Being Barnum, however, he exaggerated wildly the

virtues of every act. The fleas were advertised as 'insects that can draw carriages and carts' and it was only when the punters had paid their money that they discovered that the conveyances were suitably minuscule. At the other end of the scale, a live hippopotamus was also exhibited in the museum. It would have been a big enough draw in its own right but Barnum could not resist billing it as 'the great behemoth of the Scriptures'.

In three years Barnum paid for his museum and expanded it beyond even his wildest dreams. With his incredible imagination and sense of the bizarre, he entertained millions. Still seeking fresh phenomena to tempt, tantalise and astonish audiences, the super-showman then made a find that would turn out to be one of his greatest – tiny Tom Thumb. Barnum's half-brother, Philo, tipped him off that a remarkable midget was being exhibited at Bridgeport, Connecticut. Barnum dropped everything, raced north and examined him. He discovered a bright, five-year-old boy of amazingly minute proportions. The boy had been born on 4 January 1838 weighing nine pounds and had developed normally until the age of six months. Since then, however, he had not grown another inch. Barnum signed up the little fellow on the spot for $3 a week.

The midget was called Charles Stratton. With his showman's flair, Barnum renamed him General Tom Thumb and made him his number-one attraction. Not content with the truth, Barnum billed the child as 'a dwarf of 11 years of age just arrived from England'. He taught him to act 'autocratic, impudent and regal' and dressed him in various guises, from a mini-Cupid to a Roman gladiator to Napoleon Bonaparte. The partnership between the six-foot showman and tiny Tom was a remarkable one which developed into an enduring friendship. As Tom Thumb grew into adulthood, he remained a perfectly formed midget, two feet tall and weighing 15 pounds. What he lacked in size, the brilliant little man made up for in personality. With patter, songs and dances devised by Barnum, he made theatrical history – and enough money to ensure his and Barnum's passport to even greater fame abroad.

The crowds overflowed when Tom Thumb and his supporting cast appeared at a London theatre, and a command performance was given at Buckingham Palace, where even Queen Victoria was amused. There were audiences with King Louis-Philippe of France, Queen Isabella of Spain, King Leopold of Belgium and other European royals. With sell-out performances, and with gifts from the crowned heads, the three-year European tour made Tom Thumb and Barnum very rich. Their association would continue for 30 years, and it was the warm-hearted midget who came to Barnum's aid when fate dealt the entrepreneur a flurry of blows.

Back in the United States, Barnum had grown richer still with his sponsorship of Jenny Lind, the 'Swedish Nightingale'. But in 1855 disaster befell him. Always a soft touch for his friends, Barnum had underwritten a dying enterprise, the Jerome Clock Company. When his friends plummeted into bankruptcy, they took Barnum with them. The next blow was the burning down of his home, Iranistan. The palatial mansion and international showplace exploded into flames after a painter dropped a lighted cigarette.

The greatest blow, however, came in 1865 when Barnum's precious American Museum was also destroyed by fire. Wild animals escaped on to the streets of New York, an orang-utan being recaptured in an office block. A gallant fireman single-handedly carried the 400-pound Fat Lady to safety but the seven-foot 11-inch World's Tallest Woman had to be lifted free with the aid of a derrick. It all made huge headlines; Barnum saw to that.

No one was killed in the museum blaze but the loss of its half a million cherished exhibits was heartbreaking for Barnum. The damage was put at $500,000 but the insurance covered only a fraction of it. Barnum faced ruin. At this point Tom Thumb stepped in and revealed himself to be as big of heart as he was tiny of frame. He helped finance a new European tour which was the beginning of Barnum's second fortune. By 1870 the showman had repaid his creditors, rebuilt his museum and opened his newest, bigger, better-than-ever circus.

When Barnum formed a partnership with James Anthony Bailey in 1871, the Barnum & Bailey Circus reached its zenith with a three-ring spectacle that became part of circus tradition. 'The Greatest Show On Earth' travelled across North America in its own railroad cars, adding new words and phrases to the English language – such as 'jumbo', 'ballyhoo' and 'white elephant'.

Barnum's white elephant was called Toung Taloung and had to be repainted every time it rained. More enduring, however, was a mighty elephant which he purchased from London Zoo in 1882 and inspirationally renamed Jumbo. The animal was advertised as 'the only mastodon on Earth, whose like the world will never see again – a feature crushing all attempts at fraud'. Thereafter the creature gave its name to everything from jumbo-sized burgers to jumbo jets. On one occasion Jumbo seemingly felt so overworked that he embarked on a sit-down strike. Unwilling to leave England, the pachyderm refused to enter his van until Barnum bribed him with a barrel of beer. Jumbo died in 1885 after being hit by a train during a tour of Canada.

Meanwhile, Barnum's beloved wife Charity had become an invalid, and she died in 1873 after a series of strokes. Sick with loneliness, he took a new wife 10 months later: a lovely young English girl named Nancy Fish. Barnum was 64 and Nancy 40 years younger, but she remained a devoted wife and friend until his death at the age of 81.

When it became evident that Barnum's end was near, the *New York Evening News* did a remarkable thing. With the showman's permission, they published his obituary in advance so that he could read it. The headline announced, 'Great And Only Barnum: He Wanted To Read His Obituary And Here It Is!' Laughing, Barnum and Nancy read it together, and it was close to his bedside when the 'Great And Only' died. He left a fortune of $5 million – finally proving his great adage: 'There's a sucker born every minute.'

THE ALCHEMISTS
FOOL'S GOLD

A fool and his money are easily parted and this applies particularly to a greedy fool. Those who are already wealthy yet desire more are even likelier targets. And those who fall for the lure of gold are perhaps the greatest gift to the confidence trickster. Alchemists, those medieval chemists who believed they had the Midas touch, tried desperately to turn common metals into gold – and even the realisation that this could not be achieved did not prevent them from taking money from those who still believed it could.

Tricks of the alchemist's trade were reported in a paper read in 1722 at the Royal Academy of Science in Paris. It described, for instance, how fraudsters would use a double-bottomed crucible. The upper surface was of wax painted to resemble the lower surface, which was of iron and copper. Between these surfaces, the alchemist would put gold or silver dust. When the pot was heated, a lump of 'gold' would magically appear.

In the early eighteenth century, Frenchman Jean Delisle claimed to be able to 'turn lead into gold and iron into silver by merely heating these metals red-hot and pouring upon them in that state some oil and powder he is possessed of, so that it would not be impossible for any man to make a million a day if he had sufficient of this wondrous mixture'. Delisle was invited to Paris by Louis XIV to prove his gold-making technique. Knowing he would be exposed as a fraud, Delisle kept making excuses. Eventually he was arrested in 1711 and taken to the Bastille. He was told to make gold or he would spend the rest of his days in jail. Failing health led to his death in a Bastille dungeon.

The French king's successor, Louis XV, was also infatuated with the search for a magic formula for precious metals. He fell victim to probably the greatest alchemy hoaxer of all time, the mysterious Count Saint-Germain, whose story is told earlier in this section. Alchemy was an art that reached its pinnacle of plausibility in the eighteenth century yet it was still being practised in the early twentieth century.

One its arch exponents was Hans Unruh, a cheat who preyed on the rich and aristocratic. This was his sales patter to them: 'I must ask you to treat what I am about to tell you with the strictest confidence. This is not a secret to be shared but one we must keep strictly to ourselves. It is very important. And it could be dangerous.' Thus Unruh addressed an audience of aristocrats assembled in a Munich hotel suite. As they listened intently to him, they began to believe that they were recipients of the most golden of opportunities ever likely to come their way. As long as they told no one else the amazing secrets he was imparting to them, they were destined to become incredibly wealthy.

All eyes were now unblinkingly on the stranger who had invited them to witness his magical demonstration. Unruh picked up a salt cellar from the table in front of him and brandished it before the captivated audience. From the contents of this little salt cellar, explained Unruh, would come what everyone in the whole world lusted after – pure gold.

Some guests coughed awkwardly. One stifled a laugh. Unruh waited until he once more had everyone's attention, then continued. He was a scientist, he told them, and he had discovered how gold was made. It came from the depths of the earth, where it was created by a chemical action on ordinary salt. If some method could be discovered to reproduce this chemical change artificially, unlimited quantities of gold could be manufactured worldwide. And anyone with the knowledge would be very wealthy indeed.

'And I am the man with that knowledge,' said Unruh. 'Please realise how privileged you all are that I choose to share it with you.' He paused to allow his words to take effect. Some among the gathering wondered whether they were listening to a fool wasting their time yet dared not speak out for fear they might miss a money-making miracle. Others simply sat in silent disbelief. Whatever their private thoughts, the audience were by now becoming more interested in what Unruh had to say.

They once more found it hard not to laugh out loud, however, when Unruh picked up a lamp stand and held it high with a dramatic flourish. He told them research had proved that if you treated salt with a special form of light it would turn into pure gold. Now came Unruh's practical demonstration. He took hold of the salt cellar and gently tapped some of its contents on to a steel plate. Then he took the lamp stand and held it in such a way that the shade completely covered the salt.

He switched on the lamp and waited a few moments.

When he finally removed the shade, the onlookers were speechless. There on the plate where grains of salt had once been were bright, glittering flecks of gold dust. To emphasise the value of the little pile, now the object of several pairs of money-hungry eyes, Unruh scooped it up and tipped it into a small pouch.

By now, any disbelief the aristocrats had been harbouring had turned to pure greed. Unruh had his guests under his spell. This was the moment to explain that he was, in fact, a struggling scientist. If those present wanted to exploit his miraculous discovery, initially they would have to be his financial backers. A great deal of money was needed to provide the vital equipment for this very special kind of gold prospecting.

'You are wealthy, of proven integrity and have a great sense of responsibility,' Unruh told them. 'You have all been specially selected for this opportunity. I wish you all to become shareholders in my enterprise. Perhaps you would like to go away and think it over.' But the guests did not need any more time to consider what all this meant. They wanted to be part of Unruh's gold-making project right now. Sums equivalent to thousands of pounds were handed over to Unruh that night. The rich departed happy in the knowledge they would become even richer – and Unruh left knowing he had just pulled off an extremely clever con trick.

Had his greedy spectators bothered to check the gold before them more closely, they would have realised things were not as they seemed. There was no gold at all, just fine scrapings of brass, but in the right light it looked just like the real thing. Unruh had simply concealed a trickle of this dust in the lampshade, and when he tapped the shade the 'gold' showered down on the salt.

VIRGINIA WOOLF AND FRIENDS
THE EMPEROR OF ABYSSINIA

The urgent telegram that was delivered to the battleship HMS *Dreadnought*, pride of the British Navy, at anchor in Weymouth Bay, Dorset, on 7 February 1910, sent its officers into a frenzy of activity. Addressed by the Foreign Office to Admiral Sir William May, Commander-in-Chief of the Home Fleet, the missive warned of an imminent visit to the ship by the Emperor of Abyssinia and his entourage.

There was barely enough time to send a greeting party to Weymouth railway station before the dignitaries arrived, accompanied by an interpreter and a Foreign Office official. Despite the short notice, their reception was impressive. A red carpet stretched from the train down the platform and through the station concourse. Beyond was a guard of honour which they graciously inspected. A launch then took them to the *Dreadnought*, which was bedecked with bunting. There was a slight hiccup when the national anthem of Zanzibar was played instead of that of Abyssinia, but no one took umbrage. Equally unfortunately, a gun salute had to be cancelled at the last moment because no one knew the number of rounds protocol dictated to honour a foreign emperor. Nevertheless, the party was ceremoniously piped aboard

304 ◀ THE STING

and senior officers donned full dress uniform to accompany them on a tour of the mighty ship.

The guests were delighted. Indeed, they could hardly contain their glee. For they had achieved the purpose of their visit with unforeseen ease – and made utter fools of the Royal Navy. The 'Emperor of Abyssinia' and his entourage were a group of London high-society dilettantes led by Horace de Vere Cole and his cousin, novelist Virginia Woolf.

In retrospect, it seems incredible that anyone could have been taken in by the motley party. They overacted their roles to a ludicrous degree. Their faces were stained with make-up, they had false moustaches and spoke in a made-up language. They shouted 'Bunga bunga' to one another whenever anything of interest caught their eye. Despite the banquet laid before them, none of the hoaxers ate. Cole explained that their religion precluded them from breaking bread at sea. The real reason, however, was a warning by one of the group, theatrical make-up expert Willy Clarkson, that eating or drinking would ruin their disguises.

Clarkson had done a good job. The costumes and make-up fooled everyone. Their first test had been at London's Paddington Station when Cole, in top hat and morning coat, announced himself as Herbert Cholmondesley of the Foreign Office and imperiously demanded that the stationmaster lay on a special train to convey his royal guests to Weymouth. It was Cole who had sent the telegram to the *Dreadnought* and it was he who had persuaded six of his friends – Clarkson, Woolf, her brother Adrian, artist Duncan Grant, sportsman Anthony Buxton and judge's son Guy Ridley – to perpetrate the elaborate hoax.

They feared exposure only twice during their day's visit to Weymouth, ostensibly to join celebrations for the fourth anniversary of the launching of the *Dreadnought*. The first occasion was when they were introduced to an officer who was related to Virginia Woolf and who had met Cole on several occasions. The officer looked them both in the eye but recognised neither. The second crisis was when Buxton sneezed and blew off half his moustache. He stuck it back on again before anyone noticed.

At the end of their visit the hoaxers tipped the ordinary seamen who had carried their bags and posed for press photographs before reboarding their train for the return journey to London. Even then they did not let their guise slip. Before dinner was allowed to be served on the train, Cole demanded that it stop at Reading so that white gloves could be purchased for the waiters.

Unfortunately for the impostors, word of their exploits was leaked to the newspapers. Questions were asked in the House of Commons about this appalling breach of security by the Royal Navy. The hoax was described as 'an insult to His Majesty's flag'. Sir William May had to suffer children shouting 'Bunga bunga' at him in the streets of Weymouth. There was even talk of jailing the perpetrators of this ambitious confidence trick.

Horace Cole was indeed sought out for summary punishment. Two naval officers armed with canes arrived at his house threatening to avenge the honour of the navy by giving him a sound beating in front of his household. Ever the smooth talker, however, Cole persuaded them that they could beat him only if he could beat them back. The three men then crept off to a backstreet where Cole and the officers ceremoniously but gently caned one another in a display of Edwardian drama. Afterwards they shook hands and went their merry ways.

The hoax had cost Cole and his friends £4,000, a tidy sum in those days, but they declared it money well spent to expose the gullibility of officialdom and to prick the pomposity of the military hierarchy. Virginia Woolf felt she had another reason to look down her nose at mankind and she ultimately used the hoax in a 1921 short story, 'The Society'.

CYNTHIA PAYNE
MADAME CYN

'Madame Cyn' was a brothel-keeper with a difference. Her chirpiness and cockney sense of humour meant that, far from being vilified as a vice queen, she became something of a folk legend in Britain. And when the whip-wielding madam appeared in court for the first of two infamous sex-party cases, even the prosecution had to admit Cynthia Payne managed 'a well-run brothel'.

When Payne was arrested in 1980, she was running her sex business from a four-bedroom house in Streatham, south London. Then aged 46, discreet and with wide experience of the pleasure game, she counted vicars, barristers, several peers and an MP among her regular customers. They would buy £25 worth of 'luncheon vouchers', which could then be traded for the girls of their choice plus generous helpings of food and drink. For each voucher, the women – dubbed 'dedicated amateurs' by Payne – were paid a £6 fee. The atmosphere was more like a jolly swingers' party than some seedy whorehouse. When the police raided 32 Ambleside Avenue they found no fewer than 53 men enjoying (or waiting expectantly for) their sexual entertainment. Seventeen of them were in an orderly queue on the stairs – each clutching his luncheon voucher.

At Payne's trial, police said they had watched 32 Ambleside Avenue, an ordinary house in an ordinary street, for 12 days and had counted 249 men and 50 women go in and out. In defence, her lawyer said that her clients were so respectable that after the police raid they had simply donned their bowler hats, picked up their briefcases and returned home as if they had spent a hard day at their offices. There had been no complaints recorded and Payne's neighbours were under the happy misapprehension that she was no more than an affable housewife with lots of friends. Court reports of the sexual high jinks were lapped up by a fascinated public. One regular partygoer was Squadron Leader Robert 'Mitch' Smith, who was also Payne's lover. Although he had his own flat in Purley, Surrey, the Squadron Leader spent most of his time at 32 Ambleside Avenue, even giving guided tours of the neat, suburban house.

Despite Payne's 'tart with a heart' nature, her cheerful plea of guilty to running a brothel and juicy tales of queues to bedrooms, the judge did not see the funny side of the case. He sentenced her to 18 months in prison and a £2,000 fine for running a disorderly house. Payne also admitted three charges of controlling prostitutes and was fined £650 on each charge. She was used to being penalised in her chosen career. And the indignity of being hauled before a court was not new to her. In March 1965 she had appeared before Marlborough Street Magistrates Court in London and had been fined £10 with £6 costs for keeping a brothel. In October 1966 she was in the same court again, facing the same charge. She was fined £30 with £10 costs. In 1973 it was back to Marlborough Street. This time her brothel-keeping cost her £50 with £22 costs. She was back in court yet again a year later after her flat in Great Portland Street was raided and sexual items were found. A £200 fine was imposed, with £29 costs.

Then came her highly celebrated 1980 court appearance, which landed her in prison. She immediately appealed against her sentence. Despite a public outcry, backed by some MPs, that the prosecution had been a total waste of public money, the appeal judge refused to quash the sentence altogether. He said: 'This is conduct which is outrageous.' And of the (generally middle-aged) ladies involved in the luncheon-voucher trade, he said: 'Some were common prostitutes, others were married women who were on the premises for the purpose of earning pin money.'

Payne remained in jail but her sentence was cut to six months. She served only four months of it before being released on 20 August 1980. Madame Cyn was swept away in a Rolls-Royce to sip champagne while she negotiated press contracts and publishing deals. She never expressed an ounce of regret for what she did but said: 'I'd like to think I'll be remembered for running a nice brothel, not one of those sordid places like they have in Soho. I should have been given the OBE for what I did for the country.'

Seven years later Payne was to hit the headlines again. Her colourful antics were turned into a film, *Personal Services*, and it was a party, which she said was held to celebrate the film, that had her once more falling foul of the law. On 22 January 1987 Madam Cyn put on a plain, black dress and, looking more like the Queen Mother than a madam, turned up at the Inner London Crown Court to answer charges not unfamiliar to her: 'Cynthia Diane Payne, you are charged that you, being a woman, on May 30, 1986 and on diverse dates between December 1, 1985 and May 30, 1986, for the purposes of gain, exercised control, direction or influence over a prostitute, namely

Leigh Richmond Rogers, in a way which showed that you were aiding and abetting the prostitution of the said Leigh Richmond Rogers.'

There were nine other charges relating to other girls. Payne listened carefully. She had heard it all before. Only this time it would be different. This time she was *not* admitting the charges. Defiantly, and with her permed head held high, she answered 'Not guilty' to each charge. The court was told: 'Some of you may have heard of Cynthia Payne before. If you have, so far as the prosecution are concerned, you can put out of your mind anything you may have heard of her, seen of her or read of her.' The Crown's case seemed straightforward enough. It alleged that at Payne's parties prostitutes were present, that invitations were selectively given out, various sexual performances took place and that, so inadequate were the four bedrooms, a downstairs room and even a bed in the garden, large queues of sexually eager couples had to wait on the stairs.

The police had their own hero in this tale of sex for sale. He came in the rather overweight form of Police Constable Stewart Taylor, infiltrator of the parties, recipient of many lewd suggestions and witness to many sexual acts performed in Payne's home. PC Taylor, under the false name of Peter Tollington, had pretended to be a long-forgotten friend of Payne in order to gain entry to her parties. His first introduction into Madam Cyn's social circle was at a jovial gathering on 13 December 1985. PC Taylor said most of the men at the party were aged between 50 and 60, with one or two younger ones 'thrown in for good measure'. He then went on to describe what happened at that party and two subsequent ones.

Keeping up the pretence of a swinging partygoer, PC Taylor allowed himself to be regularly taken into a bedroom by one of Payne's girls. Each time, he said, he told the girl he was impotent and preferred just to talk. Each girl was given £25 for her time. Taking his undercover duties very seriously, PC Taylor also watched various cabarets, such as lesbian encounters and striptease dances.

To improve his chances of getting a conviction, PC Taylor took along his 'brother-in-law Harold' (or more accurately PC Jack Jones) to the next two parties. Again there were tales of half-naked women, men being caught literally with their pants down and propositions by a string of women. The policemen's evidence took a bizarre turn when the court heard that, to add realism, 'Harold' had been presented as a part-time transvestite who owned a guest house in North Wales. The undercover cop attended Payne's parties wearing make-up and a cravat. The incriminating point the two policemen wanted to emphasise was that on all occasions, in line with other male partygoers, they each gave Payne £30. This she strongly denied.

Overseeing the whole operation had been Sergeant David Broadwell of the Obscene Publications Branch. He told the court that at the first party officers watched 59 men and 28 women come and go; at the second, 45 men and 20 women; on the third, the night they raided Payne's house, 35 men and 23 women had knocked on the door. The raid came after a special signal was given from 'inside'. Sergeant Broadwell and other officers said that throughout the house they had found men and women in various stages of undress and performing a wide range of sexual activities.

One encounter with a couple caused guffaws in court. With his voice not altering as he gave his evidence, Sergeant Broadwell said: 'The girl jumped to her feet and shouted. In doing so, she knocked the male person into the bath. His trousers and underpants were around his ankles.'

The good sergeant completed his evidence with the help of a large plastic sack containing whips, belts, chains, leather items and a dog collar.

When Payne took the witness box, she said that she simply loved giving parties. Indeed, two of them had been to celebrate the film about her. 'I live for my parties,' she said. 'But I don't charge any more, although I did ask the men to bring a bottle. If they forgot, they gave me money towards restocking the drink.' Payne admitted she knew sex took place at her parties but said she certainly did not run a brothel any more because it was against the law. She told the court: 'There is a free and easy atmosphere in my house and people feel uninhibited. They do what they like. Sex makes people happy.'

The defendant had the court almost gasping with her matter-of-fact tales of her sex slaves — men who didn't attend the parties but who turned up to clean for her stark naked in return for the odd caning. She lost her composure only once, when the death of her long-term lover Squadron Leader Smith was mentioned. He too had liked being whipped, and kept his 'equipment' in a cupboard at his Purley flat. Payne started to cry when the court heard how her lover had lain dead on the floor for two weeks before being discovered.

Tuesday, 11 February 1987 saw a crowded court. The jury and packed public gallery had heard evidence from police, prostitutes and loyal pals of Payne. Now a verdict had to be reached. While the jury was out, the accused cheerfully signed 'Sexplicitly Yours, Cynthia Payne' autographs. When they returned, they announced that they had found her not guilty on all counts. The trial had lasted 13 days and cost £100,000. The judge ordered that the £4,808 Payne had contributed towards her legal aid should be returned to her, together with costs. There was now only one thing for 53-year-old Madam Cyn to do. Return home and hold a party – under the sign that hung prominently on her wall:

My House is CLEAN Enough To Be Healthy
And DIRTY Enough To Be Happy!

WILHELM VOIGT
CAPTAIN OF KÖPENICK

A detachment of five soldiers under a corporal were returning to their barracks in the north-west Berlin suburb of Plötzensee one autumn day in 1906 when they turned a corner and encountered an officer who ordered them to halt. Imperiously, he told them: 'I am Captain Voigt and this unit is now under my command. Wait here.' Within moments another four grenadiers arrived on the scene and they too were ordered to join the line-up. 'Fix bayonets,' said the man dressed in officer's uniform as he marched them all off to the nearest railway station.

But 'Captain Voigt' was no officer; he was Wilhelm Voigt, a 57-year-old cobbler living in eastern Berlin with his married sister and commuting daily to work in Potsdam. Wilhelm was also a small-time crook who had spent 27 years in prison and looked certain to return there. That sorry destiny was again determined for him when he stopped at the window of a second-hand clothes shop and spotted the neatly pressed uniform of a Prussian guards captain.

Voigt spent an entire week's wages on the uniform and spent some days practising the arrogant walk of a Prussian officer as he roamed the streets of Berlin. Astonished at how impressive he looked despite his bulging stomach, the moustachioed cobbler began to assume the role perfectly. He had learned to mimic the speech and mannerisms of officers while mending their boots as an apprentice. Now he found that he could bark orders at passing soldiers and, for the first time in his life, he saw people leap to action when he addressed them. The German awe of uniforms and people's willingness to accept directions unquestioningly from anyone in authority gave Voigt the idea for his greatest scam.

That is how Wilhelm Voigt came to be marching through the streets of Berlin at the head of a platoon of soldiers. The soldiers didn't know what they were doing but they never expected to be told. So, when they arrived at a station on the Berlin circular railway, they did not argue when their captain ordered them aboard a train for the town of Köpenick, a dozen or so miles away. He ordered the corporal and the privates into a workmen's carriage while he himself relaxed in a first-class compartment.

The train was bound for Köpenick but Voigt ordered his men to disembark at a stop five miles earlier. He reckoned it would be more impressive if he and his men marched into town. And so it was that, after two hours' march, the group arrived in the main street of Köpenick and halted outside the town hall.

The kindly captain gave each of his men one mark and told them to find an eating place but to be back at the same spot within the hour. The nine men returned as ordered and Voigt placed two of them on guard outside the town hall while marching the rest inside and up the stairs. Arriving at the office of the mayor, Voigt burst in and announced to the startled dignitary: 'You are under arrest!'

'On what authority?' asked the mayor. 'Where is your warrant?'

'My warrant is the men I command,' was the perfunctory

reply as the phoney captain called the borough treasurer and told him to open the safe. The official handed over the town's entire treasury of 4,000 marks and was rewarded with an 'official' receipt. The mayor, his wife, the deputy mayor and the treasurer were then gathered together in the street under the guard of the nine soldiers. Voigt, meanwhile, was requisitioning three vehicles in which to remove his captives. One was a small cab, in which the captain deposited himself and the cash box. The soldiers and their prisoners filled the other two vehicles, which, on Voigt's orders, were driven off to a police station 15 miles away.

Voigt then roared off in a cloud of dust with his 4,000 marks. His first stop was Köpenick railway station, where he had taken the precaution of depositing a change of civilian clothes. With his military disguise wrapped in a parcel under his arm, he took a train back to Berlin. He arrived at his lodgings at roughly the same time that the soldiers and their prisoners arrived at the police station and waited for their captain ... and waited ... and waited.

The news of the confidence trick was flashed around the world. It was a pantomime that reflected badly on the impressionable nature of the German character – and sorely tested the German sense of humour as the Prussian military became a laughing stock. However, the Kaiser, himself a Wilhelm, was reported to have roared with laughter when he heard of the stunt. He told an aide: 'Such a thing could only happen in Germany.' And the newspaper *Berliner Tageblat* said that the culprit, if found, should not be punished but rewarded for teaching the Germans a lesson.

Oddly, that is almost what happened. Ten days after his visit to Köpenick, Voigt was arrested in a dawn raid on his slum room, where he was quietly drinking a cup of coffee with about half of the stolen money still stuffed in his pocket; the rest had been spent. He was allowed to finish his breakfast while detectives removed the bundle of military clothing from under his bed. After being marched to the police station, the now-famous crook was fêted and given a bottle of port.

Voigt's trial was a sensation. More than 10,000 people applied for entry to the court. The judge's penalty of four years' imprisonment was deemed harsh by many – including the Kaiser, who, in an unprecedented intervention, pardoned him halfway through the sentence. He was released in 1908 and discovered that a play had been written about his exploits, *The Captain of Köpenick*. He asked for and received free seats for all his jailbird friends. Until his death in 1922, Wilhelm Voigt lived a life of comfortable retirement in Luxembourg – on a pension allotted to him by a rich German dowager with a fine sense of humour.

PHILIP ARNOLD AND JOHN SLACK
THE 'DRUNK' PROSPECTORS

On a summer day in 1872 two old-timer gold prospectors sauntered into the Bank of California in San Francisco. Philip Arnold and John Slack had every reason to feel happy with life for, as a greedy bank teller was to discover, they were bearing a wonderful hoard. Arnold and Slack slammed a drawstring sack on the counter and demanded that it be kept in the bank's safe, then, satisfied that their 'deposit' was in safe keeping, the two grizzly old prospectors wandered off to find a saloon in which to celebrate their good fortune. Watching all this was a teller with a strong feeling that here was a chance to cash in.

As soon as Arnold and Slack were out of sight, he peeked into the sack. He was expecting to see a handful or two of gold. Instead, his eyes focused on more stunning, sparkling uncut diamonds than he had ever seen before in his life. The startled teller picked up the bag and ran into the office of bank boss William Ralston, who had become wealthy through dubious deals but was always on the lookout for fresh ways of increasing his fortune. After examining the diamonds, he now had visions of becoming America's Diamond King.

Promising the teller a suitable reward for his troubles,

Ralston told him to seek out the two prospectors straight away. Ralston himself joined in the search. It took three anxious days before the prospectors were tracked down. Arnold and Slack were extremely drunk and wanted only to drink some more. They could not understand what Ralston wanted with them. Ralston could not understand what they were saying and had to stay with them, patiently waiting for them to sober up.

After much coaxing, and with Ralston's promise of financial backing, Arnold and Slack eventually told the bank chief that they had found a diamond field 'bigger than Kimberley'. But they had not acquired title to the land yet and so refused to tell him exactly where it was. They would, however, allow anyone who wanted to see the diamond field to do so – as long as their visitor made the entire journey blindfolded. Ralston, his imagination swimming with diamonds in unbelievable quantities, agreed. But he didn't fancy making the journey himself, and instead sent his mining engineer, David Colton, to accompany the two men. Three weeks later, Colton was back. He could hardly contain himself. Everything Arnold and Slack had said was true. Colton held a fistful of diamonds under Ralston's nose. A deal was struck.

Ralston paid Arnold and Slack $50,000, put another $300,000 aside for any expenses incurred, and pledged them a further $350,000 when they started producing their promised harvest of diamonds. By now word had spread about the prospectors' land. Everyone wanted to be part of the scheme. Others who contributed money included Baronet Anthony de Rothschild, the editor Horace Greeley, General George B. McClellan and Charles Lewis Tiffany, founder of the world's largest jewellery business.

To ensure that there was nothing untoward about what

Colton claimed to have seen, Ralston sent along a group of witnesses to Arnold and Slack's gold field. The group travelled by train to Rawlings, Wyoming, where they were then blindfolded and taken on a long and hard journey through wild range land. When their blindfolds were removed, the visitors felt they were dreaming. Ant hills in the valley shimmered and sparkled with diamond dust. Not only that: diamonds as big as a man's thumb were scattered across the ground

When the party reported their findings to Ralston, his plans changed. He no longer wanted to be part of Arnold and Slack's team; he wanted to get rid of them and take every single diamond for himself. He threatened the two prospectors with legal claims, saying they had no rights. He bullied them into backing down from the deal they had made with him. Apparently worn down by Ralston's harassment, Arnold and Slack agreed to accept $700,000 for their share of the diamond field. They were then told to leave town.

News of the diamond 'Klondike' soon spread around the world. But one man did not believe the story. Eminent geologist E.W. Emmonds had never found any evidence of diamonds in Wyoming and decided to investigate the prospectors' story for himself. Using his knowledge of the area, Emmonds worked out the location of the alleged diamond site – and smiled when he saw how close it was to the railway line. It did not take him long to work out that all those taken to see the site had simply been led round and round in circles. The ant hills were man-made and, on close inspection, there was also something strange about the 'diamonds'. They showed marks of having been chipped at by a tool. Emmonds could reach only one conclusion: the stones had been placed at the site, scattered liberally around to give the impression that the site was rich with the gems.

When word of the hoax came out, Ralston was a laughing stock. It was later discovered that Arnold and Slack had painstakingly set up a clever con. They had gone to Europe and spent their life savings of $35,000 on buying hoards of fake gems. They had increased the number of gems even more by using a lapidary tool to split each 'diamond' into pieces, then they had spread them around the carefully chosen site.

Public sympathy was on the side of Arnold and Slack, who were widely admired for pulling such a clever trick on the rich and greedy, and the two men escaped prosecution. Arnold went to Kentucky, where he founded his own bank. Slack was never seen again. And what of the greedy, grasping William Ralston? Three years after he had embarked on his dream of running the world's biggest diamond syndicate, Ralston the universal figure of fun saw his financial empire collapse.

REVEREND HAROLD DAVIDSON
INTO THE LIONS' DEN

The Reverend Harold Francis Davidson was a whoring clergyman who 'rescued' distressed prostitutes, was caught on film with naked schoolgirls and ended his days being eaten by a lion. He is certainly one of the strangest men ever to don a Church of England cassock.

Born in Southampton in 1875, Davidson was groomed for a career in the church by his clergyman father but as a pupil at his school in Croydon he discovered what he considered to be a latent talent for acting. At 19 he spurned his father's entreaties and went on stage as a stand-up comic, albeit with a scrupulously clean act. Later he went on to win rave reviews for his performance in the title role of a touring production of *Charley's Aunt*.

Yet, even as he earned the applause of his audience, Davidson's thoughts were very often with the work of the Church. He took to visiting vicars in whichever town his touring company happened to find itself, to ask if they knew any old folk who would like to hear the Bible read out loud. He acquired his interest in helping fallen women after persuading a suicidal teenager not to jump into the Thames. The girl was given some money to return to her home and Davidson went on his way wondering if his true gift wasn't, after all, to do God's work.

By his twenty-second birthday he had made up his mind to join the Church. He studied holy orders at Oxford's Exeter College and, though he took five years to pass the three-year degree course, emerged to a curacy at Holy Trinity Church, Windsor. Eight years later he was moved to St-Martin-in-the-Fields, in London, but within 12 months he was on his way to the country to take up a lucrative living with a salary of £800 a year.

At the turn of the nineteenth century, the quiet village of Stiffkey, Norfolk, was a picturesque though otherwise unremarkable paradigm of rural life. It was the kind of place where locals joked to one another about nothing ever happening; where the only chance for a gossip was at the public house or the church; and where the word 'scandal' simply did not rear its ugly head. Until, that is, the Reverend Harold Davidson arrived on the scene. At first the new incumbent seemed the perfect village vicar. He ran a comfortable home with his Irish-born wife, Molly, an actress he had met at Oxford. She bore him four children. But gossips suggested she didn't really enjoy the role of vicar's wife and the marriage gradually became rocky. By 1913 Davidson was spending most of his working week in London, returning home only to conduct Sunday services, for which he was habitually late.

The reverend's work with poverty-stricken boys in London's East End won him much acclaim, including the congratulations of Queen Mary herself. But in his private life Davidson's odd sexual urges were already beginning to emerge. As chaplain to the Actors' Church Union, he took to lurking in female dressing rooms while actresses stripped for quick costume changes. After several women complained, he was banned from a number of theatres.

During the First World War, Davidson saw service as a Royal Navy chaplain. He appears to have been best remembered for arranging his church parades at times calculated to inconvenience his superiors. He was also the subject of an embarrassing incident in Cairo in which he was arrested during a police raid on a brothel. Davidson insisted he was merely trying to track down a prostitute who was passing venereal disease among the ratings.

After the war he returned home to discover his wife was pregnant with the child of one of his friends, a colonel he had allowed to live in the vicarage. The marriage was long past saving and Davidson returned to his old habit of spending weekdays in London. More specifically, his nights were spent in the company of prostitutes – he picked up about 200 a year – and naive young girls. His approach was almost always the same. The woman concerned would be told she looked like a well-known film star and then invited to join him for tea. He got few refusals. Most of the girls saw him as a harmless, quirky old man who just might provide them with some useful contacts in show business.

As the years went by, more and more of Davidson's protégées were invited to stay at the Stiffkey vicarage. Predictably, it didn't go down well with his wife Molly. The family had hit hard times because of Davidson's disastrous business investment in Australian mining and she didn't see why they should have to support all these 'lame cats'.

In retrospect, it is amazing that Davidson managed to maintain his job as a country rector for so long. He was eventually trapped by an outraged local magistrate, Major Philip Hammond. Villagers were now gossiping about

'Davidson's girls' and there were regular sightings of them grappling with local youths in a ditch or haystack. Hammond had had enough. He called in the Lord Bishop of Norwich and made a complaint under the Clergy Discipline Act, legislation which allowed wayward vicars suspected of immoral acts to be hauled before a consistory court. The Bishop at first believed Davidson's work with prostitutes was totally legitimate. But, to play safe, he employed a private detective to check out the reverend's personal life. He could hardly believe the results. The investigation dossier made clear he had to act immediately to preserve the good name of the Church.

Davidson's trial began on 29 March 1932 at Church House in London. The judge, chancellor of the diocese of Norwich, F. Keppel North, presided over weeks of evidence in which a string of nubile young women told how the rector had pestered them under the pretence of caring about their future. However, the prosecution could produce only one, Barbara Harris, who would accuse him of actually molesting her. Throughout the hearing, Davidson himself was a poor witness. Just as his defence counsel, Richard Levy, would score a point in his favour, Davidson would undo the good work by appearing contradictory or fatuous. At one point he even denied knowing the meaning of the word 'buttock', a claim which visibly irritated the judge.

His cause was lost when he denied that photographs existed of him with the naked 15-year-old daughter of an actress, Mae Douglas. The girl, Estelle Douglas, had wanted to do some modelling work and Davidson had arranged the photographic shoot. Like lightning, prosecutor Roland Oliver produced a picture showing the girl, her bare bottom towards the camera, posing with a shawl draped around her neck. Davidson's hand was on her right shoulder. Looking flustered and shaken, Davidson hit back by saying the picture was a fake 'touched up' in the darkroom. Then he tried to argue that the shawl had slipped out of his hand 'accidentally without my knowledge'. Finally he came up with the ludicrous excuse that Estelle been wearing a bathing costume under the shawl a few minutes before the photo was taken. He had not noticed that she had taken it off.

On 8 July 1932 Davidson was found guilty on five counts of immoral conduct and ordered to pay costs. A little over three months later, on 21 October, the Lord Bishop of Norwich announced the rector's defrocking. Davidson, he said, was 'entirely removed, deposed and degraded' from his offices as priest and deacon.

Desperate for cash, Davidson returned to show business – though only just. He earned a living by displaying himself in a barrel on the promenade at Blackpool and would proclaim his innocence to any gawking tripper who happened to pass by. 'The former Rector of Stiffkey,' he would bawl, 'has been placed in his present position by the authorities of the Church of England who failed in their Christian duty towards him. The lower he sinks, the greater their crime.' It was an awful way to earn a living – and it got worse. Davidson varied his act by fasting in a glass box, appearing frozen in a custom-built refrigerator and being roasted alive in a see-through oven while being stabbed with a pitchfork held by a dummy demon.

Eventually Blackpool tired of him and in 1937 he found himself moving to a similar sideshow serving the holidaymakers of Skegness. He played the part of Daniel in the lions' den, a considerable act of courage considering that he was terrified of animals. But Davidson's days as a freak act were numbered. On the evening of 28 July, fortified by strong drink, he entered the lions' cage and began poking them with a stick. One of the beasts, Freddy, attacked him and dragged him round the cage by the neck. The audience thought it was all part of the act, until they saw blood oozing from his wounds. Davidson was eventually rescued by the lion tamer's assistant and a member of the public. They were too late to save him. Two days later he died in hospital.

So ended the life of one of England's most bizarre clergymen. The arguments over whether he was a pervert or not have never been settled, nor is there ever likely to be conclusive proof. Yet perhaps the most likely explanation was put forward by the author Tom Cullen in his book *The Prostitute's Padre*. Cullen suggested that Davidson suffered from some kind of mental disorder which saddled him with multiple personalities. Cullen quoted the rector's long-standing friend J. Rowland Sales, who was convinced Davidson lived out a part-fact, part-fantasy existence as three distinct personas. One was the kindly clergyman Uncle Harold. Another was 'Little Jimmy', who mischievously spent all his spare time getting Uncle Harold into trouble. The third was 'the Bunco Kid', an unashamed confidence trickster. Davidson, it was argued, spent his life in a kind of purgatory, torn between all three of his complex identities. In the end, however, it seems to have been the Bunco Kid who won.

GIUSEPPE BALSAMO
COUNT CAGLIOSTRO

Giuseppe Balsamo was born into an impoverished Sicilian peasant family in 1743. As he mixed with the nobility of Europe, however, he preferred to be known by the grandiose title he had bestowed on himself: Count Alessandro Di Cagliostro. One further title was generally applied to this strange character: 'The King of Liars'. Balsamo began his career of criminality by stealing from his own family and from the church poor box in his native village. With sufficient money to flee Sicily, he briefly became a monk before being defrocked as a noviciate for unexplained 'blasphemies'. He then attached himself to the coat tails of the Greek alchemist Altotas, and practised the ingenuous art in Egypt until the supply of gullible investors ran out. Back in Italy, he settled down to a life of lucrative crime.

Balsamo married an incredibly beautiful girl he discovered living in rags in a slum area of Rome. His bride, Lorenza Feliciani, was 14; he was 26. Quite what Lorenza first thought of Balsamo we will never know. He was once described thus: 'While not actually handsome, his face was the most remarkable I have ever seen. His eyes were indescribable – all fire and yet all ice.' But once Balsamo proposed to Lorenza, her interest grew. She saw him as her way out of the gutter. And he most certainly saw her as the beautiful bait that would hook wealthy victims. Despite her background, and because of her obvious attractions, Lorenza became Balsamo's key to the higher echelons of eighteenth-century Roman society. After a stint of passing counterfeit coinage – and a sideline dabbling in the production of phoney aphrodisiacs – the couple embarked on a tour of Europe.

Their first stop was France, where they met the world's most famous lover, Casanova. Balsamo and Lorenza's confidence tricks had earned them money enough to mould themselves into the roles of aristocrats. And Casanova immediately fell for their charade. To him, they could belong nowhere else but within the circles of high society. It is not known whether Casanova worked his infamous seducer's charm on Lorenza. But it is certainly likely. What is known is that Lorenza was seduced by a Monsieur Duplessis when her husband was in jail over unpaid debts. So outraged was Balsamo that he complained to the highest authorities and Lorenza suddenly found herself in prison.

Amazingly, the couple forgot and forgave. Realising that as a twosome they were a force to be reckoned with in the world of deception, they agreed to stay together. And so, now calling himself Marchese Pellegrini, Balsamo set off back to Italy accompanied by Lorenza. The next 10 years were spent masterminding a series of spectacular confidence tricks which were to take them as far afield as North Africa. The couple returned to London in 1776. With a string of victims on their tail, it was now time for a change of name. They became Count Alessandro Di Cagliostro and Countess Serafina. To add a little colour to their background, Balsamo said he had stolen the countess from an oriental harem and made her his wife. No one challenged the unlikely origins of such an aristocratic lady. Neither did they question the couple's source of wealth when rumour spread that the count could turn common metals into gold.

So the couple were welcomed into society and enjoyed themselves immensely. They wore rich clothes and extravagant jewellery. They had liveried servants at their beck and call. And they rode in elegant coaches pulled by beautifully turned-out horses. In fact, the count and countess's sole wealth was the £3,000 they had made in their foreign escapades.

Balsamo wangled himself an introduction to the Freemasons and found the secret society to be the perfect setting for his faker's magic. He virtually took over the London lodge of which he was a member, claiming powers of second sight and soothsaying. It was not long before he was made Grand Master of his lodge. And that bizarre but envied position was to open many doors for him throughout Europe. In Paris he had a lot of fun creating the 'Egyptian Rite of Freemasonry' and appointed himself Grand Cophta. It also meant he was in charge of collecting membership fees and monies paid in relation to the lodge's strange initiation ceremonies.

With no one daring to usurp Balsamo's power, he soon created a leading Freemasonry role for Lorenza too. She was appointed the new Queen of Sheba in charge of a female lodge. This was a controversial move, not just because of Lorenza's new-found authority, but because up until now the Freemasons had been a strictly male order. But it was not surprising that the wealthy élite of Parisian society flocked to their 'queen'. Lorenza would earnestly take duchesses and fellow countesses aside and confide in them that, although she looked only 30, she was, in fact, 60 years old. A magic elixir concocted by her husband had held back the years.

Her rich and noble confidantes swore to keep the 'queen's' secret — in exchange, of course, for bottles of the age-defying potion. It also encouraged men and women followers alike to part with their money for other powerful remedies. They could not help but be impressed by the personal attention of the count, who even carefully wrapped the pills he prescribed in fine gold leaf. The cunning count made sure he gave out nothing that was dangerous. Indeed, any of the magical cures bought by his wealthy patients could have been obtained from a doctor at a fraction of the price. For they were simply herbal remedies.

The Grand Master was fast winning a reputation as a genius in the field of medicine. It was inevitable that his fame would spread. His presence in many countries was demanded. In Leipzig, Germany, Balsamo got quite carried away, declaring that if the local Freemasons' lodge failed to observe the Egyptian Rite, its master would incur the wrath of God. Coincidentally, the master killed himself shortly afterwards and there was mass hysteria at Balsamo's divine powers. In the Baltic state of Courland, nobles wanted to make Balsamo their king. He sensibly declined the invitation. In Moscow, he recruited young boys and girls as 'soothsayers'.

Hearing of the presence of the 'count and countess', one of the Tsar's ministers begged Balsamo to cure his insane brother. At first Balsamo was reluctant, then agreed to examine him. The brother was brought before Balsamo, tightly bound to prevent doing harm to himself or others. Balsamo ordered that the man be untied and was greeted with protests. Did he not realise the patient was a lunatic, liable to attack people? The Russian wardens were eventually persuaded to release their patient – who immediately leaped towards Balsamo. The count coolly pushed him aside and instructed that he be thrown into an ice-cold river. Perhaps it was the shock of finding himself immersed in freezing water, but the madman emerged sensible and profusely sorry for his behaviour.

The count and his beautiful countess arrived in Strasbourg on 19 September 1780. As usual they made their appearance in fine style, with liveried servants on black horses. Realising that there was now no end to what people would believe, Balsamo extended and elaborated his mystical powers to an incredible degree. He claimed to have been born before the great flood of Noah; to have been a pupil of Socrates; to have been on close terms with Moses, Solomon and Roman emperors; and to have drunk wine at a wedding feast in biblical Galilee. If anyone dared to look askance at these ridiculous stories, Balsamo would whip out a bundle of letters dated 550 BC.

Balsamo continued to administer his pills, potions and promises of eternal life. To answer claims of being an impostor taking money from the vulnerable, he took daily walks distributing alms to the poor. And, despite investigations ordered by the French government into his alleged powers, no respected member of the medical profession could declare him a phoney. Confident of his hallowed standing, Balsamo boldly told revered philosopher Lavater: 'If your science is greater than mine, you have no need of my acquaintance; if mine is the greater, I have no need of yours.' Lavater immediately became one of the great count's disciples.

Another recruit of Balsamo's was Cardinal de Rohan, confidant to Queen Marie Antoinette, wife of Louis XVI.

Balsamo's initial attitude towards de Rohan was as insulting as it had been to Lavater. When de Rohan sent a servant to him to demand an audience, Balsamo sent the message: 'If the prince is ill, let him come to me and I will cure him. If he is not ill, he has no need of me and I have no need of him.' De Rohan was enraged by the impudence but was nevertheless curious enough to pay Balsamo a visit. The two men forged a close friendship. Balsamo cured de Rohan's brother, Prince de Soubise, of scarlet fever when all other doctors had failed. This won him Godlike adulation, with his face appearing on snuff boxes, buckles, rings and other jewellery.

However, Balsamo's closeness to de Rohan was also to be his downfall. Balsamo and Lorenza had decided to go to Paris to escape increasing hostility from more orthodox physicians. There they learned that de Rohan had fallen out with Marie Antoinette and was desperate to win favour once more with the French queen. The couple became embroiled in de Rohan's plot to steal a diamond necklace he knew she coveted. The plan involved forging her signature, and when Louis XVI was informed, he ordered that de Rohan, Lorenza and Balsamo be thrown into the dungeons of the Bastille.

At a subsequent trial the count and countess were cleared of all conspiracy charges and were given their freedom. They left the Bastille in a parade of thousands of cheering followers. But the scandal had left its mark on the hitherto unblemished reputation of this amazing aristocratic couple. For harsh interrogation had forced Lorenza to reveal one too many secrets about her husband's success – and the news quickly spread that gullible innocents throughout Europe and across the world had been victims of a cruel impostor.

Despite their phoney titles, Lorenza and Balsamo were no longer fêted by the rich and noble classes. Louis XVI eventually ordered that they leave France, never to return. The couple spent aimless months wandering around Europe, their relationship slowly falling apart. For with the trappings of their former grand life long gone, Lorenza saw little attraction in her husband.

Lorenza persuaded her husband to return to Rome in the hope that some of their old tricks might win them back their glorious lifestyle. It was 1789 and Balsamo believed that creating a new Egyptian Rite Masonic Lodge could be the answer to their prayers. It was a monumental mistake. Any Roman Catholic joining the sinister world of the Freemasons was subject to excommunication as a heretic. Three years later Balsamo was seized by the papal police. On 7 April 1791 he was found guilty of heresy and sentenced to death. This time Lorenza did not stand by her husband. She denounced him in the hope that her life would be spared. Her sentence was to spend the rest of her days locked away in a convent, where she died in 1794.

Balsamo survived, however. The Pope commuted his death sentence to life imprisonment and he was taken to the dungeons of the castle at San Leo. He died there on 26 August 1795, it being rumoured that he had been murdered. The fake mystic, Masonic Grand Master and medicine man who claimed to be immortal had reached the end of his cheating life at the age of 52.

THE TRODMORE SYNDICATE
THE RACE THAT NEVER WAS

Some scams are as complicated as they are devious; others are almost artistic in their simplicity. One such was the infamous Trodmore Hunt horse-racing scandal, the beauty of which was that the conspirators did not need to fix the race – because they didn't even bother to run one. The Trodmore conspiracy was dreamed up in 1898, during a period when there were few firm guidelines on the way horse races were run in Britain. Scores of small race meetings were held around the country, often organised by the local hunt to raise money. They might be held at irregular intervals. If the crowds were large they might be repeated the following year; if poorly attended, which was more usually the case, they might not. A clerk of the course would write to one or all of the racing publications asking them to print race cards and results. Bank holidays being a favourite date to stage minor meetings, the sporting press usually found itself inundated with requests at this time. The newspapers resigned themselves to printing as many cards as possible in the hope of keeping everybody happy.

Monday, 1 August 1898 was a bank holiday and when, a few weeks before, a letter arrived at the offices of *The*

Sportsman from the Trodmore Race Club no suspicions were aroused. The missive politely requested that the journal devote space in its pages to announce the club's first full meeting and to add the Trodmore card to the list of those printed in advance of the holiday. According to the letter, the first race would start at 1.30 p.m. and the last at 4 p.m. The request was neatly written on high-quality notepaper with a lavish, printed letterhead in the name of the 'Trodmore Race Club of Cornwall' and was signed by 'G. Martin, Clerk of the Course'.

The editor inserted the race card without a second thought but did not at that stage concern himself with getting hold of the results of the day's racing. Before that became a problem, however: a second letter arrived at *The Sportsman*. It was from a reader who said that, having noticed the Trodmore Hunt card in the editor's illustrious journal, he planned to attend the meeting in Cornwall. He would be happy to wire the starting prices and full results to the newspaper if he was paid a small consideration for his time and trouble. The editor agreed.

The trap had been set and the sporting journalists had fallen headlong into it. For there was, of course, no such person as Mr Martin, no helpful reader – indeed no horses, no jockeys and no race planned whatsoever. There were, however, an awful lot of bets to be placed. And, but for a bizarre quirk of fate, the bookies would have been seriously stung, a gang of fraudsters would have got seriously rich and no one else would have been any the wiser.

The crooked syndicate who had concocted the scam found the latter part of their plan – the actual placing of sufficient wagers – to be the most difficult. A huge amount of money had to be wagered on the fictitious race to make the operation worthwhile, yet it would have to be distributed in small sums to avoid suspicion. The larger bookmakers, who generally dealt on credit, could not be used because they took time to pay out the winnings. So the phoney punters had to rely on small-time street bookmakers, who, out of commercial necessity, were a naturally suspicious breed.

Even then, it was judged foolhardy to slap large wagers on horses running in a meeting no one had ever heard of. So a large-scale map of London was pinned to the wall and divided into segments. Each punter was assigned a sector in which he would seek out every street bookie and place with him a small bet on the Trodmore race. In a further attempt to avoid suspicion, the dodgy punters were ordered to adhere to the following strict code of conduct:

1. Approach each bookmaker once only, so that no one bookie would get two punters wanting to bet on the same minor race.
2. Bet not only on the Trodmore card but on one other race meeting as well.
3. If any bookmaker raises questions about the Trodmore meeting, show him the relevant page of *The Sportsman*.
4. If he remains suspicious, the golden rule is to smile sweetly and walk away.

It would only have taken one bookmaker with a reasonable knowledge of the geography of the West Country to have discovered that there was no such place as Trodmore. As it happened, no bookie consulted a map and by 1 p.m. on Bank Holiday Monday, 1 August, every penny of stake money – several hundred pounds, at the very least – had been wagered. The following day the results of the five races were duly published in *The*

Sportsman, along with the starting prices. The winners were: Reaper (5-1 nap), Rosy (also 5-1), Spur (2-1), Fairy Bells (7-4), Curfew (6-4) and Jim (5-4). It was a most undramatic list, none of the odds being sufficiently long-priced to make the bookies uncomfortable. Even so, the largest stakes had been on the 5-1 nags.

This was the point at which fate took a hand in this extraordinary charade. Journalists at *Sporting Life* had spotted the Trodmore results in *The Sportsman*, the paper's rival, and had swiftly copied them for their own issue the following day. The syndicate had deliberately not contacted *Sporting Life* for fear that doubling the number of people involved would have also doubled the opportunities for errors. Their caution was well justified. For in their haste to reproduce the Trodmore results for Wednesday's paper, a printer at *Sporting Life* wrongly punched out the starting price of Reaper as 5-2 instead of 5-1. Whereas most bookies had paid out on Tuesday on the basis of the results in that morning's *Sportsman*, a few who had been hit hardest delayed for as long as possible. When Wednesday dawned, they naturally checked the odds in *Sporting Life* and found them different – which made the slow-paying bookies feel edgy and the early payers distinctly angry.

Suddenly the most obvious check was made, as to where in Cornwall lay the racecourse of Trodmore. Map makers, Post Office officials and bemused Cornishmen were all consulted, to no avail. Trodmore did not exist. The police were called in and the finger of suspicion was pointed at the editor of *The Sportsman*, his printers and even the sub-editor who had been ordered to insert the card. There was no proof against any of them, although the consensus of opinion was that the plot had been hatched by a group of Fleet Street journalists. By this time, however, the crafty conmen who had formed the Trodmore syndicate had smartly vanished — along with all the profits from the 'Race That Never Was'.

DONALD CROWHURST
MAN OVERBOARD

Donald Crowhurst paid the ultimate price for a fraud born of ambition, greed and need. He was a man with a dream, who hoped to be remembered as a brilliant sailor and navigator. Instead, he is remembered as a conman. Crowhurst entered a round-the-world yacht race in the face of fierce competition from the best sailors of the day. He needed not only the kudos but also the £5,000 prize money to pay off his creditors. However, he woefully underestimated his own talents of seamanship and, when he realised he could not win the race, he set an outrageous course in unchartered waters. He took short cuts, gave false radio readings and maintained a bogus logbook. Crowhurst thought he could cheat his way to victory. But, when even that course became flawed, he committed himself to a watery grave.

Born in India in 1932 to a railway superintendent and a schoolteacher, Donald Crowhurst returned to Britain at the age of 15 and lived in Reading, Berkshire. He began careers in the Royal Air Force and the army but left both under a cloud. His RAF days ended when a prank, during which he rode a motorcycle through a barrack room, went wrong. Later he was compelled to resign from the army after being caught trying to steal a car. In civilian life he found a niche as an electronics engineer, got married and developed a consuming passion for sailing. He even invented a radio direction-finding device for sailing boats which he christened the Navicator. The idea was finally snapped up by Pye Radio.

After that he turned his attentions to circumnavigating the world. Inspired by the success of Sir Francis Chichester, who sailed single-handedly around the world in 1967, Crowhurst set his sights on the Golden Globe race, sponsored by the *Sunday Times*. With a specially built trimaran called the *Teignmouth Electron*, he was determined to sail his way into the record books. The first hint of the difficulties he would encounter came when he took the vessel by sea from a shipyard in Norfolk to Devon. Instead of the expected three days, the trip took two weeks. If he was alarmed by the excessive vibration suffered by the trimaran when it got up to speed, he cast his doubts to the back of his mind. It left him little more than a fortnight to prepare for his epic voyage. It wasn't enough time to repair the leaky hatch covers. And such was his haste to beat the race deadline for entrants on 31 October 1968 that he left a valuable box of spares on the quayside, not to mention piping to pump out the flooded hatches.

Crowhurst was plagued with mishap upon disaster as he progressed at a painfully slow pace. His biggest problem was to keep out water. Soon he was forced to revise his early estimates that it would take him a mere 243 days to complete the course. He could have and should have turned back. But foolish pride, together with lingering ambition and the need for money, made him go on in the face of mounting odds. Within six weeks he began to complete a second, false logbook glamorising his pace. He stopped radio contact with race organisers for months at a time to maintain his cover. He even put ashore in Argentina to make some repairs, strictly against the rules of the event. This misdemeanour wasn't discovered until much later.

Instead of rounding the treacherous Cape Horn, Crowhurst lingered in the South Atlantic before doubling back on himself, monitoring the progress of his rivals on radio. Robin Knox-Johnston was in the lead position set to scoop the Golden Globe as first past the post. But the £5,000 prize money for the fastest competitor was still up for grabs as all the yachts had set sail on different dates. Crowhurst pitched himself back into the race when the second-placed Nigel Tetley was homeward bound.

Suddenly he realised that, if he won, his logbooks would be scrutinised and his falsifications would shine out. He decided to settle as runner-up to the first two genuine competitors, happy that it would bring him valuable kudos. But disaster struck when Tetley was forced to abandon his sinking boat 1,200 miles from home. Crowhurst could not help but win the first prize for the fastest passage – until the judges surveyed his concocted logbooks.

Crowhurst was acutely aware of the shame and dishonour that would follow. His feelings of guilt were compounded when congratulatory messages began pouring across the radio waves. It was then that his nerve broke and his fragile emotions lay in tatters. Coupled with the loneliness of life on the open sea which he had endured for nearly seven months, it was enough to drive him mad.

Entries in his logbooks which were later found and examined prove his agitated state of mind in those last few months. The final entry was made on 1 July 1969 at 11.20 a.m. No one knows precisely what happened to the tortured Crowhurst. It is thought he jumped overboard to meet a watery end in the Sargasso Sea, close to the Caribbean. He was probably clutching the bogus logbook which would have illustrated his deception beyond all doubt. His body was never recovered.

Nine days later the Royal Mail ship the *Picardy* found the *Teignmouth Electron* adrift in the Atlantic. Aboard, crewmen found three logbooks, plenty of food and fresh water but no sign of Crowhurst. The news was seen as a tragedy at home. But doubts had already been raised by the chairman of the race judges, Sir Francis Chichester, about Crowhurst's apparent bursts of incredible speed and his long lapses of radio silence. It was enough to put two *Sunday Times* reporters, Nicholas Tomalin and Ron Hall, on the trail of a scandal. They probed the logbooks and pieced together the sad story of Donald Crowhurst's blighted bid for fame.

The news of the fraud sent shock waves through the world of sailing, hitherto known for its good repute and robust ethical code. Still, there were many who stopped short of outright condemnation out of respect for the man who paid the ultimate price for his sham. Robin Knox-Johnston, who finally won both the Golden Globe trophy and the prize for the fastest passage, handed over the cash to an appeal fund for the lost sailor's wife and four children. 'None of us should judge him too harshly,' the victor remarked. But, in the end, no one judged Donald Crowhurst's shoddy actions more harshly than he did himself.

JIM BAKKER AND JIMMY SWAGGART
A FALL FROM GRACE

'As the Lord giveth, so he taketh away.' In the case of television hot gospeller Jim Bakker, the Lord gave him too much and eventually had to take it *all* away. Bakker was head of an organisation called PTL. It stood for Praise The Lord, but it also spelled money. Throughout the 1980s boom in tele-evangelism in America, Bakker reached the very top of his vocation by a tear-stained style of Bible-punching which had the viewers sending in untold millions of dollars. Peak viewing – and therefore peak earning time – was *The Jim and Tammy Bakker Show*, an extraordinary double act of syrupy sweetness and light featuring the preacher and his blonde, bronzed, mascara-daubed wife.

PTL's income was $129 million in 1986 alone. The money went to support its own TV station, networked across 1,200 channels. PTL also owned a 2,300-acre theme park, dubbed the 'Christian Disneyland', complete with hotel and shopping mall, which drew as many as six million visitors a year. Bakker, however, hid a secret from his generous flock. In 1980 he had taken a church secretary, Jessica Hahn, to a hotel in Clearwater Beach, Florida. Small but perfectly formed, Bakker allegedly drugged and had sex with Jessica, then said a short prayer before returning to the pulpit to admonish his flock for not following God's ways.

The scandal lay dormant for seven years until, on 19 March 1987, Bakker announced that he was the victim of a 'diabolical plot' to oust him from his seat of power. Hinting that his television rival Jimmy Swaggart was jealous of his supreme position as America's number-one TV evangelist, Bakker said he had been 'wickedly manipulated' for the benefit of 'treacherous former friends'. The little man then resigned in order to fight these irreligious slurs, leaving colleague Jerry Falwell to run PTL as a caretaker until he and Tammy were able to return to take their rightful place.

Falwell was made of sterner stuff, however. He thoroughly dug into PTL's dealings and discovered a black hole of funds being sucked into the personal accounts of the Bakkers. There was also the question of approximately a quarter of a million dollars paid into an account to which Miss Hahn had access; it sounded very much like hush money.

While Jim and Tammy Bakker were off the air, supposedly marshalling their defence against these scurrilous allegations, they appealed to Jerry Falwell for a subsistence allowance. Falwell was astonished at their 'shopping list' of demands: $300,000 a year for him, $100,000 for her, a lakeside home in South Carolina, fees for attorneys and wages for security guards and a maid. Plus perks. 'I don't see any repentance there,' said Falwell. 'I see greed, the self-centredness, the avarice that brought them down.'

Bakker and his attorney, the Reverend Richard Dortch, were defrocked by the PTL in May 1987. The ensuing scandal went into overdrive, as the participants went their different ways. Hahn posed nude for *Playboy* before becoming a saucy chat-line DJ, while Bakker became the subject of a government inquiry into his fundraising gimmicks. It was estimated that over a three-year period the Bakkers had between them pocketed an amazing $4.8 million from PTL. The Internal Revenue Service, angry that so many tax-free donations had been misdirected, revoked PTL's charitable status. Bakker was indicted for fraud, along with his lawyer.

Retribution on the phoney men of God was slow in coming. But in August 1989 Dortch, having agreed to testify at the forthcoming Bakker trial, was jailed for eight years. Bakker, meanwhile, was still to be seen in public, making tearful appearances before the television cameras as he was wheeled back and forth for psychiatric tests. The Bakker trial itself suffered further delay when the preacher was found cowering like a whipped cur on the floor of his lawyer's office.

By way of defence, the lawyer, Harold Bender, assured the court that his client was 'a man of love, compassion and character who cares for his fellow man'. The judge was unimpressed. Finding Bakker guilty on all 24 counts, he sentenced him to 45 years in jail and imposed a $500,000 fine. For once at least, the tears that flowed down Jim Bakker's cheeks were perhaps warranted.

And what of the rival preacher whom Bakker had first blamed for his downfall? Fellow tele-evangelist Jimmy Swaggart was a braggart. He boasted that, unlike Bakker, he was incorruptible, and most of his flock believed him – until they heard what he got up to in a seedy New Orleans motel room.

Prostitute Debra Murphee was regularly employed by

Swaggart to perform obscene sex acts while he watched from the comfort of an armchair. Murphee went along with the lucrative sex games until the preacher suggested that she invite her nine-year-old daughter to watch also. The mother, who had a record for prostitution offences in two states, announced that she was so disgusted that she felt obliged to go public with her story. She recreated Swaggart's favourite poses for *Penthouse*, and the 16 pages of explicit pictures were deemed so hot that they had to be sealed in each copy of the magazine. Murphee also went on a national media tour to publicise her revelations.

Swaggart had, like Bakker, exposed his tormented soul before the television cameras when in 1988 he tearfully confessed to 'a moral sin'. He did not specify what it was but newspapers speculated that it involved the hiring of prostitutes for pornographic acts. Finally, in 1991, he was stopped for driving his car erratically – and was discovered to be sharing it with a prostitute and a pile of porn magazines.

Because of such perfectly understandable 'moral sins', Swaggart's local church, the compassionate Louisiana church of the Assemblies of God, was inclined to deal with him leniently and recommended a minimal three-month suspension from preaching. The national church was hardly much tougher and ordered him banished from the pulpit for a year. Swaggart, however, unwisely defied the ban after only a few months on the grounds that his absence would destroy his $140 million-a-year worldwide ministries. He was immediately defrocked by the Assemblies of God.

Murphee faded from the scene after a proposed movie deal about her meetings with the dirty preacher failed to come to fruition. Swaggart, meanwhile, saw his television empire dwindle from tens of millions of viewers to mere thousands. The self-appointed mouthpiece of the Lord was merciful towards himself, telling his congregation that God had forgiven him for his sins, adding piously: 'What's past is past.'